I0794116

NEVILLE GODDARD'S FINAL LECTURES

NEVILLE GODDARD'S FINAL LECTURES

Edited and introduced by
MITCH HOROWITZ

MEDIA

MEDIA

Published 2022 by Gildan Media LLC
aka G&D Media
www.GandDmedia.com

NEVILLE GODDARD'S FINAL LECTURES. Introduction copyright © 2022 Mitch Horowitz. All rights reserved.

No part of this book may be used, reproduced or transmitted in any manner whatsoever, by any means (electronic, photocopying, recording, or otherwise), without the prior written permission of the author, except in the case of brief quotations embodied in critical articles and reviews. No liability is assumed with respect to the use of the information contained within. Although every precaution has been taken, the author and publisher assume no liability for errors or omissions. Neither is any liability assumed for damages resulting from the use of the information contained herein.

Front cover design by David Rheinhardt of Pyrographx

Library of Congress Cataloging-in-Publication Data is available upon request

ISBN: 978-1-7225-0099-3

10 9 8 7 6 5 4 3 2 1

Contents

Introduction

Into the Silence: The Final Year of a Mystic

"To outgrow is to die. You die to one state and you move into another state."
—Neville Goddard, May 5, 1972

It is difficult to speak of Neville Goddard's final lectures since we possess a valuable but incomplete record of the teacher's public talks from the last year of his life, 1972.

The speaking catalogue that survives is thanks to Neville's fateful decision to grant listeners blanket permission to record his lectures, which brought dramatic new exposure and listenership to his work in the digital age. Neville's career as a public speaker began on February 2, 1938, in New York City, and he was soon delivering talks at metaphysical churches and in auditoriums on both coasts and throughout the nation. The advent of portable consumer audio technology made possible the recording of his presentations mostly from the mid-1950s through the final two years of his life, with the plurality in the late sixties.

Today, the lecturer's words—resounding in his clipped, mellifluous speaking style—are a source of fascination and study for seekers worldwide. His message, always consistent yet fresh in delivery, was that your imagination is the creative force symbolically called God in the Bible—a book not of historical events and tensions between man and divinity but rather a blueprint of your own psycho-spiritual development and self-realization. Everything that you experience, Neville taught, is the out-picturing of your emotionalized thoughts and mental images.

The 1972 lectures transcribed and assembled in this volume reflect Neville in the full bloom of his vision as a practical mystic and radical re-interpreter of Scripture. It is critical to understand that Neville's thought system—on full display in the work collected here—significantly broadened after 1959, a year that, starting on July 20, opened the seeker to a series of revelatory awakenings, which he recounted in his 1961 book, *The Law and the Promise*. But this cycle of spiritual unfoldment actually began three decades earlier. In an undated lecture from a posthumous 1977 collection of Neville's talks, *Immortal Man*, the teacher said:

> Let me share with you my experience back in 1929. I did not know how literally true the Bible was until it began to unfold itself within me. I was a dancer, living in a hotel. Early in the morning, maybe about three-thirty or four o'clock, I was taken in spirit into the Divine Council where the gods hold converse. There I saw an angelic being at an open ledger. She turned and looked into my face; then, taking a quill pen, she made a note in the open book.
>
> From there I was taken into the presence of Infinite Love, the Ancient of Days just as described in the 7th chapter of the Book of Daniel. He looked at me and asked, "What is the greatest thing in the world?" I answered in the words of Paul, "Faith, hope and love, but the greatest of these is love." With that he embraced me, our bodies fused and we became one body.

> Paul tells us, "He who is united to the Lord becomes one spirit with Him. One body, one Spirit, one hope, one Lord, one faith, one baptism, one God and Father of them all, who is above all, through all and in all." In that Union I felt infinite love without loss of my identity. I was still individualized, but I have never known such intensity of love; God truly is love.
>
> Thirty years later, in the summer of '59, that Union, that graft began to bear fruit. It took thirty years for the graft to take. Then the gift of God began to move downward from that which was collective to me the individual. For He said, "Let US . . ." (that is a collective being) ". . . make man in our image." Then the heavenly gifts come down from that which was collective to that which is individual.
>
> You can analyze the gifts. Infinite power. No man on earth knows this power until he has tasted of it.

Neville furthered this narrative in *The Law and the Promise*, where he recalled being "taken in spirit into a Divine Society," and then restored to earth "tormented by my limitations of understanding." As noted, these limitations began to lift in July 1959 when the teacher underwent a mystical rebirth, or resurrection, emerging from the womb of his own skull, the inauguration of what he called "the Promise".

Following that experience by five months, in December 1959, Neville first encountered the biblical figure of David—who addressed him lovingly as "Father," confirming the teacher's Oneness with God. Four months later, in April 1960, Neville experienced the opening of his body by a bolt of lightning to reveal a Divine luminous fluid within, representing the living water of creation.

He described it this way in his January 31, 1972, lecture, "What Is Man?":

> And when man is turned around by a complete splitting of the temple, for the curtain of the temple is torn in two from top to bottom,

> and at the base of your spine, you're going to see a golden, pulsing liquid light. And as you see it, you're going to know that you are it. You're looking at yourself and yet, it is formless and you fuse with it, and then you become that fiery serpent, and up you go into the rain and it vibrates like thunder. Then you are completely turned around. The energies that went down into generation are now turned up into regeneration.

As noted, Neville called this cycle of rebirth the Promise—a process of self-realization that awaits all individuals as they come to understand, fully and experientially, that they are Christ clothed in the flesh, he taught.

In Neville's 1966 essay "Resurrection," the title piece of his final book, the teacher added one further stage to his realization. He described the fulfillment of Christ's three-and-a-half-year ministry on earth with the Holy Spirit descending upon man in the form of a dove, bringing complete and final union with God. In a 2016 preface to the book *Resurrection*, I calculated that Neville may have experienced this fourth stage in January 1963. As I was working on this anthology, I received confirmation in Neville's own words that the experience occurred on January 1, 1963, which you will encounter in his lecture collected here, "God's Son."

* * *

None of these experiences can, of course, be fully understood using our traditional points of reference. They are neither strictly ordinary nor strictly belonging to some ethereal or spirit realm. These events, concrete and literal in Neville's teaching, are revelations of a Greater Reality—an actuality that comes into focus with the unfolding of your true nature. "The finding of David, everything said in that book, I have actually experienced in a spiritual sense," Neville further said in his lecture "What Is Man?" on January 31, 1972, "but when it came to me, it was just like this room, just as real. It was a cubic reality."

As I was completing this introduction, I received, as I often do, a propitiously timed letter from a reader. He asked if I had personally undergone this experience—and is it the same for everyone? I replied, "I have not had the experience that Neville describes. He does speak of it very literally, so I would take him at his word—yet, personally, I never feel that the individual seeker is bound by any liturgy or marker related by another." The search is exquisitely personal.

* * *

I have been describing the Neville who you meet in *Neville Goddard's Final Lectures.* It is the writer-speaker in complete philosophical ripeness of outlook. For some listeners, however, the more radically mystical nature of Neville's latter-day teachings proved too great a stretch. Or at least an unwelcome distraction from his more practical work on the creative forces of the imagination. At times, audiences in later years shrunk.

A longtime student of Neville's, Freedom Barry (1921–2014), who appears in lectures IV and XV, recalled at a 1996 workshop that Neville's account of his mystical rebirth, or "Birth From Above," specifically put off some listeners.* Freedom reflected on a daunting series of lectures Neville held in Los Angeles; he did not say specifically when they occurred but his description suggests Neville's latter-day presentations:

> That hall was full when he opened. It held three hundred people there in the Fine Arts Auditorium at the Wilshire in Los Angeles. That hall was full, and he told this shocking story in the most literal terms of being born through the skull of his head as a womb opens.

* Weekend retreat, Cambria, CA, September 14-15, 1996.

> And the next night, that was on Monday, the next Thursday, there were thirty people. The next Monday, there were twelve. He kept telling it, and so after the third night, and the audience was down to twelve, Freddy Messenger, who was his agent, he said, "Neville, you've got to stop telling that story or you'll have no audience at all." He said, "Then I'll tell it to the bare walls." And Neville would have. That's the beauty of it, and he almost did.

Neville was not above joking about such things. In the opening lines of his lecture "Justified States," delivered on April 3, 1972, he remarked, "Tonight, we will take both the Law and the Promise. Just a little while on the Promise, that you may not be concerned." It is also important to note that Neville neither renounced nor neglected any of the practical principles he developed earlier in his career. He made no revision of his teaching about "the Law" or the mind's reality-shaping powers—including in areas of traditional attainment and success. In the January 31, 1972, lecture that I quoted earlier, Neville reassured his listeners:

> Tonight, if you are here for the first time and you expected something entirely different, then let me give you a short portion of the Law. You are living in a world that really is a psychological world. All things take place in the imagination of man—all things. And so, because they do take place there, let them take place there first before you expect to see them on the outside. So, assume that you are the man that you would like to be, believe that you are, try to catch all the feelings that would be yours if they were true. Give it all the tones and the feeling of reality. And then sleep. Go sound asleep in that assumption that you are already the one that you want to be. Try that, and I assure you from my own experience, what you have assumed that you are, you'll become. You have already become what you are because you want to assume that you are it. Everything

> in the world is just like that. It's all imagination and all that you behold, although it appears without, really is within, in your own wonderful human imagination of which this world of mortality is but a shadow.

Apropos of practical methods, Neville offered what I consider some of his most compelling personal advice in the lecture "Feel After Him," delivered on an unknown day in February 1972. In this talk, the teacher shrewdly identified the prurient *pleasure* we often feel when indulging in negative emotions and the *desire* to complete the expression of an explosive emotion, such as the venting of anger or resentment. "And if perchance you catch yourself imagining what you do not wish to experience," he said, "stop it, stop it right there and then, and don't give it an extra second. It may be you are in the midst of an emotion and you'd like to complete the emotion and tell him off completely. Don't. Stop it. Break it. And that causes a sort of a mental, well, a mental abortion, a mental miscarriage. If you break it without exploding the emotion."

* * *

In these final lectures, Neville also revealed aspects of his private life and how he responded to disappointing or bitter episodes. In particular, he described a painful event that he experienced as a drama student, entirely new to city life, when at age seventeen he migrated from his native Barbados to study theater in New York. In the lecture "Ends, Ultimate and Temporary" delivered on March 17, 1972, Neville described suffering humiliation by his teacher but using the experience as a goad to something greater. Bear in mind that the youthful Neville probably spoke in a rounder, more rural Anglo-Caribbean accent, which his instructor deemed a career-killer:

> My own disappointments in my world led up to whatever I am doing today. When the teacher in my school, I could ill afford the $500

> that my father gave me to go to this small school in New York City, and she made me the goat. She called me out before an audience of about forty students. And she said, "Now listen to him speak. He will never earn a living using his voice."
>
> She should not have done that, but she did it—but she didn't know the kind of person that she was talking about. Instead of going down into the grave and burying my head in shame, I was determined that I would actually disprove her. It did something to me when she said to me, "you will never earn"—to the class, using me as the guinea pig to show them what not to do—and so, she said, I spoke with a guttural voice and I spoke with this very heavy accent, and I will never use my voice to earn a living . . .
>
> We all went to this school and this teacher simply singled me out to make some little, well, exhibition of what I should not be doing in class. But I went home and I was so annoyed that I had lost my father's $500 or $600 that he gave me for the six-months course, but I was determined that she was false, that she was wrong. So, I went to the end. I went to the end and actually felt that I was facing an audience and unembarrassed that I could talk and talk and talk forever without notes, no notes.

Today, Neville is, of course, one of the most highly regarded spiritual orators of the twentieth century. Many of his vast range of digitized lectures, delivered extemporaneously and without notes as foreseen in his vision, amass hits in the hundreds of thousands. And his reputation, based on the number of listeners and readers, shows only signs of growing. Indeed, when I started writing about Neville in 2005, his ten books were limited to a handful of unremarkable-looking backlist paperbacks. As I write these words in 2022, reprints of his original books and new collections of his essays and lectures number in hundreds of editions, many of which have entered multiple reprints.

Since I am noting Neville's personal life, I must also clarify the nature of his death. Conflicting accounts exist. The most widely heard is that on October 1, 1972, Neville "collapsed and died of an apparent heart attack" at age sixty-seven in his West Hollywood home, as reported in *The Los Angeles Times*.*

In actuality, Neville's death certificate from the state of California provides a different record, which squares with an account from one of his intimates, driver and friend Frank Carter, who was the last person to be with the mystic on the night of his death (Neville's wife was hospitalized at the time). Neville's daughter Victoria, or Vicky, summoned Carter to the teacher's home to consult with the coroner the morning of October 1 when his body was discovered. In the coroner's presence, Carter witnessed a massive amount of blood around Neville's corpse and a contorted expression on his face, as though he had choked and bled out.**

According to his death certificate, Neville died of a rupture of the esophageal varices—i.e., swollen or enlarged veins—leading from the throat to stomach with subsequent hemorrhaging, hence the profusion of blood and appearance of choking. The cause was liver damage or cirrhosis. That condition generally results from long-term alcohol abuse. "The coroner kept asking me what happened," Carter recalled, "he said, 'Was Mr. Goddard a heavy drinker?' and his daughter said, 'Well he used to be, but not lately.'" At a dinner party the night before, Carter recalled, Neville did not even finish a full martini, nor did the men have anything further to drink when he dropped Neville off at home. Yet Neville often spoke of enjoying alcohol, including a bottle of wine each day with lunch. In one of the lectures in this anthology, "Feel Chosen," delivered on an unknown day in 1972, he remarks, "I had my full bottle of wine today with some cheese for my lunch, and thoroughly enjoyed a bit of wine and, oh, a section of Edam."

---

* "Neville Goddard; Religious Topics Author-Speaker," October 4, 1972

** *Neville Goddard: The Frank Carter Lectures* (Audio Enlightenment, 2018)

I do not view the teacher, or any artist, in a lesser light for his probable cause of death, and I realize, too, that there exist symbolical or extra-physical interpretations of Neville's passing, some referenced by Carter, which I honor in the outlook of every mature seeker. Carter notes that Neville's face was covered by a napkin, removed by the coroner for the driver to view the body. "He reached down and picked up the napkin and showed me," Carter said, "and there was the image which I had seen in my dream all those years before." Carter recalled once dreaming of the death of Judas, as told in the first chapter of Acts, where the King James translation reads, "his bowels gushed out," similar in Carter's mind to the profusion of blood he witnessed around Neville's body. After sitting up much of the night following his haunting dream, Carter phoned Neville the next morning and said, "Neville you are Judas." The teacher immediately agreed. "Judas," he replied, "betrayed the Messianic secrets."

Regarding the napkin over Neville's face and its removal—which I always found a peculiar element of Carter's telling—in a March 6, 1972, lecture in this volume, "John the Crown of Scripture," Neville says of the opening of Christ's interment chamber:

> So, when they came into the tomb and found it empty, they found the linen clothes, then they found the napkin removed from the linen clothes. The napkin that had covered his head. And here it was removed from the linen clothes. The linen symbolizes the body. This is the linen clothes. Removed from the body, but it was covering his head, is a napkin. Well, the ancient word *napkin*, which we translate napkin, meant more than simply what you and I use today, where you speak of a napkin, a dinner napkin, a cocktail napkin, or a cemetery napkin. That seems the limit of a napkin in this twentieth century or when our Bible was translated. But in the ancient days, it meant more than that. The napkin was simply that which is the afterbirth. An afterbirth, if you see the afterbirth, then something

was born. So, he tells you something was born by removing the napkin from the linen clothes. As in birth, you always remove the afterbirth. And that was what they found.

That's all symbolism proving that something was born—and what was born? God was born.

It should also be noted that Neville referred to his own demise occurring, as it did, in his sixties. In a lecture delivered November 21, 1969, titled "Enter the Dream," he said: "In my own case this little garment seemed to begin in 1905, but it was always so. It was always growing into manhood and departing in its sixties. Always appearing, occupied by God, moving towards a certain point and then disappearing."

Neville's remains are interred at a family plot in his native Barbados in Westbury Cemetery in Bridgetown, Saint Michael, also the burial place of his parents, Joseph (1874–1959) and Wilhelmina (1880–1941), his older brother Joseph (1918–1974), and his second wife, Catherine Willa Van Schumus, nicknamed Bill (1907–1975).*

* * *

Returning, where we began, to the teacher's philosophy, the older Neville added a critical caveat to his observations about the causative powers of imagination. The self-revelation of your mind's creative power, and the worldly attainments resulting from it, are mere markers and steppingstones, pieces of evidentiary proof, in the progress

* Neville's death certificate lists cremation as the funerary choice. His body was transferred to Chapel of the Pines Crematory in Los Angeles by Pierce Brothers mortuary. Neville observed in the lecture titled "John the Crown of Scripture," delivered on March 6, 1972: "Cremating the body is only simply quickening the pace that's going to take place if you put yourself into the ground, for there you slowly decay, while the furnace will make it a quick process, but it's the same dust." As referenced, a gravesite and headstone exist for Neville (e.g., see https://www.findagrave.com/memorial/196711330/neville-lancelot-goddard); the burial plot presumably contains his ashes. Cremation as a spiritual and funerary practice was introduced, or reintroduced, to modern Westerners in 1876 by Colonel Henry Steel Olcott, cofounder of the Theosophical Society. See "How the Occult Brought Cremation to America" by Mitch Horowitz, *Huffington Post*, September 9, 2013.

toward realization of your greater nature. Discovery of your true spiritual self, of your identity as the Creator, Neville taught, is the pyramidical capstone of life, of which mentally out-pictured experiences and fulfillments form a catalogue of evidence culminating in the mystical realization of the Promise.

Hence, discovering yourself as the creative force called God is, in Neville's philosophy, the ultimate purpose of existence. Should this purpose go unfulfilled in your present incarnation, he said, you will receive eternal recurrences in order to reach it. This is no cause for existential dread over *Groundhog Day*-like repetitions. Rather, Neville said, the unrealized individual is reborn or reincarnated in young-adult form, possessed of peak physical vigor and vitality, and destined to reexperience life in the same world, with the opportunity to settle struggles left unresolved from the previous incarnation. This, like other aspects of the Promise, is a *sui generis* element of Neville's teaching, which every seeker must personally evaluate.

All of these steps, Neville taught, lead to the individual, still distinct and recognizable, finally rejoining the source of Creation—his or her true Self; a Self that lay forgotten and awaiting rebirth within the cavity of the skull or Golgotha. As the Creator willingly went to sleep within human flesh to experience man, his beloved, this divine Self, forgotten in the descent of crucifixion that begins the life journey, gets remembered, reawakened, and reborn from the base of the skull. The final sign of realization, noted in several of these lectures, is a holy dove descending upon you, completing your full awareness of Self.

Like all of Neville's teachings, these ideals are truly known only through individual experience, a point the teacher constantly urged on listeners. "Test me," he would say. "Do it this very night." In Scripture, we hear about the days of creation but not the *length of time* that a day—or night—occupies. Perhaps in Neville's challenge, a night can be seen in both quotidian and existential terms. Viewed in a certain way, a night may be a lifetime without awareness. This is the ground on which your testing begins.

As Neville spent most of his sixty-seven years attempting to illustrate and live out his philosophy of infinite potential and greater awareness, so are we, in this record of the teacher's final year, invited to dedicate ourselves to the same effort. *Ecce homo.*

—Mitch Horowitz
New York City

* * *

Further Reading:

Magician of the Beautiful: An Introduction to Neville Goddard by Mitch Horowitz

The Ideal Realized: Practical Instructions from Neville Goddard edited and introduced by Mitch Horowitz

Infinite Potential: The Greatest Works of Neville Goddard introduced and edited by Mitch Horowitz

Miracle: The Ideas of Neville Goddard by Mitch Horowitz

Daydream Believer: Unlocking the Ultimate Power of Your Mind by Mitch Horowitz

Lecture I

Faith Is Loyalty to Unseen Reality

January 28, 1972

You should find tonight a very helpful message. We're told that, "Faith is the assurance of things hoped for. The conviction of things not seen." By faith, we understand the world was created by the word of God, so that things which are seen were made out of things which do not appear. If you see it clearly, you will see that faith does not give reality to unseen things. It is loyalty to the unseen reality that gives meaning to the word faith. All things exist, eternity exists, and all things in eternity, independent of creation.

So, on this level, the shadow level, we do not see the reality. We do not see the source, the cause of it all. That's where we are called upon to exercise faith, loyalty, to unseen reality. It really is the abandonment of self. It's an act of self-commission. A man cannot commit himself to what he does not love. And Scriptural faith is faith in God. So, any idea that we have of God, which does not spontaneously call forth out of our heart the feeling of love, is not a true idea of God. For the whole basic matter is that God is love. I speak from experience. I stood in the presence of Infinite Love. And it's man.

So, I do not have the problem that others would have concerning this presence that is Love. I can yield to him instantly, or I know he exists. I know he exists in me. I also know he exists in you, but you may not be aware of it. I can only ask you to believe it; and yield completely to this presence within you, for by him all things are made. And without him was not anything made that is made.

So tonight, we will show you what I have done in the past with great success and how it operates. Now, if I wanted something in this world, and who doesn't, I would formulate an act, which would imply that I have it. And then in my imagination, I would simply, having performed that act, I would *yield completely* to this being within me to execute it. I would fall off into sleep convinced that he heard me, that he saw my act in faith, for we are told in that same 11th chapter that I quoted when I first started, the 11th chapter of the Epistle to the Hebrews, that we must come to God believing that God exists. For unless we believe that he exists, we cannot please him.

So, who would draw near to God must believe that he exists. Without faith, it is impossible to please him. And so, if I took the 13th chapter of Corinthians, Paul's wonderful hymn, *In Praise of Love*, and paraphrased it, "Though, I speak in tongues of men and angels. And though I had the power of prophecy that I understood all mysteries and all knowledge. And though I gave all that I have and gave it away. Though I gave my body to be burned and had not faith, I cannot please him." *I cannot please him without faith*. Because I am not on the surface level of my being, I am not going to do it. I simply yield completely to him having acted. It's an act of self-commission. I perform the act. What act? I act as though I had what I sought. I act as though I heard that you have what you asked of me. I perform an act and then I yield completely to that depth of my own being who is God and allow him from that depth to externalize it for me, as he tells us in the 55th chapter of Isaiah, "Your ways are not my ways. As the heavens are higher than the earth, so are my ways higher than your ways."

So do not ask how it's going to be done. All I have to do is to completely yield to this being within me, for he has ways and means that I, on this level of my being, know not of. I rise then under compulsion. And under this compulsion, I go through a series of events, which will lead up to the fulfillment of that to which I yielded. I assume that it's done. And then I commune with myself and give thanks within me that it is done. And it works in every way, even in the most marvelous things like this, for instance. My friend, he's here tonight. He didn't think he could make it tonight, But I got his letter this week. He said, "Last week, having heard you over the years and having received a hunger from your interpretation of the Scripture, what we are told in the Scripture, in the book of Amos, 'I will send a famine upon the world. It will not be a hunger for bread or a thirst for water but for the hearing of the word of God.'" When that hunger comes upon you, not a thing in this world can satisfy you, but an experience of God.

Now he said, "I am a stockbroker and things have been very, very slow since the bottom of 1970. The market has risen, but people with money will not come into it because, undoubtedly, they were burned prior to this. Yet the market is really healthy today, it's growing and growing and growing. Yet, I must confess things have been slow. I have a wife, I have a daughter who is a minor, I have obligations in life. And yet, in spite of the fact, I should really think of these things first, the hunger for an experience of God supersedes all other hungers. And so, I went home from your meeting and I said to myself, 'I commune with myself'—for you taught me to believe that the self, the depth of my own being is God, that sensible awareness that is God. I said, 'God, you sent this hunger upon me, a hunger for an experience of you. Give me, I said in the 86th Psalm, show me a sign of your favor, just a sign of your favor.' Well, I had a dream, which I did not recall until Friday morning on the way to my office. As is my custom, I turned on your tape. I carry a tape with me and on my way to the office. I turn it on and I listen to that first. Something there clicked within me and the memory returned. And I remembered the dream of the previous night. And the dream was this. I found myself in an ancient world. I knew from the feeling, from the atmosphere, from everything about it, it was an ancient world. And suddenly a youth popped up over a wooden fence and leaned against a post and instantly I knew that he was David. Here is David. I knew he was my son, yet he didn't speak, I didn't speak, but it didn't come until I was driving on the freeway, driving to my office. I have no memory of the previous experiences that you say one must have prior to the coming of David. So, I'm a little bit confused. Was that an apparition? Was that a foreshadowing of the event that must take place?"

I will say to him now, as he in his office, yes, it's the most wonderful foreshadowing. For when it happens, you'll be so stirred, you'll awaken from the state. It won't happen that way. It will happen out of your own skull. Your skull will explode. That's how it happens. The whole thing is contained within man, within the skull of man. And when David comes in the true form, he actually comes after an explosion in your own skull as though the whole thing came to an end. And then when the whole thing settles, he stands before you. And he calls you Father and you know he's your Son and he knows you are his father. And then by this relationship, you know you are God. So, this is the most marvelous adumbration, for sharing in a not altogether conclusive or immediately evident way, but who knows the time it could happen now in the fullest of itself tonight, tomorrow. I am not going to predict when it's actually going to happen. But I do know it will happen. He's been given a sign. Show me a sign of thy favor and the sign came.

So, I tell you tonight's subject is on faith and faith is something that we must all grasp the significance of. For without faith, it is impossible to please him. And if he makes all things, good, bad, and indifferent, and makes them through faith, find out the mystery of faith. Now, faith does not give reality to the unseen things. It is *loyalty to the unseen reality* for all things exist. If you only saw it, everything in eternity exists, man exists. Man is part of the eternal structure of the universe. He doesn't grow out of a worm as our evolution is saying. Evolution is confined to the affairs of man not to the creation of God.

Yes, I take a hoe and then I turn from a hoe, digging the little land with a hoe into a tractor. Then I'll find something far better than the tractor. So, I will swim across the ocean or rather swim across a little river. And then I will find a raft that will take me. Then I'll find a little boat that will take me. Then I'll put a sail on it and that'll do better. Then I will take something more than the sail and I'll find something with steam. Then I'll go beyond the steam and I'll find nuclear energy. And this is simply evolution in the affairs of man. So instead of walking across the continent, I now fly across the continent. That's evolution in the affairs of man, but there is no evolution in the creation of God. It still remains a theory, a marvelous theory, and we are all under compulsion to study it and, all right, to pass our lessons in evolution as though the thing was proven. There isn't one single bit of evidence in the world to support the theory, the hypothesis of evolution, not one. Yet, it's compulsory in all the universities of the world as though it had been proven—in the affairs of man, yes, but not in the creation of God.

Man, as he is, and all things as they are, there are eternal parts of the structure of the universe. Eternity exists and all things in eternity, independent of creation, which was an act of mercy. So, when God said, let us make man in our image, man existed. He didn't say, let us make something and call it man. Let us make man, man existed, in our image. And God became man. There's no way to make him in his image until God actually becomes man. So, God became as we are that we may be as he is. And he's not pretending that he is a man. He has to completely forget that he is God and lose all memories of his power that is God, and take upon himself, the weaknesses and the limitations of man. And in this, he now is pouring himself into his own likeness, which is God. He's raising within himself that which he became, redeeming everything in his world. That is the power that is God.

Now, while we are here as man, you want to be and you name it. You want to be successful in the world of Caesar in dollars and cents, nothing wrong with it. You want to be a successful doctor, successful lawyer—I don't care what it is you want to be, well then, formulating in your mind's eye, what would it be like if it were true? How would you see the world if you were now the man that you would like to be? See it in your mind's eye and then yield yourself completely to the depth of your own being. How do I do that? You fall asleep in the assumption. I dare to assume that I am the man that at the moment reason denied and then fall asleep in that assumption, leaving it completely to the depth of my own being to externalize it in my world. I will wake tomorrow morning under compulsion to do certain things, which I had not formulated, I hadn't determined. I'll find I'll meet the right people. I'll do this. I'll do that. I'll do the other. And it all adds up towards the externalization of my assumption. Just as in his case, he now has a sign of God's favor. The depth of his own being responded to his abandonment. It's a complete self-abandonment. And I can't commit myself to what I do not love. I can't do it. So, if my idea of God does not bring forth within me the sense of love, well then, I have the wrong God.

If I know that he's even full of love, believe me, he is, but the day will come, you'll have the actual experience and you will know that God is all love. I stood in his presence, and God is man. The world says God is not a man, he's an impersonal force, they'll say; he is this; he is that—God is man. The Ancient of Days, without beginning, without end. As is said concerning David, although he was a youth, he seemed to have no beginning, no end. He seemed like the Ancient of Days. And yet he was young, as described in the book of Samuel. Here is this youth, just as described in the book of Samuel, the 16th chapter, the first Samuel. That's the one I saw. That's the one you are going to see. Well, where is he now? He's within you. "He put eternity into the minds of men. Yet so that men cannot find out what he has done from the beginning to the end." That's what he put into the mind of men. That's what he put there, the Father and the Son. God himself entered death's door, the human skull. And he laid down in the grave, the human skull. And he is dreaming the dream of life that man is dreaming.

And in the end, he will awake. And when he awakes, he is the being in whom he ended. The being in whom he awakes. So, you are John, he awakes as you. And because he was a father before he entered you, when he awakes as you, you are a father. And because his son, before he entered you was David, when you awake, your son is David. David of Biblical fame is the son of God. That's the Messiah. That's the Christ. That's the power under wisdom of God. So, within you is that power, within you is that wisdom to do anything that you desire in this world.

So, this is the faith of which I speak. How do I do it? You can sit right here and you go to bed at night. As you're told in the 4th Psalm, "Commune with your own self, upon your bed and be silent." You don't commune with another. You commune with your own self—that's God. For the self of man is God. When you say *I am*, that's God, there is no other God, but you don't see him. Now, he is becoming visible. The darkest night in the world was when God became invisible. He told the story to all of us before we set forth, then he became invisible and took up his residence in us.

He became invisible and in us he is, *I am*—my own wonderful human imagination. That's God. So, I don't see my imagination but I see objects in space. For imagination is the reality that is causing these objects in space. So, I see the fruits of its activity, but I do not see *it* because it is invisible. The day will come, I will see it. I have seen it. He is the Ancient of Days just as described in the seventh chapter, the book of Daniel, and also in the book of Revelation, just as he described: he has no beginning, no end. He is the Ancient of Days. But he's Infinite Love, there's nothing but love. Yet he will wait on us just as swiftly and as indifferently when the willing up is evil as when it is good. For it is he who does all things. He said, I kill, I make alive;

I wound; I heal. I do all these things and none can deliver out of my hand. So, if the willing man is evil, he will execute it; if he is good, he will execute it—because there is no other creator. So, it's entirely up to man, what he imagines. What am I going to imagine? But remember when I imagine, I must imagine, and then completely yield. That is faith. For by faith, we understand that the world was created by the word of God. What word? A spoken word? You're told in the beginning was the word and the word was with God and the word was God; was God himself and his son—and his son is David. I have found in David, a man after my own heart, who will do all my will, any will, good, bad, or indifferent, is that power in you for he is defined in Scripture as the power of God and the wisdom of God.

So, the power and the wisdom to create anything in this world are housed within man. That is David. When man comes to the end of the journey, there's an explosion within his head and then that power and that wisdom of God comes out personified as that eternal youth, who is his son. His son is David. And you are the one who awakes and you are the Lord. The Lord called Jesus. So, who is Jesus? An eternal question. I read in the morning's paper, rather yesterday morning's paper, that the Archbishop of Canterbury spoke, the first Archbishop ever to speak at St. Patrick's in New York City. And the Cardinal introduced him. He had a standing ovation, they turned the crowds away. The Cathedral was filled to capacity. And this Archbishop of Canterbury, he spoke to the crowd and he went up to Riverside Church and he spoke there. He had seen in the interval, he saw *Jesus [Christ] Superstar*; well, I haven't seen the play. And he commented on it. He didn't quite describe it. He said, at intervals, it comes close to a certain

Christian faith. There are certain passages in it he thought offensive, but they did not say who is Jesus. Neither did he, the archbishop; he didn't say, who is Jesus?

Who is Jesus? I'll tell you. *Jesus is the man in whom the will of God is fulfilled.* And that will be true of every child born of a woman. Jesus is the man who accomplishes the work that his father gave him to do. And when he accomplishes that work, *he is his Father.* Man matures when he becomes his own father. And the day will come, everyone will awake, and he will be the Father. And that is when he fulfills the will of God as we are told in Jeremiah, the 23rd chapter. The word is wrongly translated, anger. "The anger of the Lord will not turn back." That word, anger means breathing forcefully, a forceful breath. It doesn't have to be an angry breath because you're breathing forcefully. The word *breath* and the word *spirit* are the same in both Hebrew and Greek. So, the spirit of the Lord will not turn back until it has executed and accomplished the intents of my mind. In the latter days, you'll understand it clearly.

From the very end, you'll understand, he will not turn back because he has a purpose. The purpose is to transform man into God. As God, not something just to reflect him, but *as God.* So, you came down, you are the Gods that came down. You are the *Elohim.* You've been taught to believe you're a worm. You came out of the swamp and then suddenly you became a tadpole and you became something else. And finally, you find yourself a man—forget it. You are the Gods who came down from heaven and assume the restriction, the limitation of man, this is the limit of contraction and you assumed it. And you are going to fulfill a definite purpose in man. While you walk the earth as man that predetermined plan will erupt within you. And the whole thing will unfold within you, beginning with the resurrection. The resurrection did not take place in the Near East in some little place where they're looking for it now. It takes place in man. Man is where God is buried. The Holy Sepulcher is the skull of man. It's not in the

Near East. The Bethlehem that they are talking about is in the skull of man. Zion, the holy place, where he dwells—that's the skull of man. And the whole drama unfolds within man.

And man awakens within himself to find himself completely sealed within his skull. And he comes out like a child being born out of his own skull. And then a few months later comes an explosion in his skull and that compartment that contains the Son of God, who in his will, who in his wisdom, releases the Son. You would not let my soul remain in hell, said he, in the 16th Psalm. So, he brings him up. He resurrects his Son and the Son is David. And David, looking at the Father, and the Father for the first time knows who he is, memory returns. And the Son was the one who revealed him to himself.

So, the whole drama unfolds within man. And the whole thing is contained within the skull of man; has nothing to do with anything on the outside. They're looking in vain, all the archaeologists, and they bring back all this nonsense. I was on TV one night with one archaeologist and then a Baptist minister and a Seventh Day Adventist minister. And here I am, all these groups around me, and this man brought a piece of cloth. And he said this is taken from the tomb of Christ. I said are you kidding? No, he was sincere, he was very serious. He's an archaeologist. This is where, in some strange way, light has impressed upon it, this cloth, the image of Jesus. I said you are an archaeologist. And he was brought there with a Seventh Day Adventist and here's the other fellow, he is a Baptist, and I have no degrees. None of these things that these fellows have. I said to the archaeologist, tell me, do you look like that picture? He said, no, that's the picture of Christ. But don't you know Scripture? It does not yet appear, what we shall be. But we know that when he appears, we shall be like him and shall see him as he is. Do you look like him? You'll never see Christ save you'll see him in yourself. You are the Lord, Jesus Christ. The Baptist then said you've just taken from me 2,000 years of Christianity. I said I can take it from you, I should. Because if it's true, I can't take it from you. And if I have taken it from you, well, then it's good I've taken it from you. He didn't like that.

All this nonsense, this piece of cloth, mind you—well that's what our great writer said, Mark Twain. He went across Europe. Now, as he traveled, they brought pieces of cloth. This was taken from his robe and this, the piece of wood that was taken from his cross. He said, if you took all the wood together, it could build a huge house. And that was the cross he bore on his shoulder on the way to Golgotha. Take all the little pieces of cloth together. They could actually clothe an army, and people fall for it. Can you imagine that? They're looking at the holy cloth, holy piece of wood. There is nothing outside of man. The whole drama takes place within man. He has nothing to do with anything outside. You're living in a world of shadows and the drama is within.

So, let us now get back to this simple approach of faith. Do you know what you want either for yourself or for another? Construct a scene which would imply the fulfillment of your dream; just construct it. Enter into it just as though it were true. Feel what it would feel like if it were true. And give thanks to the one who is going to execute it. It's your own being, I grant you, but he is the depth of your own being. He is the Father. You haven't yet found him, but he is the Father. And you are now on the surface of your being, so fall asleep in the conviction that things are as you desire them to be in confidence that he will execute it. I use the word *he*, it's yourself. But for clarity's sake, I say he, because you're not aware of him as yet. You will be one day. Everyone will be aware of their being. And because that being has one son and that one son is the son of all, *we* are one. There's only one. There aren't millions of gods, only one God; but the one God is made up of brotherhood and we are the brothers, raising ourselves to the level of the one God. And that one God has one son and the son is David. And I've been sent to tell you this and tell you I will and must. If only a few hear it, what does it matter? You hear it with conviction because I tell you the truth; they will laugh.

I am not here to set up some little "ism." I am not here to speculate and try to set up some little philosophical setup that may work. No, I want no church, no "ism." Just to tell you who you are. And you will tell it to others and others will tell it because, in the end, you're going to prove it to be true. You can't rub it out because it is true. All that I have told you is true. I'm not speculating. I'm not theorizing. I stood in the presence of the Infinite Being and Infinite Love. And he embraced me. And he sent me, after he embraced me. Therefore, love embraced me. Therefore, guided by love. We became one body. As we are told in Scripture, he who is united in the Lord becomes one spirit with him. So, in the end, there's only one body, one spirit, one Lord, one God and Father of all, who is above all, through all, and in all. So don't go looking for him in any so-called holy place in the world. People are misled morning, noon, and night by so-called holy men—forget it. Man comes to you telling you he is a holy person, turn around, and start running.

All these holy fellows, they just simply meet you and meet another crowd, and next thing they do, they run to the bank. What was in your pocket? Just pick that one fellow here, he is flying off to Switzerland. He was in Spain after having collected a fortune. They found $300,000 on him. And he was at the Maharishi that came up through this country; it wasn't the Maharishi, it was his secretary running off to Switzerland where you'll put it into your Swiss bank. And all the people fall for it, morning, noon, and night. And so, if you're taken over, you hate to hear it because people hate to know that others know they were beguiled. And so those who gave their fortunes to him, $500 to teach them how to meditate, of all the nonsense in the world. Teach you how to meditate? It's just a simple, simple thing. You don't meditate on your navel. You don't meditate on any of these things whatsoever. You know what you want. What would the feeling be like if it were true? What would it be like? Assume the feeling of the wish fulfilled. Well, anyone can do that. A child can do that. What would it be like if it were true? That's meditating. Now yield completely and the being within you will take that and externalize it for you.

Meditating on your kundalini and all this nonsense. It hasn't a thing to do with it. And going into so-called diet. Diets will not commit you or commend you to God. He gave you a palette, didn't he? Well then, exercise the palette, too. And so, I'm going to go on a certain diet. A friend of mine went on the diet of things that you should only feed parrots, but she isn't a parrot. Eating pumpkin seeds, eating all these things. If you really enjoy them. But don't tell me that you really enjoy them. Of course, you could acquire a taste for anything. I don't. So, you can't. But exercise that God-given gift: it's a palette, and simply enjoy it.

So, to come down to the night's message on faith. By faith, the worlds were created by the word of God. Faith does not give reality to the unseen things. *Faith is loyalty to unseen reality.* For this thing exists. All things exist. I tell you of my own experience that the entire world that is unseen to this world exists now, it actually exists, not out there beyond the stars, right here. It's all existing right here. And the day will come that you will actually awake and you'll be able to step into these unnumbered sections of time.

A thousand years ago has not passed away. And two thousand years from now is not something that is going to suddenly form itself, *it is now.* And you are simply in a section of time. And the day will come when you'll be able to move into any section of time. All these things exist now. And the purpose of it all is simply to awaken. And when you awaken, who are you? You are the author of it all. You are God, God the creator. And God, the creator is a Father. And the Father-Son is simply the sum total of all the experiences of humanity, fused into a single being and that single being personified is David. There is no other Christ. David is the Christ. The anointed. Listen to these words in the 89th Psalm, "I have found David." These are the words of the Lord speaking. "I have found David. With my holy oil

I have anointed him." The anointed one is the Messiah. That's what the word Messiah means. And Messiah means the same as Christ; it's the identical meaning. Now go down a few verses and come to these: "He shall cry unto me." That's future. What I just quoted is an accomplished fact. "I have found David. With my holy oil, I have anointed him." That's done. Now, "He shall cry onto me, thou art my Father, my God, and the rock of my salvation." That's future. It will happen to everyone, but the whole thing has already been accomplished.

Now it's completely contained within the skull of man. That's where the whole drama is unfolding. And when it unfolds, you are God the Father and your son is David. If the whole vast world rose in opposition because they were taught differently, it will make no difference to me whatsoever. They have accepted some mis-concept of the great story, as told in Scripture. The New Testament only interprets the Old. The Old is the foundation. The New interprets the Old. Christianity is the fulfillment of Judaism. But Judaism is the foundation, that is the tree. And Christianity is the fruit of that tree. And so, to bring something else into it is stupid. Where in the Old, which is the tree, it is stated who is the son of God, and Scripture cannot be broken. And who is the one who is anointed with the holy oil of God? Is it not David? Rise and anoint him. This is he.

"And then the spirit of God came upon him mightily, from that day forward, never lost a battle. For I have found in David, the son of Jesse, a man after my own heart." And Jesse means Jehovah exists. Everyone one day will know he is the Father of David, therefore, he is the Jehovah who exists. That is what Scripture is teaching. It is not secular history. Until a man stops looking at it as secular history, he is not going to understand the Scripture. But to come back to our wonderful approach tonight. You want a better job? You want more money? You want this, you want that? Don't be ashamed of it. Who gave you the urge? Your Father did. You have the desire. It came from the depth of your own being so he can execute it. He only asks you to have faith. Faith in what? Faith in him, have faith in God. All right, where is he? He's my own wonderful human imagination. I cannot see the fulfillment now, but he will do it, for now assume that I am already the man that I want to be and yield completely to that assumption and fall asleep, just completely fall asleep and completely forget it.

A lady who is here tonight, she called me up on the phone here just a few days ago and asked something of me. I will not tell you, it's too personal. But she asked me to please pray for a certain thing. It's so simple. I sat in my chair after I spoke to her on the phone and heard her tell me, but she came back tonight and told me. Yet it has happened. She is here, she's seated here tonight, drove all the way from San Bernardino to tell me the story. And it simply worked. What did I do? It didn't cost me anything. Are we not told in the 55th chapter of Isaiah, "come buy wine, buy milk, without money"—cost you nothing. What does it cost anyone to have faith in God? Why put a price on it? Why charge anyone? It costs nothing.

Lecture II

What Is Man?

January 31, 1972

There's a little poem by Robert Penn Warren, just take the last line of it. Speaking of the Lord, he said, "He stared into the dark pit of self, whence all had sprung./ He said: *What is man that I should be mindful of him!*"* What is man? It is in you, the individual that the great things happen, the kingdom of God comes to you in you. The Davidic tradition has its root and its fulfillment in you. The whole is actually contained within the individual. We think this whole vast world is so real. Let me tell you that to believe that the visible kingdom is unreal and that the invisible kingdom is real is the supreme act of faith. To this faith, the kingdom of this world has already become the kingdom of our Lord and of his Christ. The terms Christ, messiah, and anointed are interchangeable terms.

When you read them in the Bible, they're all interchangeable. They're all synonyms for the savior. Christ is called the Son of God, so is

* Neville is quoting from "Interjection #5: Solipsism and Theology" published in *Or Else: Poem/Poems 1968–1971* by Robert Penn Warren (Random House, 1974).

the anointed, the son of God. And so is the Messiah. It means the same thing. So let us see now who this Messiah is and what he is and where he is. I tell you he is in you. So, when Paul tells us, do you not realize that Jesus Christ is in you? Unless of course, you fail to meet the test. He separates Jesus from the Christ. He speaks of Jesus as the Lord, but no one can say Jesus is Lord, except by the Holy Spirit. He speaks of Jesus as the Lord and then Christ as another. So, in the book of Revelations, you speak of the Lord and of his Christ to tell you that he is the Father.

You can read that in Scripture, but how are you going to know that Jesus is the Father? He tells you, "I am the Father; who sees me, sees the Father." If he's a father, he has a son. At least he has a child. Let us turn to the book of Acts. You'll find this in the fourth chapter. "Oh, sovereign God who made the heaven and the earth and the seas and all within them, who by the mouth of our Father David, thy servant did say, why do the nation's rage? And why do the people imagine vain things against the Lord and his anointed?" *Against the Lord and his anointed.* Now in the King James Version of the Bible, that word *anointed* is translated as it should be, *Christ.* For the Greek is *Christos,* "against the Lord and his Christ," not the Lord, Jesus Christ, but the Lord Jesus and his Christ, his son, the word translated, *servant,* thy servant, David. The Greek poet means *son.*

As told us in the second Psalm, for he is quoting now the second Psalm, what I've just quoted is from the second Psalm. He attributes the author of the Psalm, at least the one who wrote it, to David. He says David is the author of the Psalm. Now, here we find in the 18th Psalm, one also says that David is the author. "Great triumph you give to your king and show steadfast love to your anointed, to David and his descendants forever." The anointed is the Christ. He is the Messiah. He is the son of God. Now let us turn to this statement, concerning the root, who is going to open the Bible, who is going to give it meaning? And John began to cry, as we are told in the fifth chapter of Revelations, "He saw the book, but it was sealed with seven seals.

And the wise one asked, who can open the book? Who can break the seal?" When no one in heaven or on earth, or below the earth, could answer that he could, John began to weep and then this wise one said to him, "Weep not. Know there is one. One from the lion of the tribe of Judah, the root of David. He has conquered. He can open the book and its seals."

Now, who is the root of David? Go to the end of the book, "And Jesus said to the angel, say unto John, I am the root and the offspring of David, the bright morning star." He is the root. He's the father of David. He's also the offspring. So, the grandfather and the grandson are one and the same being. "I am the root and the offspring of David." David remains the son of God.

Then what is this offspring that comes out of you? He's buried in you. One day you're going to experience it. Out of your own being will come, not another, will come you. And you will know you are the father of David because you'll see him and he'll call you father. And you will know he's your son. And there'll be no uncertainty as to this relationship. It's all buried in man. So, "What is man that I should be mindful of him?" These are not the words of the Scripture. These are the words of the poet. For the words in Scripture, the Psalmist is asking the question, "What is man that thou art mindful of him?" But the poet turned it around and said to put words in the mouth of the Lord, who said, "Why should I be mindful of man?" Because the whole is contained in man, this whole venture is already done. It's all in man. The kingdom of the world has already become the kingdom of our Lord and of his Christ because it has been accomplished and it's being accomplished in the individual, one after the other.

It has been fulfilled in me. All that is said in the Scripture, I have actually experienced it. The finding of David, everything said in that book, I have actually experienced in a spiritual sense, but when it came to me, it was just like this room, just as real. It was a cubic reality. There's not a thing, I would say, gossamer about it, the whole thing was real. One step after the other unfolds itself within the individual, that's who you are. Now, it came after this one could break the seal. So, he gives meaning to Scripture. Scripture began to take on a meaning, after the lion of the tribe of Judah who had conquered, who was the root of David, discovered David, for only the son can reveal the Father. No one knows who the Son is except the Father. And no one knows who the Father is except the Son and anyone to whom the Son chooses to reveal him. So, until David comes, you've been taught to believe that Jesus is the son of God. You have been taught to believe that Jesus Christ is like an extra title. That Christ is like a surname, Jesus Christ. It isn't so at all. It is the Lord Jesus and his Christ, who is the son of God, for Christ is the son of God. And the son of God is David. That Davidic tradition is buried in you individually. And you're going to fulfill it to the very end. So, all the kingdoms of the earth will vanish. They'll leave not a trace behind them, but this everlasting divine history is all contained within you and you are going to fulfill that history of salvation. Every jot of it, not one little thing will you miss. And then you will know why God is mindful of man, because the whole secret of God is contained within man. God himself is buried in man.

In the Scripture, he is called, in the Old Testament, Jehovah; in the New he is called Jesus. But this is the same being buried in man. And his son is with him. The whole drama is a relationship between father and son. And one day you will find him. If the whole vast world rose in opposition, it would make no difference to me, for I am speaking from experience, I am not theorizing. I am not speculating. I'm telling you exactly what I have experienced. And the day will come that that which is now imprisoned within you after you are born from above, this body of yours will be split in two, from top to bottom. And the Spirit that has been held captive through the ages will be set free. And when he's set free, he ascends like a fiery serpent. So, the ancient teachers in the second century of the Christian world, they spoke of this being, the Christ in man, as the suffering serpent and also the serpent in the wilderness. You will find it in the work of the second century. That serpent in the wilderness that was called a savior. One looked upon it, he was saved. You don't look upon it, you experience it. And all that is now taking place here.

When he opened the eyes of the blind, he said, what do you see? He said, "I see men, but they look like trees walking." *I see men, but they look like trees walking.* That's a perfect vision. If you saw a man, as you see them on a chart minus the skin and saw all the great nerve centers and all the nerves of the body and all the blood vessels, all the veins and all the arteries, all anchored in the brain and all turned down, you'd see an inverted tree. It looks just like a tree but inverted. Now, the day will come when it's going to be turned up. And the root will remain the same, it's the brain, but then the tree grows up. It's now turned down into generation; it will be turned around into regeneration.

I recall my vision of maybe twelve years ago, that man is now gone from this world. He was second in the Labour Party when [Clement] Attlee (1883–1967) was prime minister. And I saw him in this wonderful vision one night. I came with a group of men, all turned up. They were like human stags, antlers reaching up almost to the sky, growing out of the brain. And he took a branch and placed it on his head, thinking it would give him the same power that they enjoyed. And he ran and jumped and fell flat on his face. Went back again, he couldn't quite understand how they could cross a chasm with no difficulty whatsoever. There was not a thing in the world beyond their power to bring it captive to them. They could cross the ocean without any difficulty. As this thing grew, with enormous power. And every time he tried it, he failed. He was trying to do what everyone in the world tries to do, *to do it from without.* All the outer ceremonies, all the outer rituals, all the outer degrees that men give each other—it doesn't work that way at all. It all comes from within because the whole thing is within. And when man is turned around by a complete splitting of the temple, for the curtain of the temple is torn in two from top to bottom, and at the base of your spine, you're going to see a golden, pulsing liquid light. And as you see it, you're going to know that you are it. You're actually looking at yourself and yet it is formless and you fuse with it, and then you become that fiery serpent, and up you go into the rain and it vibrates like thunder. Then you are completely turned around. The energies that went down into generation are now turned up into regeneration.

I came through the Palace Hotel lobby soon after that experience. I had not mentioned it to my audience in San Francisco. An artist, a very great artist, was sitting in the lobby, she was waiting for me. I had an appointment. And so, I came through the lobby. As I came through, she was writing and scratching like mad on a piece of paper. And there she was and she held her hand and asked me not to talk to her, not yet. And she kept on making a quick sketch and then she gave me the sketch and she had drawn me. And coming out of my head were the antlers. She said, "Neville, they went beyond the ceiling." It's a three-story ceiling in the lobby of the Palace. "You came to the door and nothing stopped it. You came right through. There was no obstruction, and yet I could not stop but see. I saw these things coming out of your head like antlers going through the ceiling and not a thing could stop it." Well, I had the experience. I hadn't told it because if you tell these things, they think the man is insane. Why go and spend your money listening to it? Yet all these things are true. Here is the story of the 22nd chapter of Isaiah. He's now going to speak of the one who can break the seal. And in this chapter, you'll read it in the 22nd and 23rd verses of the 22nd chapter of Isaiah, and here he speaks of the root of David. He speaks of this one who will now receive a peg. He's going to fasten him sure, a secure fastening. He's going to hang the key of David on his shoulder. And that one will rule for a time. He will rule as God. Then the peg will break and all the burdens of

Israel will fall from his shoulder, but he will have that burden to carry for a while.

And then this night I found a room, not quite as large as this, but square with one door leading into it. And I am seated on the floor talking to twelve men. I am discussing the word of God and explaining the word of God. Suddenly one of the twelve jumps up quickly and leaves the room. And I knew exactly what he is going to do. I knew he was going to reveal what he had heard. But I'm speaking of a different kingdom, not the kingdom of this world. I am talking of the kingdom of God, implying, naturally, in that you're king. It's a kingdom, it's a realm, and you are king. He leaves quickly and he had no sooner gone through the door than a handsome man about 6' 6" entered, beautifully arrayed in the finest clothes. All the purples and all the lovely things of the period of, say, the first century. He comes through the door and he walks like a soldier, straight as an arrow, and he goes to the extreme end. He turns just like a soldier at a right angle, walks to the extreme end again, the same military turn. And he walks to the center and then he comes down, like it's here, and he stops in front of me. But as he entered, he was such an important character that the thirteen of us or rather, the twelve now because one was gone, we stood up and stood at attention as he entered. He was that important a figure. He came in front of me and as he did so his attendant handed him a mallet and then a peg and then he hammered the peg into my shoulder, blow after blow. It wasn't painful, but every blow I could feel, but it wasn't painful. Then he took a very sharp instrument that the attendant handed him and with one quick sweep he severed my sleeve. And then he took the end of it and he pulled it this way and discarded it. It was a beautiful baby blue color. I recall looking at it and seeing how altogether lovely it was, what fine material. And then he stretched his hands out and formed the cross, just like this. Then he embraced me. Then he kissed me on the right side of my neck and I in turn, kissed him on the left side, I mean on the right side of his neck, and then the whole scene dissolved and there's the fulfillment of the Scripture. Everyone is going to have it. Everyone will have the opportunity to exercise that power, to exercise that authority. All will have it because the whole drama is contained within the individual.

I'm not speaking of you in the plural. I'm speaking of you in the singular. That's why I say, he is mindful of you because his whole secret is contained in you. And when the whole thing is unfolded, you are God the father. And because he is a father, there is a son and his son is David and David calls you father. That is the story, and everyone is going to have it. So why should I be constantly concerned about the realm that really is unreal? I've seen it, that ancient history as the world teaches its ancient history, it isn't secular history, it is divine history and it is forever. For David and his descendants forever. Now he is the anointed. He shows steadfast love to his anointed, to David and his descendants forever. So, I am the root and the offspring of David.

The root is the graft. You take a bud from the Tree of Life and you simply graft it onto the Tree of Knowledge. When the time for it to bear comes, it will bear the fruit, not of the Tree of Knowledge. It will bear the fruit of the Tree of Life. That's what a graft does. So, you graft a tree, you find a good stump, a good tree, a solid tree. And from a tree of your choice, you take a good bud, a good graft, and you implant it into that tree. And then in time it grows, and it bears, and you watch it. It's not going to bear the fruit of the tree on which it is grafted. It's going to bear the fruit of the tree from which it was taken. And we are all taken from the Tree of Life. That's Jesus. I am the resurrection and the life.

And here is the sacrifice, the whole tree. And we are now grafted with the Tree of Life. We do not differ in any respect from the parent tree when we grow. It's the same strength, the same power, the same wisdom, the same everything that the parent tree has. If you've ever seen a graft, my mother had wonderful roses. She was passionately fond of roses, and I can see my mother now grafting. That was the one job she wanted to do for herself. The gardeners would clean the yard they would dig and they'd fertilize, they'd water. When it came to grafting, that was mother's choice. And she wanted to do her own grafts. She selected the graft. She selected a strong tree that would bear it. And when that graft took and began to bear the rose, it was the rose of the tree from which she took the graft.

So, you've been grafted, as you've been told in the book of James. Received with meekness the implanted word, which is able to save yourselves. So no longer will you be eating of the Tree of Knowledge, which is turned down into generation. When it's completely taken and the time is right for it to bear, you're going to bear the same fruit as that which is recorded in the gospels concerning Jesus Christ. So, when the arm was unveiled, as you're told in the 52nd chapter of Isaiah, "To whom has the arm of the Lord been revealed? Who will believe our report?" You have to take it on faith. If a man goes into the desert, the wilderness, for forty days and forty nights, and he is alone and he's tempted, and then the evangelists write the temptations down in detail, how would they know unless they were told? How on earth would they know unless they were told by the one who had the experience? How would anyone know the experience of the descending dove unless told? Where it's actually told in the book of Mark, the earliest gospel, that it was seen by him alone. No one saw or experienced it but the one who had the experience. So, he had to tell it. I have told the experience. And these things happen over a period of time. And these things reveal to you who you are. I could tell you from now to the ends of time that you are God. I could tell you that you are the father of David. But I can't really convince you. You have to have the experience and the experience you will have. Christ is a witness to the truth of God. I am a witness to the truth of Christ, for Christ is the anointed. And the anointed is David. I have found David with my holy oil. I have anointed him. Where is the Christ child? Where is the Christ youth? Forever and forever, he plays that part. And one day when you awake, you are the Lord because you are the father of David. You'll never know you are the Lord unless David calls you father. And when he calls you father, there is no uncertainty as to the relationship. It's like memory returning. And the whole thing comes back. So, the memory of the bud was so great it produced the parent stock. The whole thing came back. If God is a father, and then I take from that tree, which is a father, and implant it upon this that is barren, when that bud takes and it grows, I must be a father. I must bear the same flower, the same fruit, that the tree brought from which I took the graft. So, we are all engrafted with the word of God. And all will bear this fruit of God.

And then you enter an entirely different world, clothed differently, for flesh and blood cannot inherit the kingdom of God. These bodies cannot function in that world. It's an entirely different body. And I call that body *heaven* for wherever you are, clothed in that body, everything is perfect. You could pass through hell. It would cease to be hell while you walk through. It would be transformed in harmony with the perfection that springs within you. You couldn't go anyplace and see anything but perfection because you are perfect. Your body is perfect. It's immortal. It never vanishes. It never withers. It's the immortal you. And one day you will see it. It will come out. When you are clothed in it, you feel as though you are clothed in fire and air, and you do not raise a finger to transform anyone. In your presence, they are transformed. If they're blind, you do nothing. You show no compassion. You do nothing. The blind sees in your presence. The deaf hears. The one without the arm, the arm comes back, and fits the socket. The one without a foot, the foot comes back, and fits the socket. And wherever you go, everything is made perfect.

Not a thing can die in your presence because you are the God of the living. You are the resurrection and the life. And that's your future. That's your destiny. I will be long gone but you'll be telling the story.

And those after you will get it from you and they'll tell the story and they cannot deny it because time will prove it to be true. Or you can deny it now in words, but you can't deny it in Scripture. Bring me the Bible, if you think you know the Bible, let us open the Bible together, and I will confirm everything I've told you in Scripture. It's all there, but man has been, well, taught a strange lesson. And he's completely confused these characters. And now he sticks one on the outside and worships it. Don't do it. As in the very end, they fell before him. He said rise, you're a man. I'm a man just like you. You wanted no worship because in the end, when you awake, you are God.

There is only God in the world and his son. His son is his will. He does all the father's will. And so, the day will come, you will know that he is the witness to the truth of God. And you'll also know that you are the witness to the truth of the son because you saw the son and you know he does exist. He has been resurrected. And his name is David; not a David, *the* David, the only David. And no one has to tell you until he stands before you. And it's absolutely as I've told you, just as I've described it.

Tonight, if you are here for the first time and you expected something entirely different, then let me give you a short portion of the Law. You are living in a world that really is a psychological world. All things take place in the imagination of man—all things. And so, because they do take place there, let them take place there first before you expect to see them on the outside. So, assume that you are the man that you would like to be, believe that you are, try to catch all the feelings that would be yours if they were true. Give it all the tones and the feeling of reality. And then sleep. Go sound asleep in that assumption that you are already the one that you want to be. Try that, and I assure you from my own experience, what you have assumed that you are, you'll become. You have already become what you are because you want to assume that you are it. Everything in the world is just like that. It's all imagination and all that you behold, although it appears without, really is within, in your own wonderful human imagination of which this world of mortality is but a shadow.

Bring the whole thing into this world. So, you lose it—you can repeat it for the reality never disappears. This is the shadow world. You bring it back by contemplating the state and assuming the state once again and feeling that you are now what you want to be. And bring it right back into your world. Man thinks it's gone and gone for good. No, the eternal forms are forever. They never disappear. One day you're going to have this experience. You will see man differently. You will see everything differently. And when you see it, and you are in control of your own being, you're going to see the whole vast world is dead, actually dead. And you are the living reality of the world. Everything round about you is frozen as though it's made of clay. And you will know it because once you see it and the whole thing is still, time stands still. Then you'll release that activity within you that you froze and everything will be animated and continue to fulfill its purpose. And then you'll realize where the animation was, it was all in you. The cause of it all, was all in you.

So, he was perfectly right when he changed the little words around, I mean, the poet that I quoted in the beginning. He stared into the "dark pit of self, whence all had sprung." For that's where it springs, it comes out of the self. But now, men came out, they're all dead, and he buried himself and he and his son are one. So, he buried the reality in man. And man became a living being. And by his presence, he turned death into sleep. And then he dreams the dream of life. And this is the dream of life. The day will come and the dream will come to an end. When it comes to an end, you will awake as the dreamer and the dreamer is God.

It seems sacrilegious, doesn't it? But I am telling the truth. You're not a little worm, you never were a little worm. You came down from heaven and only he can ascend into heaven who came down from heaven. No one has ever ascended who did not descend. You descended. Read Scripture carefully and you'll see the preexistence of the one spoken of in Scripture as Jesus and the son Christ. Read the 17th chapter of the book of John: "Return unto me the glory that was mine before that the world was." He's asking for the return of a glory he held with the father before that the world was. "Father, I've accomplished the work thou gavest me to do. Now glorify thou me with thine own self, with that glory which I held with thee before that the world was." Is that preexistence? In this world, his splendor was set aside; he now asked for the return of that splendor for he's done the work that he came to do and having finished it, he's returning and only he could ascend who descended.

And so, if you have not descended, you can't ascend. No one has ever ascended but he who descended. But I am telling you, you did descend. We all came down together. One man fell carrying all. He chose us in him before the foundation of the world. And if one fell, then we all in him fell. One was crucified, all were crucified. So, we are the ones who hang upon the tree. Are we not told in Acts, "And they're hanging him upon a tree"? Now we are told in Deuteronomy, "Cursed be everyone who hangs upon a tree." And then in Galatians, "He took upon himself a curse because he was hanging upon a tree." Well, this is the perfect tree. It is a perfect tree. "And when the eye was open, he saw men like trees walking." This is where Christ is hanging. And he's buried in everyone until you awake. And when you awake, you are the Lord and the father of Christ. You are the Jesus spoken of, and you have a son and his name is David. He is the Christ. So here, these are the trees on which Christ is crucified. The Cosmic Christ because he became humanity. Not one little man but humanity. Every child born of a woman is God crucified. That's where the drama begins. It begins at Golgotha. That's when God became man. And then man becomes God at Bethlehem. Man reverses that. He thinks the crucifixion comes last. No, it begins the drama. Paul said, "I have been crucified in Christ, nevertheless, I live, yet not I, Christ lives in me and the life I now live in the flesh, I live by faith in the Son of God who loved me and gave himself for me."

So, I have been crucified with Christ. That's what he said. Now, he who is united with the Lord becomes one spirit with him. And if I have been united with the Lord in a death like his, I shall certainly be united with him in a resurrection like his. So, the resurrection is taking place morning, noon, and night in the world, but not everyone is called to tell it. Many a one goes this night to sleep, not to wake here anymore, who possibly had the experience, but never had the urge to tell it. But I was called. I was embraced by the risen Lord and sent. Therefore, I have to tell it. And tell it I must and I will. But I'm telling it as I've experienced it. Not as teachers tell it today; I cannot go along with that. I was raised with that but then I found it wasn't true.

And then when I had the experience, found confirmation for the experience in Scripture, and there it is. Great triumphs he gives to his king and then he speaks of the steadfast love. He shows steadfast love to his anointed, then names it to David and his descendants forever, for you are coming out of humanity. That which is buried in you is coming out of humanity. And who is it? The father and son. I am the root and the offspring that is now the father of David, is the root of David, and the offspring of David, is the grandson of that father. But they are one. He said, I am the father of David, called it root, I am the root—and I am also the offspring. So, I am the fruit that is born by reason of being grafted unto humanity.

And it comes out and you are that being. You are the Lord or the root of David, for David calls you father. And no loss of identity, may I tell you. No. Although there's only one body, one spirit, one hope, one Lord, one faith, one baptism, one God and Father of all; still in spite of that oneness there is no loss of identity. We are one body, yes—and yet you are individualized and you will be individualized forever and forever. But clothed in your glorious body. I'll know you. But this will be like a dream. For we have gone through the experience of the dream of life. We won't carry it with us. We will leave it behind. It was essential to the work that the father had planned for all. So, we fell—it's told us in the 82nd Psalm, "I say you are gods"—meaning you—"all of you, sons of the most high, nevertheless, you will die like men and fall as one man, O ye, princes." And so, we all fell. One man fell and became fragmented. And we are the fragmented being. Now, we're being gathered together one by one. He calls us, calls us back into the one body, the one spirit. So, you'll see why God is mindful of you. You are precious in his sight. Not one can be lost. Couldn't lose one because then something would be missing in the body of God. And he could not allow one to be missing. Not one will be lost, not one in all my holy mountain said the prophet. So, take it home and dwell upon it. You'll find that the things you need tonight badly in the world of Caesar, they'll come. Your father knows what you need. You dwell upon the spiritual things and the earthly things will come. They'll all come.

You don't have to do anything on the outside. Not a thing on the outside, no special diet, no special ceremonies, rituals. My daughter works for Channel 28. And she told me to look at something last night, which I did. And here are all these, they call themselves followers of Krishna, all dressed up in their robes, all like nightgowns of ladies. The hair is completely shaved with a little pigtail coming out of the skull and then paint right down the nose and paint across the forehead and [David] Susskind (1920–1987) was the commentator. And he interviewed them and suddenly they all jumped up and started chanting Krishna, Krishna, Krishna. Now they say they have a master. They show the picture of the master. They follow the master blindly. And it's all for Krishna. He said, why all the dress, you are so conspicuous when you walk the streets dressed as women and all your robes, and then you walk down Fifth Avenue and you go bowing to people, they don't know who you are, you frighten them, you scare them. So, that is something on the outside. And they think they're really doing a great job. But he had them on for a little over an hour. It was amusing. They're strict vegetarians. That's all right, but that's not going to get them into heaven.

Lecture III

Feel After Him

day unknown, February 1972

New ideas require many reiterations and restatements before they become part of the generally accepted currency of thought. The idea that I've been trying to get over since I started back in 1938 is still new. It comes as a shock to anyone who hears it. And even after you've heard it for years and years, and think you're living by it, I've discovered that one is not really living by it. It has not yet become a part of their thinking. And it is that *imagining creates reality.*

I say this because I identify imagining with *God in action.* To me, *man is all imagination* and God is man and exists in us and we in him. The eternal body of man is the imagination. And that is God himself. If by God, I mean the creator of the universe, the maker and the master of the whole vast universe and I identify that creator with the human imagination, *then man should be more careful as to what he's imagining.* So, I can give lip service to the statement *imagining creates reality.* And yet if I'm observant in the course of a day, if I observe what I'm imagining, I would find unnumbered moments in my life, in one twenty-four hours or other, the waking eighteen, where I am imagining things I do not wish to experience.

If I really believe that imagining creates reality, I would be more careful, more concerned about what I'm imagining. So, I will give it lip service and say imagining creates reality and go blindly on imagining anything other than what I want to create, beginning with the morning paper and reacting to things that you do not know, whether they be true, they could be planted by some press agent, planted by some lobbyists. You do not know. And here we react as we read and then we go through life in just twenty-four hours and find that most of the twenty-four hours we spend imagining what we *do not wish to experience.* If man would only look upon the world as a world of appearance, behind which the reality of imagining lay, he would find the truth, he would find God.

As it is totally told in the 17th chapter of the book of Acts, now it's a story, whether it was historically true or not, it doesn't really matter. It's trying to push a point to the fore. It is said that the men of Athens spent all day in the marketplace looking for a new idea, either telling one or hearing one. Then came upon the scene one called Paul. And they wondered, what has this babbler have to say? What is his new idea? And he told them the idea of Jesus and the resurrection. And we are told the Epicureans and the stoic philosophers mocked him and scoffed at him. Others say we will hear more about this later. And he said to them, and this is all ironical if you read it carefully. He said, "Oh men of Athens, I see in every way you are very religious. For, as I passed by, I observed the objects of your worship." Right away that's irony, the objects of their worship. Then he said, I noticed this inscription over an altar, "to an unknown God." What you, therefore, worship, unknown, I declare to you. Then he tells them of the only God, the God that created everything and he's not a God of far off. He is indwelling, he is within every single being in the world, the God of the universe, not made with hands. You wouldn't find him in a temple, in a church, in a cathedral, or the little objects of your worship that you make of man with your own hands and then worship him and call him Apollo. But hear the God that I speak of is within everyone. That's the God of whom I speak. That's the God that raises from the dead.

Well, they laughed and they mocked him. Then we are told he went on from Athens to Corinth. What he performed there, no one knows, whether Athens ever took him up because they were the wise men. They were called the very learned men of the day. We have them today, too. They scoff at anything that is not part of their great voluminous works. But I am telling you, if as Paul said to the Athenians, if you would only feel after him, you'd find him. If you would feel after him, you would find him.

Find what? Find the God of the universe. For he gave us not the spirit of the world but the spirit of himself. That spirit of himself in man is man's own wonderful human imagination. When you say, *I am*, that's God, the one and only God, and there is no other God, therefore he's in every man, every woman, every child born of woman. It is the God in that being that allows that being to breathe, live, and experience what we call life in this world. That is the immortal you. So, the eternal body of man is the imagination. And that is God himself. The one we speak of in the New Testament as Jesus. That is God. But where is it? Something on the outside? No, he is in you. When you say *I am*, that's Jesus.

Now the world is taught differently, therefore, it comes as a shock when they hear it, they don't want to hear it. They will listen if it could simply improve their life in this world, get more money, do things that they want to do, and still hold onto this little object on the outside. So, he spoke, "I observed the objects of your worship." Well, man does that with what they call Jesus. They take their human hands, they make a mold of something, they call it Jesus, put it on a piece of wood, or put it on something else, stick it on the wall, and then cross themselves for good luck. There is the object of their worship. Something they made themselves. The maker is greater than the thing made, no matter how wonderful it's made, certainly the artist is greater than his work. And so, we make all these things and put it on the outside and then bow before it and worship it. I tell you your own wonderful human imagination is God; that's God. Now, if I would only observe this and keep it in mind, I should be able to put Paul to the test. He said, "Feel after him and you'll find him." Blake said, "Imagination is spiritual sensation."* Spiritual sensation, but how would I "feel after him and find him?" Well, first of all, he does all things good, bad, or indifferent. And he waits on me just as indifferently and as swiftly when the willing me is evil as when it is good because he's creative power.

He kills, he makes alive, he wounds, he heals—all things are done by the one creative power. There isn't another God who is evil and one that is good. One that is altogether loving. And one that is altogether hating. No, only one power. And that power is the human imagination. So how will I then feel after him? What would the feeling be like if it were true? What true? That I am the man that I would like to be. What would the feeling be like? Test it, for all things are made by him, and without him was not anything made that was made. But now if I had dared to assume that I am now the man that I want to be, and I persist in that assumption, watching my mind morning, noon, and night. So, anything that I find myself dwelling upon that is in conflict with that assumption, I ignore it, I put it aside. I will be faithful to this divine vision, the vision of myself. So anytime I catch myself daring to feel less than the thing that I'm feeling or trying to externalize in my world, I simply stop it and go back to that assumption that I am the man that I want to be. If I persist in it and it becomes a fact then I have

* Blake wrote this in a letter of August 23, 1799, to the Rev. John Trusler (1735–1820), an English minister and patron of the arts, including to Blake, with whom the poet exchanged several critical letters.

found him. I don't observe imagining as I do objects in space. I am the reality that is called imagining. So, you don't *see* God because God is spirit, but you *see the results* of his activity in you. He's active in you as you imagine. You're completely free to imagine good, bad, or indifferent. So, you simply select what you want to imagine. Would you like to be—and you name it. But you say, I don't have the background for it. I do not have any of the qualifications for it. It doesn't really matter. If imagining creates reality, you do not need the qualification that the world thinks you need. All you need do is simply to boldly assume that you are the man, the woman that you would like to be. And if it proves itself in performance, then you have found him.

So, Paul said to the Athenians, "Feel after him and you'll find him." Well, I have seen it numberless times in my thirty-four years of teaching. I started back in February of 1938 and here I am, this is February of 1972, and I'm yet to see it fail—if we, the operant power, apply it. It doesn't apply itself. We are the operant power. For in man is God and God is man's own wonderful human imagination. So, if I dare to assume that I am the one that I would like to be, well, that's God who's doing it.

So how will I turn then to God tonight? Say a half-dozen people asked of me tonight, it takes no time, they voiced their request. It's a statement made in the book of John, the Epistle of John: "If we know that he hears us in whatever we ask of him, we know that we have already obtained the request made of him." Well, when they're talking to me, they say, I would like so and so, instantly it comes within the frame of my golden rule. It's something I would like myself. If I were in their present state of consciousness, I would like that. It doesn't violate my rule. It doesn't injure someone. It doesn't take from anyone. Well now, did I hear it? I heard it. Well, if I and my Father are one, well then, my Father heard it. I do not know the means that will be employed to bring it to pass, but I can't deny that I heard it. If I heard it, and I and my Father are one, well, can I not now say to my inner being, "Thank you, Father"? You heard it because I heard it, for if we know that he hears all that we ask of him, then we know we have already obtained the request made of him. So, as they say to me, I would like so and so, well then, I heard it. I do not know as a man called Neville how it's going to happen. I do not know. I'm not going to suggest what they do or what they should do. I only know that I heard it and if I heard it, my Father heard it because he and I are one. He is my own wonderful human imagination. So, I could actually say within myself, as though we were two, "Thank you." You heard it because I heard it, and then allow the depth of my own being to devise the means necessary to bring it to pass. And that I am not responsible from that moment on, I do not call them up and say, "Did it happen?" I do not get in touch with them and write them and say, "Tell me, how are things coming?" It's not my concern. I did what was asked of me. And all it was asked of me was to hear and use my imagination lovingly on their behalf. Well, I did it in the twinkle of an eye. You don't have to go into some sweat to do it. I don't have to go to some church and do it, go to some synagogue and do it, or some so-called holy place. Wherever I stand should be holy because the Father is within me. And where can you go to a more holy place than where God is? If I know God is my own wonderful human imagination, then where can I go that could be more holy than wherever I am, no matter where it is?

So, the request is made, I heard it. And then having heard it, I give thanks to the being within me, who has the means, the wisdom, and the power to externalize it. Knowing that the entire outside world, that all objective reality, is solely produced through imagining. What is now proven in the world was once only imagined. Try to deny that, try to deny it. There isn't a thing in this world that you can say that's real that was not first only imagined. So, I say to everyone here, take the statement, "Feel after him and you'll find him." He didn't say you may find him. Feel after him and you'll find him.

But these ideas are so new and yet they aren't new, they go back into the Old Testament. Here, we find the word for *imagination* used as the word *potter.* Well, if you say the word potter, go down to the Potter's house, and I let you hear my word. So, I went down to the Potter's house and there he was working at his wheel and the vessel in his hand was spoiled. So, he reworked it into another vessel, as it seemed good to the potter to do. If you read it in the form of the story, in which it is told in the 18th chapter of Jeremiah, you will think of a man with clay in his hands, at his wheel, pumping away, making a vessel, making some kind of a, well, it could be anything, a plate. That's not it. The word potter means imagination. It's like saying to you go into your own imagination and see what you are doing with a friend. You just heard that he was in need. Are you now going to finish that and take him now into a greater need, or are you going to rework it into another vessel as it seemed good to you to do? You don't go to some Potter's house, go down to the Potter's house, and there, I will let you hear my word. So, I went down to the Potter's house and there he was working at his wheel. And the vessel in his hand was spoiled. He didn't throw it away and discard it. He reworked it into another vessel as it seemed good to him to do. So, a man, a friend of ours, he's unemployed. All right, so he's unemployed and he doesn't have the qualifications for a better job and there is no job at the moment for what he has. So what? I will rework it. I will hear him tell me that he has the most marvelous job and he's gainfully employed. What the job is, I do not know. But I can say to myself, well, if I heard it surely the depth of my own being heard it. And so, I can say, thank you. Having reworked him in my own mind's eye into an entirely different being; the same friend, but not one unemployed, he is now gainfully employed. So, feel it. If I can feel this state, I'm finding God for God is spirit.

And may I tell you, and by spirit, I do not mean some intangible thing. It actually is the human form divine. When I speak of the human imagination, it is a form, it is a reality, it is the divine form. So, the eternal body of man is the human imagination. And that is God himself. And there is no other God. He said, "I kill and I make alive. I wound and I heal. I do all things and none can deliver out of my hands." This is Scripture. But man, when he hears the word, God, he thinks there's something out in space. Where, he doesn't quite know, but something in space. If the word God, in any way, conjures within you something that is other than your own wonderful human imagination, you've got the wrong God.

If the word Jesus causes you to think of a man who lived 2,000 years ago and died 2,000 years ago and rose 2,000 years ago, you've got the wrong one. You're told Jesus is within you. If he's within me, I should find out exactly where he is in me. And then who is he? Well, I found him. He is my own wonderful human imagination. That's Jesus. And all that is said of him, every child born of woman, is going to experience, to discover he is Jesus, and there is no other Jesus. So, you're told in Scripture, in the 17th of Matthew, "In the end, there is Jesus only." Why? You're told now in the book of John, the Epistle of John, "And when he appears, we shall be like him." Because when he appears and it's only Jesus, well I have to be like him. So, within me, the whole thing unfolds itself.

And everything said of him, at least whether people believe it or not, I have experienced. And personally, I do not care whether they accept it or not. Any more than Paul did, the wise men, the Epicureans, and the stoic, scoffed at him and laughed at him, mocked him. So, he went on to Corinth. He simply did the work he came to do. So, he told the story and said you're worshiping, what? Something on the outside. And here you put an inscription over the altar, "To an unknown God." You say *the unknown*. What you know, say is unknown, I will tell you of a known God. Now take my word for it and feel after him and you'll find him. How would I find him? Well tonight if I wanted to be in New York and I put my body down on the bed tonight when I go to bed, I must assume that I am already in New York. Well, how would

I know that I am there? If I am all imagination, I must be wherever I am in imagination. Well, if I am in imagination in New York, now think of the world, think of California, Southern California, where you place the body, or do you see it on the bed as you're thinking, well then you are not in New York. Do you see it 3,000 miles away to the west of you? Well then you are in New York. For were you in New York, you would see the body in your mind's eye, 3,000 miles away in Los Angeles. And you'd be thinking *from* New York rather than thinking *of* New York. So, the whole thing is simply finding out this fantastic power, creative power in man and how it operates. For, there is no problem in the world comparable to this problem of solving the mystery of imagining. For supreme power and supreme wisdom and supreme delight is in store for the one who conquers this mystery.

So, whether you be in jail, all right, so you are in jail, and you dare to assume that you are free. You aren't going to break through the doors and be picked up and be sent to a longer term, you simply assume that you are free. Today on death row, many of them pray that their sons would not be put in the chamber, and they believe their prayers. And so, the Supreme Court brings in a verdict: no more killing of men because they kill someone. Whether you approve or disapprove, that's not the point. All things are possible in God's world, all things. So, I'm not going to pass any opinion, whether this thing is right or wrong. I'm not going to be involved emotionally as to whether they did the right thing or the wrong thing. I only know from personal experience, if I had a son there, I want him free. If he were there, he's not there, but if he was there, I'd want him free. Regardless of what he did, as one who loves his son, I'd want him free. But I am not going to pass any opinion or any judgment concerning the Supreme Court's decision. The thing is all things are possible. You tell me what you want and if it comes within the framework of what I call the Golden Rule, which is simply doing unto others, as you would have others do unto you. If it fits that frame, well then, you are on the right course.

Well then, you can't do it physically, no. You don't have the power or the wisdom to do it. But there's something in you, which is your essential being—it can do it. It knows exactly how to do it. Can you trust it? Can you trust this being within you to have heard what you heard? I heard it on this level, the request made. And if I heard it on this level, certainly the depth of my own being heard it, and on that depth, he has ways and means I do not have on this level. Therefore, I'm not concerned as to how it's going to work. I only know it will work. By simply assuming that I am already the one I want to be. And if I dare to assume it and remain faithful to it, then it becomes a fact.

So, imagining, plus this kind of faith, faith in God, and God is your own wonderful human imagination. So, *faith in God* is the way to success. You imagine it as though it were true and then you walk your way, not knowing how it's going to become true, but it will become true, and I invite you to test it, just try it, costs you nothing. And if I take from you your gods, as Paul took from the Athenians their gods, then it's a blessing. If you can lose your God, it's a good thing because the real gods you can't lose and you can never lose *being*, you can never lose a sense of I am. You can lose everything else, but you can never cease to be aware that you are; that's God. And so, if I can't take that from you, well then, I can't take the real God from you. If I can take any other thing from you and you worship it, you have the false god. And I did you service in taking anything but the reality, because I can't take the reality from you. So, all other services and ceremonies, they mean nothing, nothing. Go about your Father's business, which is yourself doing noble things in this world, imagining the best and it will come to pass.

That's why I say if it seems that I reiterate and restate night after night after night, it's essential. Because if you are perfectly honest with yourself this day and you observe what you are imagining in the course of one day, you'd be ashamed of what you imagined. And yet *you are imagining things you do not want to happen*. And yet you'll give lip service to a statement, imagining creates reality. And then one moment later, a friend of mine up in San Francisco, she was a friend of a mutual friend and they didn't get on very well, only at moments. One night, riding with her, we went down, oh maybe seventy-five miles down the peninsula for a dinner, a lovely dinner, and all the way back, this very, very heavy fog, you could hardly see a few yards before you. And she was talking of this friend of mine, who she claimed to be a friend of hers, and she would rant against this woman. So and so and so, I wouldn't even print it. You couldn't print it, it burned the page. And then at the end of her statement, she would say, "God, bless her soul." She kept up the entire seventy-five miles blasting this woman. And then she would qualify the whole thing and is all forgiven. "God bless her soul." So, she is still here, the other one has gone from this little section of time, and she's still playing the same part, *using her imagination in every way she doesn't want in this world.* And things went from bad to worst in her world. And they're still that way. And she can't for one moment believe she's the cause of the phenomena of her life. Oh no, she can't for one moment. And yet I had one long, seventy-five-mile drive with her. Well, it would take a whole lifetime to reap that harvest, what she said in that long drive from dinner back home.

So, man has a very weak memory and he doesn't remember when he did these things, but the depth in man who does not forget. We are warned in Galatians, "Be not deceived. God is not mocked. As a man sows, so shall he reap." Then we are told by the poet, "See yonder fields!/ The sesamum was sesamum, the corn/ Was corn. The Silence and Darkness knew!/ So is a man's fate born."* So, you don't recognize your own harvest, but it couldn't make a mistake. Everything is after the identical seed. You plant a seed. What seed was it? I had forgotten what it was. Well, wait until the tree comes up, you'll know because it can't be other than what was planted. If I plant an oak, well, then the

* Neville is quoting from the 1879 poem "The Light of Asia" by Sir Edwin Arnold (1832–1904).

oak is going to spring up into the oak tree. I plant that sort of acorn, that's going to be the oak tree. But if I plant something else, well then wait. If I have forgotten what I planted, wait, the harvest will show me. And man denies his own harvest. So, I'm telling you that your own wonderful human imagination is God, is the God of Scripture, the only God, whether in the Old Testament, you call him the Lord or call him Jehovah or call him God, or in the New Testament, you call him Jesus, it's the same thing. This is the creative power in man. And that creative power in man is man's own wonderful human imagination. Why repeat unnumbered stories that I've told you in the past? I could start with new ones but you know the technique and the technique is simple. If all things are created out of man's human imagination, well, then, let him start imagining what he wants to be. And if he does, success will follow him.

But in the meanwhile, try to prune the plant because when you hear for the first time that your imagination is God, it's an awful shock. Because as the poet said, "Behold this vine, I found it a wild tree/ Whose wanton strength had swollen into/ irregular twigs . . . / but I pruned the Tree,/ Then it grew temperate in its vain expense/ Of useless leaves, and knotted, as thou seest,/ Into these full, clear clusters, to repay/ The hand whose foresight wounded it."* So, when you first find the vine spoken of in the Bible, "I am the vine of eternity, I am the true vine and my Father is the vine dresser." And you discover that vine is my imagination, but then the whole thing went into leaves, useless leaves and branches. It was not producing grapes. Then I start to prune the tree by observing what I'm imagining in the course of 24 hours.

It becomes a habit. Then the next day I do a little bit better; the third day, better still; by the end of a week, I am in the habit now

---

* Neville is quoting from the 1801 epic poem "Thalaba the Destroyer" by Romantic poet Robert Southey (1774–1843).

of watching what I'm imagining. And don't wait—instantly prune it. Stop it. Stop imagining, don't indulge yourself. I have heard people say to me, "But just one more second. It's such a pleasant thing to cut him off." And so, in his mind's eye, he's telling off someone all in his imagination, knowing he's going to reap the fruit of it. Now, if you know that, you aren't going to simply spend an extra five seconds of precious time in finishing that emotion; stop that emotion and get on a new trend. And then you prune the plant. And finally, that plant's going to reward you with clean, full clusters because you wisely wounded it. And then you keep that vine going and the vine will pay enormous dividends. I know from experience. When you go to bed at night, let your last thought be something noble, something wonderful that you are now, or those you love are now, what you would like to be and drop off into the deep in that state and make it a habit. As we are told, you plant a seed and then the seed becomes an act and the act becomes a habit and the habit becomes the character.

So if I seem to repeat myself, it's because I have to, because if anyone here tonight could honestly tell me that in the course of 24 hours, they have observed what they were imagining and had not a thing to find fault with, well, I would like to hear that, and I will not call you a liar because I'm not here to judge, but it would be marvelous thing, if you could tell me that. But I know that all of us are victims of habit. And we get into the habit of these internal conversations that are not pleasant. And we think that no one observes, no one sees. So, as we are told in the book of Ezekiel, "He said, son of man, go down and see what the elders of the house of Israel are doing. So, I went down to the house to observe the elders of the house of Israel. And there they were, each in his own room, carving on the wall." What wall? The wall of your own interior, the wall of your skull. And they are making abominable things. And they say whether no one sees us, the Lord has forgotten us. They thought because they did it in the silence that no one knows when the only reality is their own wonderful human imagination. And that is fully aware of what man is doing and rewards man, good, bad or indifferent, with his imaginal act.

Now, no one can tell me that you could not tonight start to become, if you want to be prosperous, that's a relative term. What you mean by prosperous would not be what another means by it. But what you—and just take yourself—what would it feel like if it were true? Just what would it feel like? And then go about to your business feeling as though it is true, instead of spending your precious time reading about Howard Hughes, or who cares? I asked a friend of mine who asked me if I'm following the story; I said, you know, he doesn't know me and I don't know him. And I'm quite sure that if I met him, he would not really buy me a sandwich. So, what am I concerned about? He doesn't pay my rent, he doesn't buy my clothes, he doesn't contribute to my way of living, and I am supposed to be concerned about what he's doing? He doesn't interest me, none whatsoever. So, I must spend my precious time reading about Howard Hughes? My heart almost goes out to the man, Irving, who wrote the thing because the so-called wise editors of *Life* and the wise ones of the other one, got taken. And they're so wise, taken for a half-million dollars.* And so, I'm not saying that I would want to duplicate it in my life, but it almost serves them right.

To pull that upon the people and who cares about Hughes, really? What is his contribution to life? So, he has made two billion. So what? Hasn't bought you a dinner. Hasn't done anything for you. And so, what is your concern? You take the story of Scripture. See it, as it really was intended in the beginning to be seen: that your own wonderful human imagination is the God spoken of in Scripture. And by him, all things were made and without him was not anything made that is

* Neville is referencing an episode in which novelist Clifford Irving produced a fraudulent "autobiography" of reclusive billionaire Howard Hughes for which the writer received more than $500,000 from *Life* magazine and publisher McGraw Hill. In 1972, the year of the book's planned publication, Irving was exposed and convicted of fraud. He spent about 17 months in prison.

made. Start right in this room, you're wearing clothes, you're sitting on chairs, you're in a house. Everything here was first only imagined: the clothes you're wearing, the chairs in which you are seated, the building that now houses you. Everything here was first only imagined. And then it became some objective fact. So, objective reality is solely produced through imagining. Now you want to objectify something entirely different from what you have so far. Well now, change the imaginal act. To attempt a change in circumstances before I change the imaginal activity is to struggle against the very nature of things. I can't do it because my imaginal activity is producing the objective realities. And I can't change that objective fact until I change what is causing it. And the cause is an unseen imaginal activity.

As we are told, "He brings things that are not seen and calls them as though they were seen and they become seen." Things that are now seen, were made out of things that do not appear. That's what we are told in the book of Hebrews. What you now see, it was made out of things that do not appear. Well, if that is a fact, and Scripture's had it now for centuries and centuries as fact, well then put it to the test. Challenge, yes, challenge the Scripture, as you're taught in Scripture to challenge it. "Do you not realize that Jesus Christ is in you? Examine yourselves and see whether you are holding to the faith." Well, test him. Test him and see. If he is in me and he does all things, I'm going to test him. Well, I have tested him over and over and over and found him faithful. I dared at moments in my life to assume that I had what reason told me I did not, and my senses denied it, but I dared to assume that I had it, and it happened. It came out of the nowhere. It happened. So, I taught that principle to others. They applied it and it happened. But strangely enough, after someone becomes a little bit better off than they were, they reflect on it and because it always happens in a perfectly normal, natural manner, they say, "Oh, well, it would've happened anyway." And then they go sound asleep again.

You can give someone a sedative and you try to awaken them. And for a moment they're alert, seemingly alert. And while you are talking to them, sound asleep again. That's humanity. They're dreaming this dream of life. And they see the fruit of what they've imagined and deny that their imagination produced it. So, they go sound asleep again, back up on the negative state. But I'm asking you who come here and persist in coming to observe what you are doing in the course of twenty-four hours. You're not alert for twenty-four hours, but take, say sixteen hours. If you give eight hours for sleep, well take sixteen hours and try to observe what you are imagining. And if perchance you catch yourself imagining what you do not wish to experience, stop it, stop it right there and then, and don't give it an extra second. It may be you are in the midst of an emotion and you'd like to complete the emotion and tell him off completely. Don't. Stop it. Break it. And that causes a sort of a mental, well, a mental abortion, a mental miscarriage. If you break it without exploding the emotion.

So, feel after him and you'll find him. That's what he told the Athenians. But he pointed out all the objects of their worship. And every object he pointed out was something they themselves made with their hands and then worshiped it. I can see it now when I was a young man in the dancing world, there was a young girl, a pretty young girl, and she had a little figurine of what she called the Holy Mother. And before she took the stage, she would kiss it. The whole thing was to simply bring in rays from her kisses. And she really thought that gave her success. She kissed it and smothered it with kisses and on the stage she would go. And that was her little object of her worship. She thought that really was the Holy Mother. I mean, I tell you, without any criticism of the thing, most of these things are made by people who call themselves artists and are so far moved from any concept of being an artist. They're monstrous things made by the millions, not by good artists at all; but she had her little one and sitting on top of the stage at her little dresser and she would smother it with kisses and then dashed on the stage and she danced.

I went to a party once, these boys, one with a priest or he was going to be a priest and he quit to join the war, the others, they all went into the army. One came out deaf, one came out with one foot missing above the knee and an arm. And this one who was the priest, or about to be the priest, he came out with something else, didn't go back into the priesthood. But they all wore their St. Christopher medals when they dived into the pool at their home and they attributed their recovery or their so-called coming out of the army to St. Christopher. That was before St. Christopher was demoted. He's now demoted. The Pope just said there was no such a thing as St. Christopher. But before that, they attributed the entire thing to that; one with a foot missing, arm missing, one deaf, and one with TB, and that is St. Christopher. He didn't do a good job. But they're actually, were completely, I said to my wife, I said, "Darling, suppose they know what I teach? Suppose they have heard what I do? Would they have me here?" "Oh," she said, "certainly they would have you here because as far as they're concerned, you aren't saved, you couldn't be saved. You are a Protestant. So how could you be saved?" They loved my father dearly, said my wife, loved him more than they loved their own people, but he couldn't be saved because he was a Protestant. Therefore, it doesn't really matter what you do. So don't be concerned if they knew what you are teaching, they wouldn't even pass an opinion because it doesn't matter. Only what they have been taught to believe is true. And that's the only truth. Therefore, enjoy the day. So, I did. I enjoyed the day and observed all this nonsense.

So, I'm telling you your own wonderful human imagination is God; there is no other God. If you think there's another God, then you've got two gods. And if you start with two, you're going to have four, and four is going to give you eight, and eight sixteen, and then you have millions of gods. There's only one God. "Hear O Israel, the

Lord, our God, the Lord is one." And that God is *I am*. That's his name forever and forever and forever. And when you say *I am*, you are actually announcing the fact that you are imagining. That is imagination, that's God. And it's the human imagination. And it is the eternal body of the Savior. And the only Savior is the Lord, God. "I am the Lord, your God, the Holy One of Israel, your Savior. And besides me, there is no Savior." So, the Jesus of the New is the Lord, God of the Old. And where is he? In man. He gave us not the spirit of this world, he gave us the spirit of himself. And that spirit of himself is in man as man's own wonderful human imagination.

Now, let us go into the silence.

Lecture IV

Repentance: A Gift from God

February 28, 1972

I think you will find tonight's message a very practical one, something that all should really have and apply. The whole of life is just the appeasement of hunger, and the numberless states of consciousness from which the individual can think and view the world are purely a means of satisfying that hunger.

I say this because your state of consciousness is always being externalized. If you know how to move from your present state, if you dislike it, to the state you would like to externalize, then you have the secret. That is what I attempt tonight to tell you. For there are only states of consciousness pushed out—everything in this world—and all are contained within the individual.

Now, in the Bible we speak of prayer, and prayer to the world means begging—but not in the Bible. It's thanksgiving; it's praise. It's not petition. We speak in the Bible of repentance, and the world thinks that it means to regret, to be remorseful. That's not what the Bible teaches. Prayer and repentance are almost synonymous terms.

We are told to bear fruit that befits repentance. Then they say of the central character of the Scripture: "You and your disciples eat and drink with sinners." And he replied, "I have not come to call the righteous, but sinners to repentance." Leave the righteous alone. They are so self-satisfied. They like themselves, so leave them alone. The word "sin" hasn't a thing to do with breaking any moral code. The word "sin" means *to miss the mark.* That's what it means. You have a goal in life and you haven't achieved it, well then, you are sinning. You may have a billion dollars, and still are hungry for another. Well then, if you don't have the other, you are sinning.

You may keep all the so-called codes of the world imposed upon you by the priesthoods of the world—that would mean nothing as far as the Scriptures go. To repent is simply a radical change of attitude. That is what repentance means. For if I radically change my attitude towards life, I will then view the world and see the world from that change of attitude. And that change is a change of consciousness, and that change will be externalized in my world.

Now, repentance is at once man's responsibility and a gift of God. Now, let us show you what I mean by it. He said, "I and my Father are one, yet I go to my Father, for my Father is greater than I." *We are one, yet my Father is greater than I, so I go to my Father.*

How do we arrive at this strange, peculiar statement and what does it mean? In the office of the sent, I am not inferior to my essential being, the sender; but only in the office of the sent I am restricted and must live by faith. Faith in what? Faith in the sender. It is myself, the Father, for I and my Father are one. But when I am sent into this world to experience death, and to experience the restriction of man, I am seemingly inferior to myself, the sender. So, when I repent, I go to the sender—I first do what I have to do. So, I say that repentance is at once a responsibility of man and a gift from God.

Well now, what is my responsibility? I want to change my world. Well then, I ask myself, "What would I see if it were changed? How would I see the world, if my world was exactly as I want it to be, how would I see it?" Well then, see it! In my mind's eye, conjure a scene which would imply that it is true—live as though it were true—in my mind's eye. I know I can't make it so, but in the depth of my own being the Father—he has the power to make it so.

So now I go to my Father. How do I go to my Father? I first of all do what I am called upon to do—I enact a scene implying the fulfillment of my dream and then I turn it over completely in thanksgiving to him. It is myself, my essential being, but it transcends my reasoning mind. I do not know on this level how it can be done, but I do know that if I have faith in him—it is my own self—it will be done in my world. So, we are told in Scripture, *without faith it is impossible to please him.*

And those who would draw near to him must believe that he exists, and that he rewards those who seek him. I must believe that he exists, and that he rewards those who seek him.

Well, without faith it is impossible to please him. What is faith? The same chapter in Hebrews defines faith for us. "Faith is the assurance of things not seen, the evidence of things hoped for." By faith, we understand that the very worlds were created by the word of God, so that what is seen was made out of things which do not appear.

Well, in my world it hasn't yet appeared. I say it all is contained within my imagination. So, I will enact a scene which would imply that it's real. And then, within myself, I give thanks. Now, we are told the most wonderful prayer ever uttered we find in the book of John, the eleventh chapter. He stands at the gate of death. And he raises his eyes and says, "Thank you, Father, that thou hast heard me. I knew that you always hear me." Well, I can't deny that the depth of my own being is hearing what I am doing, what I am inwardly saying, so I can truly say, "Father, thank you." He certainly heard what I said. Well, is it now supported by some statement of Scripture? Yes, again in John, but now in his letter, the first letter, and in this he said, "If we believe that he hears us in whatever we ask of him, we know that we have already obtained the request made of him."

If I can simply assume that I am the man that I would like to be, well, certainly the depth of my being has seen that assumption, he has heard that assumption. Well, can I actually believe that that's all I need do? Well, I have to confess that I can't do it on this level. I am not wise enough on this level to devise the means necessary to externalize what I have assumed that I am.

Well, have you proved it, Neville? Unnumbered times. *Unnumbered times.* When I was completely shut out, on certain areas, imprisoned as it were, not in the federal prisons, but a state of imprisonment—to find yourself on an island, where you enjoyed four months of it, almost five months, but you have a commitment in America, and you have to get back; and then to be told that there is no possibility of return until the very earliest September. That would be the very earliest, and your commitment is in Milwaukee in the first week of May. What are you going to do then? No possibility—no ships are taking the passengers, and the list runs into thousands waiting all through the Indies, from Trinidad all the way up, all waiting, and you in the island of Barbados without making any provision for your return to America when you sailed for Barbados five months before.

So, what did I do? I simply sat in a chair in my hotel room and I assumed that I was on a little tender moving against the boat. Well, that was before the days of a deep-water harbor. Now we have a deep-water harbor. But then you took a small boat out to the ship waiting maybe a half mile to sea, and then you walked up a gangplank. So, I simply stepped up on the gangplank and walked up that gangplank in my mind's eye. If my mind wandered, which it did, I brought it right back to that first step and walked up again. It wandered before I got to the top; I brought it back again, and I trained it as you would a horse. The mind is an unruly animal, so I trained it, and I walked up step after step. When I got to the top, I turned around and put my imaginary hands on the rail, and I could smell the salt of the sea in the air. I looked back with nostalgia at the little island of Barbados—a mixed emotion—I am happy that I am sailing for America, and sad I am leaving behind a very large, wonderful family of mine. And then, in that mood I simply dropped off for a moment in sleep. Just a little nap.

The next day, I was called by the very company who had said, "We have no possibility of getting you out of here before at the very earliest September." And said there was a cancellation this day in America. And they offered to me in spite of the list of over a thousand people waiting.

It is not my concern why she or he or it canceled the passage. My prayer was answered. I did what I was called upon to do, for repentance is a radical change of attitude. She said, "You can't get out." Well, I said, "I'm out. I'm on a boat, and the boat is headed towards New York City." That is all I wanted to do.

So, I did my responsibility, and the second part of repentance is a gift from God. God has the way of externalizing it. What caused the woman or the man or something to cancel the thing, I was told afterward, she was afraid. She was afraid for some reason not explained to make the trip. And so, one passage was opened up and I got that one room. Because there were only two beds in it, and my little girl was only three years old—she could sleep with her mother, and I could climb up one flight and sleep on the upper bunk, and then take my eleven days back to New York City.

So, I did what I was called upon to do—that's my responsibility—to enact a scene which would imply the fulfillment of my desire, and then surrender completely to my Father, for he has the power to externalize it. I do not know how to do it on this level. I haven't the wisdom, I haven't anything on this level to do it, so my faith is faith in my Father. Faith in his power to externalize what I have done—all in imagination.

So, for me that is prayer, that is repentance. I didn't sit down and feel for one moment that I had done something wrong and that's why I couldn't get out. No sense of repentance like remorse as the world teaches. That's not repentance. *Repentance is simply a radical change of attitude*—that's what the word means. *Metanoia*—but radical, right down to the root, and you change your attitude. If I change my attitude, I have changed my state of consciousness, and because all states of consciousness are being externalized in the world, then that state will externalize itself in my world in a way I do not know.

For we are told, "My ways are not your ways. My ways are past finding out. Just trust me." So, without faith, you cannot please God, we are told. If I would come to him, I must first believe that he exists and that he rewards those who seek him. Well, I seek him in projecting for me that which I desire in this world. So, that is what I mean by prayer. Prayer is the attempted communion with God. That's what prayer is. As we are told in the fourth Psalm, the fourth verse: "Commune with your own hearts on your beds, and then be silent." Commune with whom? I do not need the mediation of any priest, any rabbi, or any heavenly being—I'm communing with myself. *The depth of my own being is God the Father.* That's my essential being, and he is one with the surface mind called Neville. And in the capacity of the office of the sent called Neville, I am inferior to myself the sender, but the sender and the sent are one. You and God the Father are one.

But in the office of the sent you are like an ambassador—you do not speak with the same authority of the one who sent you to represent him. So, I represent myself in the world of death, but the sender is greater than I, and yet I and He are one. This is what I get from Scripture, and this is what I put into practice, and this is what I try to teach and tell everyone who will listen to me. You *are* God the Father. That's who you really are, but you do not know it yet. The day is coming you when are going to know it, and you will only know it when his son appears before you. Jesus Christ is the same yesterday, today and forever.

Well, Jesus Christ, don't look upon him as one in the sense, like a surname, "Jesus" and "Christ" being the surname, no. Look upon it like Father and Son. The Christ is the Messiah—that's the son. "Jesus" is the same as "Jehovah"—that's the Father. But we put them together and we say Jesus Christ. So, we could say, "I and my Father are one." So here, look upon it simply as one, yes, but split for a purpose in this world. So, he sends himself. He sends his son. Who is his son? The one who is going to reveal him to you as God the Father. For no one has ever seen the Father, but his only begotten son, who is nearest and dearest to his heart, he has made him known. And so, who is that one? David. So, David comes into sight and here you know exactly who you are. The minute he appears, memory returns and you are God the Father. And his son who was with you before the world was made stands before you. So, Jesus Christ is the same yesterday, today, and forever, as you read it in the thirteenth chapter of Hebrews. *Same forever.* This is contained in the mind of man.

That's what we mean in the third chapter of Ecclesiastes—that "God has put eternity into the mind of man, yet so that man cannot find out what God has done from the beginning to the end." What did he do? He put himself and his son into the very mind of man. And when man has completed a journey, well, then the secret is out—the son appears, and the minute the son appears, the identity of the individual appears—that he is God the Father—that this relationship was before that the world was.

So, everyone in this world is destined to awaken one day as God the Father, and the relationship is forever. You cannot change it. So, when you are called upon to repent, for the story begins, "The kingdom of God is at hand. Repent, and believe the Gospel." Believe the good news. Repent and all the priesthoods of the world tell you that you must now moan and carry on because you must repent of things that you did. The Bible doesn't teach that at all. It doesn't. Repent—change your attitude if you would change the world. To try to change circumstances before you change your state of consciousness is to struggle against the very nature of things. You can't do it. How can you change a thing and still maintain it from the venue?

So tonight, without asking anyone's permission—you're not asking anyone to mediate for you to God—you go within and commune with your own heart: *What would the world be like if it were true that I am already the man, the woman that I'd like to be? What would it be like?* Well then, look at it and see it. If you don't see a change, well then, there is no change. Man's sense can detect motion in this world only by changes relative to something that is fixed. Well now, my present state is fixed, seemingly. Well then, I change my attitude towards the world. I let the world see me a changed man and I see in my world a change. Well, if I see a world that is changed relative to what it was, well then, I have changed.

If tonight I am financially embarrassed, what would it be like if I were not? If I were affluent? Would my friends know it? Would my wife know it? Yes, they would know it. Well then, let them know it. Where? By telling them audibly? No, you do it all in your imagination. For man is all imagination, and God is man and exists in us and we in Him. The eternal body of man is the imagination and that is God himself. That is the divine body that we speak of in Scripture as "Jesus." And where does he live? He lives in you. So, Blake says so beautifully, "Why stand we here, trembling around/ Calling on God for help, and not ourselves, in whom God dwells."* He dwells in us, so where would I go to find him? In a church? In a synagogue? In a so-called holy place? No, if I'm at the bar drinking a beer or a good scotch, that is where he is. He's in me wherever I am—that's where

* Neville is quoting from the second chapter of William Blake's illuminated manuscript, *Jerusalem: The Emanation of the Giant Albion* (1804–1820).

he is. And he is aware of what I am entertaining, and he is going to externalize what I am entertaining.

So, I change radically my state of mind and that radical change will externalize itself if I yield completely to him in faith that he has the ability to do it. It relieves me of all responsibility of devising the means that would be necessary to do it. I do not know—I'm not wise enough to know how it's going to work—I only know it *will* work.

So, everyone, if he knows this secret, is free. He is set free by the knowledge of prayer. "Teach me how to pray." Now, the Lord's Prayer is not the technique. If you know the Lord's Prayer, and it is recited week after week in all the churches of the world, but it is not as it is written in Scripture. A friend of mine who is now gone from this world gave me the literal translation of the Greek, when what we have in our Bible is a translation from the Latin, and the Latin has no aorist of the imperative passive mood, so they could not convey the sense of the evangelist. The imperative passive mood is a thing to be done absolutely and continuously. That, well, in other words: "Our Father in the heavens, Thy name must be being hallowed; Thy kingdom must be being restored; Thy will must be being done." That's how it is written. It is a play that is forever—without any reference to its duration, to its position in time, to its repetition—it's *to be* taking place.

And that play is the play of the Father-Son in man. And at the very end when the individual here is drawn into that play, he realizes it. He actually reenacts within himself the eternal play, and when that whole thing is done within him, he is fulfilled—what he came to do.

For the only purpose in life really is simply to fulfill Scripture. But while we are here in this world of tears, world of death, then we have given ourselves a law by which we can cushion the blows, the inevitable blows. For you get into a state quite often unwittingly, and you do not know you are in the state until you see it externalized, and you do not like what is being externalized.

Don't remain in it and wallow. Get out of it. Don't condemn anyone for it. Don't judge anyone, just get out of that state. You get out of the state by asking a very simple, simple question: "What would it be like if. . . ?" And then you imagine as if it were true. And that is the secret of prayer. "What would the world be like if it were true that I am now the man, the woman that I'd like to be?" And then I *dare to assume that I am it.*

Well then, I can say, "Father, thank you, for you certainly heard and you certainly saw what I did." You cannot encompass me as the deeper self of my being, something that is my essential being, and tell me that you aren't aware of what my surface mind is doing. It can't be unaware of what my surface mind is doing.

I saw in yesterday's paper that the second man to step upon the moon, his name was [Buzz] Aldrin, and when he came back from this fantastic thing, [Neil] Armstrong stepped on first, and then Aldrin stepped on second, that he came near a nervous breakdown and sought psychiatric help. And all the stories he read about their journey he said they were so false, and they all said, "I wish it were true." Not a thing *Life* magazine wrote about that journey was true.

Not what any magazine wrote was true through the eyes of those who had the experience, and then in the article, it quoted a thought of Jung, Carl Jung, and Jung said long before any man ever stepped on the moon, "It is far easier for man to visit Mars or the moon than to penetrate his own being."

So, you step on the moon, and it's a fantastic feat, but that's nothing compared to penetrating your own being and finding the cause of the phenomena of life, to find the Father in you, for that is where he is. He's not outside, and because he is not outside, he is never so far off as even to be near. For nearness implies separation.

So, I can say, "I and my Father are one." So, if he is even "near," it is not near enough. No matter how "near" it is, he has to be my essential being. For nearness implies separation, and he is not separated, because "I and My Father are one," giving me freedom to choose a state that I will enter, wisely or unwisely, but he will externalize it and show me exactly what I did. But grant me the freedom to change it—don't leave me in the state if I desire to get out of it. Yet many a person wallows in it, and wallows in it, morning, noon, and night, and they are totally unaware they are doing it. They will say, "Oh, yes," and then five seconds later they are back in that state. I have had interviews with people who will say to me, "This is what I would like, but I must first tell you . . ." Don't tell me anything! Tell me what you want—they are only states. They insist on wallowing in all the things of the past. Like the little old lady who insisted on confessing time and time again to the priest, and it was some little affair she had when she was a child, a young girl. And the priest said to her, "You know my dear, you have told me that over and over again," And she said, "Yes, but I love to talk about it." Well, that's the story, we just love to talk about all the miseries in the world. I tell you, *forget it*. Know exactly what you want in this world, dare to assume that you are it, and then yield completely. Surrender to the depth of your own being, and he has a way that you do not know, and he will externalize it in your world.

So really, in a real sense, prayer is the subjective appropriation of the objective hope. What do you hope for? Well now, subjectively appropriate it. That subjective appropriation of the objective hope is the art of prayer. For the Father knows exactly what you are appropriating. He saw it. And he isn't judging you; he is going to give it to you. He's not going to ask anything, he's going to give you exactly what you appropriated. So, I appropriated a trip when they told me you couldn't move out of this island for months and months to come. And I kept my date in Milwaukee. I arrived in New York City in the first week of May and flew to Milwaukee, and there I kept my date. So, the same thing is true for everyone in this world.

I am not unique in the sense that I differ from any child born of woman. You are unique and I am unique in the sense that we can't be duplicated. And that's why everyone has to be redeemed, because if not all, then something is missing from the whole. So, I can say faithfully to everyone, "You are going to be redeemed." You may go through hell before you wake up, but you still are going to be salvaged. You're going to be saved, everyone, because the whole makes the one. That is God. But why wait? And why have more blocks and more knocks in this world, when you can actually learn what Scripture really means by "repentance?" And don't go telling anyone that you commit a little sin, and now they must give you something to do that you may repent. Forget that nonsense. All that's nonsense. I don't care what you did, your Father doesn't hold it against you; it is the state in which you were when you committed that act. And man judges the individual and not the state. If I must express myself, judge the state, but not the individual in that state—he was simply something that fell into it unwittingly.

So, Blake could say, "You see now from what I tell you, that I do not see either the just or the wicked to be in a supreme state, but to be every one of them states of the sleep in which the soul may fall into in its deadly dreams of good and evil."* So, it falls into a state. So why condemn the man or the woman for the state into which it fell? Take it out of that state. All things are redeemable—take him out of the state. How do you take him out? Well, ask him what he would like. Maybe he doesn't want to get out of the state. If he wants to get out of that state, you ask him, "What would you like?" Well then, in your own mind's eye represent him to yourself as the man or the woman that they would like to be. And then yield completely to your Father, because he has the knowhow—he knows how to produce it in them.

A friend of mine went to San Francisco at my bidding. I taught him the Law, and as much as I could tell him of the other, part of the

* Neville is quoting from William Blake's notes to his painting, "A Vision of the Last Judgement" (1808).

Promise, but the Law, just what I am talking about tonight. Before he gave one lecture in San Francisco, it was a new city—he'd never seen it before—and he was walking around in the street, and he had a little fox terrier, so he was carrying his little fox terrier up the street, and a man crossed, wobbling a bit, and asked him for money. He said he was unemployed and he would like a little handout. He'd evidently had quite a little bit to drink as he asked. My friend wasn't judging that aspect at all. He didn't care if he'd had all the liquor in the world. He said, "I must apply this principle." And he said to the man, "I do not have any money to give you, but what I have I'll give you."

Well, the man couldn't understand what he was talking about but thanked him and walked his way. My friend did not make one step beyond that point before he did what was his responsibility. He represented that man to himself as gainfully employed and no need of help from anyone—just gainfully employed, and then he went his way with his little dog. A week later, he's walking down the street, the man crosses the street and comes up to him. He said, "I don't imagine that you remember me." My friend said, "Oh yes, I do." Well, he said, "I want to thank you for not giving me help when I asked you a week ago, because had you given me help, I would be asking you for help tonight, too. But I got so mad with myself because you turned me down and I was in that position to ask for help, I went out the very next day and got myself a marvelous job, and I'm on the job now."

All my friend did was he represented him to himself as gainfully employed. So, we are told that in the book of Acts, "Silver and gold have I none for thee, but such as I have give I unto you." You can give any gift in your imagination, so give it! And then yield completely to the depth of your own being knowing that he has the power, the creative power to externalize it. And that is what my friend Freedom did.*

* Neville is referencing Freedom Barry (1921–2014), who is quoted in the introduction.

So, anyone can do it. You don't have to graduate from some little "ism" in this world. If you want some little title, all right, get a title. We all are bought, anyway. You can put fifty dollars in the mail, send it off to India, and get a Ph.D. You want something higher than that, get something higher, but get whatever it is—all for fifty dollars. If you bargain with them, you'll get it for ten dollars. No exams, no studies, nothing. Just a little piece of paper and these people will frame it and put it up on their wall. Well, if that is not the height of nonsense! And then a big convention will take place, and you will hear so many doctors being called doctor so-and-so and doctor so-and-so each paid ten dollars for that doctorship.

Get down to the basic facts: the greatest book in the world that never changes is the Bible. But it is the most misunderstood book in the world. For it is taught as secular history and it is not secular history. It's divine history—it's the history of salvation. And these characters are not persons as you are, these are eternal states of consciousness, but they are all personified when you tell the story. And we have taken the personifications for persons, and the vehicle that conveys the instruction for the instruction, and the gross percepts for the ultimate sense intended. And as long as we can teach it as secular history, we will never know the Bible. So, I tell you, whatever you did this day, and you dislike it, turn from it into another state. Don't try to rub it out remaining in that state because you're going to do it again. You'll do the same thing over and over again while you remain in that state. You can pledge yourself from now to the end of time that "I will never do it again," to find that maybe twenty-four hours later the impulse is there and you'll do it again.

Get out of the state, and it is as though you never really did that—not in eternity. It isn't part of you because it's not part of the new state. But you are not a state, you are all imagination. Imagination is not a state. All these other things are states, but not imagination. That is the individual himself—that is God, your own wonderful human imagination. That is God. When you say *I am* that is God forever and forever and forever.

So, my name is in Him. Because my name is in Him, where should he turn if he wants to find God? But now, without faith in God, in your own wonderful human imagination, you cannot please Him. So, who would come to Him must first believe that He exists.

Well, I don't have to ask you if you aren't aware of being. You certainly are aware of being. Well, that's saying, *I am*. So, you do know that you exist to that extent. You may believe that that dies with the physical body; I tell you, it doesn't die with the physical body.

You have believed that a change of state is a change in the sense of death. No, it's not. The individual moves on from state to state to state, but states remain permanent for all others to enter into that state. I leave this city of Los Angeles and go on elsewhere, but Los Angeles remains. But I the pilgrim, I move on. And the pilgrim is your own wonderful, human imagination. That is your immortal self who cannot die. You cannot go to eternal death in that which cannot die—that's your immortal being. But you are going to remain in this world until you discover who you are.

And no one in the world can convince you to the extent that you must be convinced by the Son. When the Son appears, all arguments are over. The minute you see him you know exactly who you are, and you know that you are God the Father. It is through the son that man gains assurance that he is God. Not a thing in the world can convince him but that. I could tell you from now to the ends of time, but I can't convince you to the point that you will be convinced when you see David. And when you see David, it's *the* David, the psalmist, that sweet psalmist of the Old Testament—that's David—that is the Messiah. He is the Christ, and Jesus is the Lord God Jehovah. That's the mystery. You're dealing with a mystery.

So, David in the spirit called him, "my Lord," as a son always spoke of his father as "my Lord." Always. You do not do it today, but when this was put into the written form, sons always referred to their father as "my Lord." And so, David in the spirit, not in the flesh, called him "my Lord." Therefore, he called him "my Father."

And so, I hope you will take it seriously tonight and really live by it. It will not fail you, *I tell you, it will not fail you.* You can change your world and make it conform to your ideal state, to your dream. Tell it to those who will listen. Many will not listen, but it doesn't really matter. If they do not listen, leave them alone. Don't try to hit them over the head to make it so. But I'll tell you, spiritual growth is the gradual, I would say, transition from a God of tradition to a God of experience. And so, you will gradually grow and grow and grow—and as you grow, you *outgrow*; you will outgrow these traditions. And then you will find the God of experience. Having found him, you aren't going to let him go—you will know that all things are taking place within your own wonderful human imagination.

Now let us go into the silence

Lecture V

Divine Vision

March 3, 1972

I received a letter this week from a gentleman who attends the lectures: "Did I attend them? First of all, I love them. They make me feel so secure and peaceful and fulfilled. But it doesn't last very long. The following day, I am full of doubts again. And I wonder why? So, you talked on prayer and you showed us how you would pray. Well, I applied that. But again, the prayer is erased by my doubts the following day."

For those who were not here, here is a quick summary. The foundation is *I and my Father are one, but my Father is greater than I.* I am not inferior to my essential being called Father, but only in the office of the sent, but the sender and the sent are one. So, when I am sent into the world, I am restricted, I am wearing a garment of flesh and blood, depending on my senses, depending on my reasoning mind, which cannot fathom revealed truth. It has to depend upon the depth of its own being; for that which reason tells it, it cannot do. It must believe that all things are possible to that depth, that Father, that we call God. And if it is all possible, knowing I cannot do it on this level, I would do the normal, decent thing and give thanks to my own being for doing for me on this level what on this level I cannot do for myself.

But now the secret is how to keep that divine vision in time of trouble. When Paul said, "Oh, King Agrippa, I was not unfaithful to the heavenly vision." He was not disobedient to it. He kept it, knowing from the depth of his own being, it would be done. Well, I say to him, it is not another spoken of in Scripture when Peter says, "If my brother sins against me, how often oh, Lord should I forgive him?" We're living in an egocentric world. The whole vast world is yourself pushed out. It is not John over there, it is this; what St. Francis meant when he said, and on his deathbed, he asked the forgiveness of poor brother donkey. My body for all the hardships that I've caused it to suffer. *This limited me; I must forgive it morning, noon, and night.* So, when the Lord answered, "70 times 7," that does not mean 490 times. It means until my vision, which is 70, that is the "eye" it's an *ayin*. The symbol of the *ayin* is an eye, and 7 is a sword, until I fix it.* So, it does not wander, it does not move from one place to the other. I am not disobedient to the divine vision. When I keep the divine vision, even in times of trouble and things are all denying that it could ever happen, He is working; the depth of my own being is working from the model. I supply the model. I want this, that, and the other. I dare to assume that I have it. Having assumed that I have it, it is entirely up to me to hold that model from which he works. He will externalize it in my world if I am faithful to the divine vision. That divine vision need not be some wonderful, heavily spiritual vision; it's something based upon the world of Caesar; that's the vision. It is not yet externalized, but I know what I want. I must hold it in my mind's eye. And if tomorrow I wander, 70 times 7,

* The Hebrew letter ayin corresponds to "eye" and to the numeral 70; the Hebrew letter zayin corresponds to "sword" and to the numeral 7.

remember you come back to the model because he is working from a model and the model is supplied by you on this level, in the capacity of the sent; you have been sent into this world.

Now I say to him, that's what I would suggest to you, if you were here tonight, that you simply try to go back to the vision, because you became aware that you had wandered, not everyone is aware that he wandered. At least you are aware that you have wandered from it. You go back to it.

Now in the letter, he said, "The previous week it seemed to me that you were very critical of a multimillionaire in his eighties, who is now taking up yoga to extend his earthly days in this world. Do you mean he should have prayed instead?" No, I don't say he should have prayed instead. That was not my point. My point is this, that a man in his eighties, not a multimillionaire, he is a billionaire. A billionaire is one who has in excess of 1,000 million dollars, not a few million dollars. In any man's language, a million dollars is an awful lot of money, but a billion is a thousand million and he still wants more, and he's in his eighties; and to prolong his body, that he may gratify that hunger he's taking up yoga. And he thinks he's a very spiritual man, because he doesn't eat certain foods and he doesn't drink and he doesn't smoke. So, he is a holy man in his own eyes. But I will say this for him, he cannot, by my saying to him, you should now change your attitude towards life and want the spiritual things of life; no, the hunger hasn't come upon him. He has a hunger for Caesar's dollars. And as long as that hunger remains, he has to gratify it. So, I'm not critical of it. I use it only as an example, but I am fully aware of the fact that he has not yet had that hunger as you're told in the book of Amos; the eighth chapter of Amos, the eleventh verse: "I will send a famine upon the earth. It will not be a hunger for bread nor a thirst for water, but for the hearing of the word of God." Well, he doesn't have that hunger. So, at the age of 80-plus he still has a hunger for things in this world; but Scripture warns us in the thirteenth chapter of Hebrews and the sixth chapter of First Timothy: "Be free, let your life be free from the love of money. For the love of money is the root of all evils."

It didn't say a few evils, *all evils*. You can trace it back to what money means to man. Money means power. All the wars in the world are economic wars. When man thinks that he can lead his nation into war and get more markets for his people, more of these things, it's all economic. And so, if he thinks he can, he does it. And all wars are economic wars; they reach a certain point and they break forth into violence. But before wars come, it's still an economic war, and it's based upon the love of money.

I'm not saying you shouldn't have money. I need money to pay rent. I need money to buy clothes, to buy food, and do the normal things of life. I'll not deny that. But to fall in love with money and to want money for money's sake is simply a false concept of power. I am speaking of an entirely different power. And may I tell you all the power of this world is like a little firecracker compared to the power of which I speak. The day is coming when you'll realize this power. It's all within you. And you must arrest it. You'll feel it within you and you will arrest it. And the whole vast world that you are perceiving will stand still. It's absolutely still and dead. You can change its motivation while it's still, and then release the power within you. And it will execute the change motivation and think it initiated the change. That's power. There's not a thing in the world comparable to such power, it's all within a man. The day will come, man will have access to that power in that day, and he'll know he is God.

So, I am not criticizing the man for wanting another billion. I use him only as an example, to present it to you who come here, that you are not on that track. I trust you are not. If you needed money, certainly ask for it. And then if you do not know how to bring it into your world, then give thanks to the depth of your own being, as you are told "commune with your own heart on your bed and be silent." So, you commune in the sense, what would it be like if it were true? What would the feeling be like if it were true? Well, then you assume that feeling, you wear that feeling. That's the vision. And then that forms a mold and the depth of your own being who is your Father, who is God, the ultimate God takes that mold, and from that mold, he externalizes it because he has ways and means that the surface mind knows not of. So that's what I meant when I used this man as an example of it, but certainly not to criticize him.

You're told, and this is Scripture, "I am from above, and you are from below." He's not speaking to another, he's speaking to himself; he is speaking to this being down here, this thing. The being within me is speaking to this and it said, "I am from above and this is from below." It was born from the womb of my mother, my earthly mother. This that is speaking when I say, "I am from above," is born from above, out of my own skull. That means it is born not of blood nor of the will of the flesh nor of the will of man but of God. He who comes from above, he's above all, we are told. He who comes from the earth belongs to the earth and of the earth he speaks. He who comes from heaven is above all. So, he equates the one coming from above with the one coming from heaven.

You'll read that in the 31st verse of the third chapter of John. When you read the third chapter, jump from the 21st verse to the 31st and go on to the very end, the 36th verse, then go back to the 22nd verse and read through to the third. There was a break there, a dislocation of the manuscript. So read to the 21st and then go straight to the 31st and put those letters from the 31st to the end, in red letters. It's all part of the same speech of the central figure. He who comes from above is above all. He who is of the earth, belongs to the earth and of the earth he speaks. He who comes from heaven, he is above all. Now he tells us that he speaks of that which he's seen and heard, but no one receives his testament. He who does receive his testimony, he tells them they will put this seal to this: that God is true.

The word is going to prove itself to be true in the individual, for he has come only now to fulfill that word. He dictated these words in the depth of his own being and comes into this world and puts upon himself the limitations of the garment called flesh and blood to fulfill it while walking this earth. Fulfill it in spirit, fulfill it in himself. Now listen to the words. It's not taking place on the outside. If I tell you, "I am Mary and birth to Christ must give, if I, in blessedness for now and evermore would live"—I mean that literally. And let me see now what it is said in Scripture concerning Mary. The angel sent from the Lord appears to Mary and tells her the secret, our supernatural conception. That the power of the most high will overshadow you. Therefore, the child to be born will be called holy, the son of God. Then Mary answers the angel and Mary said to the angel, rather, she's now speaking to herself, "Behold, I am the handmaid of the Lord. Let it be to me, according to your word." And then the angel departed from her.

I am the handmaid of the Lord. In the hundred and sixteenth Psalm, the 16th verse, and it's now David speaking, "Oh Lord, I am the servant, the son of thy handmaid." He is the son of the handmaid and Mary claims, "I am the handmaid," and she's just been told that child will be born of her must be called holy the Son of God. A thousand years prior to that, if you take it chronologically, one declares, "I am the son of the Lord's handmaid." And his name is David. I am not theorizing it; I have experienced it. And so, I'm telling you that it is David, and when it actually takes place in your world, who then is Mary? Did you not give birth to the Christ Child? I know I did. I held the child in my arms, and looked into his face and said, "How is my sweetheart?" And that heavenly smile broke upon its face. And then the whole thing dissolved. And then a few months later here comes the evidence; here is David, the one who said, "I am the son of thy handmaid." Well, did he not come forth? Was it not pronounced by my brothers who were present, "It is Neville's baby?" Well, if it is Neville's baby, then I am Mary. I brought forth the Christ Child.

And yet, why now is the son calling me father? Listen to the words carefully. We are told in Genesis that a man must "leave father and mother and cleave unto his wife until they become one flesh." A man, now, if he cleaves to his wife, he is her husband, is he not? He can cleave to a woman, but it may not be his wife, but the word is *wife.* The man leaves father and mother and cleaves to *his wife* and they become one flesh. Now, in the 54th chapter of Isiah, your maker is your husband. The Lord of hosts is his name. The Redeemer of Israel is this one, the God of the whole earth he is called. But remember your maker is your husband. We are so told of Eve, she came out as an emanation from man. Therefore, who is this man now but her husband and who is that husband, but God?

So, the man, my man is my husband and that husband is God. Now, this is the emanation. My emanation yet my wife till the sleep of death is passed. Is not some woman in this world for male-female made he them and called their name, man. So here, whether you be male or female, this is the emanation of your maker and your maker is God. And he cleaves to you. You are not cleaving to him. It is he who cleaves to you until you become one. And what proof have I that you've become one? Christ is the son of the living God. If I bring forth the Son of the living God, well then, he has completed that union. For I am Mary then, for we are told that Mary is going to bring forth the Son of God. Well, if Mary brings forth the Son of God, you bringeth forth, after the cleavage has taken and they have become one, one body, one flesh, one spirit.

So here, the whole drama is unfolding itself within you as an individual. And when you see confusion in the world, it is only the confusion within you. When you see anything in the world, it is all taking place within you. It's really a soliloquy. The whole vast drama is the unfolding of the mind of the individual. So, you are the one sent and you are the sender. In the capacity of the sent, you seem inferior to your essential being the sender, but do not forget, "I and my father are one and he who sees me, sees him who sent me." If you see him who sent me then I am the sender.

And I'm telling you from my own experience, you are that very being who embraced you. He actually embraces you and you fuse, you become one. And when you see the Son, he is the image of the one who embraced you or when you were embraced by him, you felt you were one with him. He who is united to the Lord, becomes one spirit with him. So, in that union of you and the one who embraced you, you actually are the very image of that being. And David is the image of that being and you are that being, and it's all done in spirit. It's not done here in flesh at all. In spite of all the arguments of the contrary, this belongs to the world of Caesar and many men of science and philosophy will accept as an explanation nothing that comes from beyond or above this world of nature, they will not.

You can't blame them. They see it here and they've done marvelous things with it. They confine themselves to things here that they can prove. But we confuse ourselves, deeply confuse ourselves, when we simply identify the wisdom that comes from above with this wonderful knowledge that comes from below. Knowledge is science and wisdom is revealed truth. And you cannot in any way prove it to anyone. I can take the wisest man in the world who called himself the scientist and tell him what I'm telling you tonight. And the chances are he will go away and say, the man is a little bit cracked. There's no proof. You can't present the proof and he wants proof, well you can't present the proof.

There is no way of proving to anyone that the kingdom of heaven exists until you have entered it. There is no way of proving that God exists until you have the experience of God who exists. There's no way of proving to another that the Christ Child is an eternal child. That David is eternal, that he represents, he is the sum total of humanity. He is the resultant state of all the experiences that man is capable of going through. You go into this world of man and play all the parts.

And when you played all at the very end, the cleavage is taking place and he is the resulting state. He comes out as the Son of God who played the part. But while he is playing it, he's in the depths, molding your world in harmony with that mold that you offer him. But what mold am I offering him tonight?

When I say *I am* and I put a name on it, that's the mold I am offering him. If I say I am secure, I am blissfully happy, I am and I name it—that's his name I'm calling. *I am.* And then I put the mold on it. Now, I must be faithful to that vision. That's the vision, it's not yet in the world. It's a vision. And so, I must keep the vision in time of trouble and turn to him when I become aware that I'm not faithful; instead of wasting my time condemning myself for turning away, go back. He said, "Seventy times seven, you forgive your brother." And this is poor brother donkey that God himself is riding. In a few weeks' time you'll find all the churches decorated. There'll be a donkey and they will have the Lord seated on it. And then have all these things moving up to the cross. And people will think that that actually took place on the outside. Now this body is the donkey that the Lord wears and I'm riding him and many a time, he has thrown me; many a time he's turned aside. They're very stubborn animals, do you know that? I used to take a donkey on the beach in Barbados. I had one special one and he had the capacity to stop on a dime. He could run as fast as lightning and stop on a dime, which meant you went about twenty feet over his head. But it was fun. You're kids, you didn't care. You never thought of consequences. You break your neck. You got on that beach, a nice wide beach. You got on that donkey. No halter, nothing, bare back. And often he would start and you are holding on and all of a sudden *bang* and Neville goes twenty feet in front of it. Sometimes you'll come up, you have blood all over because the sand cut you. But it was fun. Go into the beach and wash it off and that's all, hoping that the mother wouldn't see it. But that animal is a symbol of this body that you and I are wearing. It is called among the animals of the world, it is called one of the most salacious of animals. All through the West Indies, these men who are seeking public office, they go through with a donkey, a donkey in the open cargo, as a symbol of their virility. And of course, all these crazy people are howling and carrying on with them because he is a strong man. That's a symbol, the donkey. But I tell you all these wonderful symbols are true, but don't worship the symbol. The donkey is your wonderful body of flesh and blood and you have to be constantly in control of it, constantly taking care of it, and simply turning to the depth of your own being when on the surface self, you can't do it.

So, when you are told "you are from below and I am from above," don't think some man feels himself superior to men, and he's telling them that they're below him. That's not it at all. It's the being within you that is from above. It is that being who will ascend; this being cannot. This being belongs to the earth and of the earth it speaks. But the being who came from heaven is the being who is from above; and the day will come because he and he alone descended, he and he alone will ascend. He will leave this world and ascend to himself from which he came. So, he tells us I am leaving the world and I am going unto my father. You'll see me for a little while and then you'll see me no more, for I am ascending unto him who sent me and you return, that very being.

But the being here is wearing a very restricted garment while he is here. And that garment is the form of a donkey. And that has been made to suffer through our mistakes in this world. So again, I say to my friend, if you are here tonight, I had no intentions of criticizing anyone; I just use it as an example to show you that there's something far, far greater in this world than the love of money. Far, far greater, as you are taught in Scripture, "Seek ye the kingdom of God and all these things will be added unto you." Not because you're going to have more and more homes. No, you'll find you don't need them. Not because you're going to get more and more billions, you'll find you don't need them.

And the day will come by eliminating all the nonsense in the world, you are freer and freer and freer. And people think by accumulating that they are freer and freer; it's by simply eliminating the unnecessary things in this world. If I bought everything that came to my door, I'd have to move out from a seven-room apartment into a fifty-room house. Only yesterday and today, a man tries to sell me now water, only five dollars a month, only five dollars a month. Yesterday someone tried to sell me the cable TV, well that's only, I think, five dollars a month. Another day, another five dollars a month. You put it all together and finally you're spending something like $200 on things you do not need, a month. And these go on and on and on. But people are told through propaganda that you need them, you must have them. Must have what? I once enjoyed a lovely, big $600 color TV set. Then it cost me a fortune to keep it going. You pay $600 for it. And all of a sudden, he tells you the tube is gone. I said, yes, well then let's have a new tube, but that's going to cost you $250. $250 for the tube. He said, yes. I said, take it away. I gave it reluctantly to my maid. I said, "Doris, I shouldn't give it to you, this is a burden because to put that tube in, it's going to cost you $250, and I'm going right out tomorrow and buy myself, a nice, small 21-inch black and white. Well, I got a 19. That's all I need it for. I do not need the huge, big color TV set. Everyone thinks he has to have a huge, big color TV set. I have a 19-inch black and white. I rarely turn it on. If a game is on and I like games, I'll turn it on. That's good enough. I prefer my Bible. So why must I be always keeping up with the Joneses?

So, I only use this story to illustrate a point, keep yourself free from the love of money. For the love of money is the root of all evils. It's the cause of all the wars in the world; that love of power. It is a symbol of power. And the power of which I speak puts all the power of this world into nothing. You can't conceive of any power in this world that you could use to make humanity stand still and you change its motivation. And yet within your own head, you have that power.

And you look upon the world as you see it, and suddenly you stop the activity within your head and all activity stops, and they're not independent of your perception of them. You think they are, but they're not. They're all yourself pushed out and they're animated by the activity within you. And you are carried away by the things that they're doing, as though they're things completely strange and different from what you are doing within yourself. And it's not so. And if you stop it and then you release it and everything moves on to fulfill its purpose, but you can change its purpose. And then you will know you are on the very verge of being born from above, where this is your right, this is your power, and you entered an entirely different world. And when you're asked by others, describe that world to me, Paul tells us, "Eyes have not seen nor ears heard, nor has it entered into the hearts of men the things already prepared for those who love the Lord." How could you use any image of earth to describe that world? You can't do it.

When I tell you that I actually have gone by thousands and thousands waiting for me to come by and they were all broken members of humanity, blind, lame, halt, withered. You name it, they were there. And I didn't raise a finger to make one of them better. There was no compassion that possessed me. I simply glided by, a radiant being; one of fire and air, and that I glided by off the earth. I didn't walk. I simply glided. Everyone was made perfect. Eyes came out of hiding and filled the empty sockets. Arms that were missing, came out of hiding and filled the empty sockets. And those who could not walk, they jumped for joy. Everything became animated and perfect. And when the very last one was made perfect, this heavenly chorus that accompanied me, sang out, it is finished, the last cry on the cross. So, these are the last words of the cross, it is finished. And then I felt myself once more congeal into this body.

I have never worn that I know now in this little section of time, I have not had the experience of wearing a straitjacket, but I have seen men put in straitjackets. And so, I know the confinement that they must feel in a straitjacket. Well, this was just like a straitjacket. That's how confining this body is. After you've experienced the freedom of this heavenly immortal body that is yours. It is radiant, it's immortal, and that body is yours. And the day will come, you will complete the journey in these garments, and then that body will come out. But when that body comes out, you, the sent, will return to yourself, the sender, and you and I will rejoice together in a heavenly sphere that you cannot depict by using any image on earth to describe it. It can't be done because eyes have not seen it and ears have not heard it. And how can you tell it until he brings you where those who have gone there have been. Can't do it. I am here to encourage you to set your hope fully upon this grace that is coming to you. It is coming. No power in the world can stop it.

You came down deliberately. No one took your life. They're going to tell it on the second day, rather on the second day of April is Easter. So, two days before that, they're going to tell a story, which isn't so at all. How a man was crucified by people who would not believe him. It isn't so. The crucifixion took place in the beginning of time. And when you are born of woman, that's when you are crucified here. But I was crucified with the Cosmic Christ in the beginning of time. And then I came down into this world and my mother gave me a garment of flesh and blood. And that's the cross I wear. That's my slave. I'm a slave of that cross. And I can't command anyone to perform any of its normal, natural functions for me. I have to perform them myself, eat myself, assimilate, and eliminate, and no one in the world can do it for me, no matter how much money I have and how powerful I am and what I am. I have got to perform the normal, natural functions of that brother donkey.

So, I'm riding that towards the end. And they're going to weep and say a certain group, a certain race, crucified a man. Didn't do it at all. Have we not read the Bible? No one takes away my life. I lay down of myself. I have the power to lay down and the power to take it up again. So, he confesses that no one has ever taken away his life. And yet for 2,000 years, we perpetuate the lie and tell that story over and over and over. And it isn't so at all. Read it in the gospel of John; the most profound book in the New Testament is the gospel of John. No one takes away my life. I lay it down myself. I have the power to lay it down and the power to take it up again. And so, I have laid it down myself willingly to enter this arena. And at the end, I can say what Paul said, "I have fought the good fight." It is a fight. I have finished the race. I have kept the faith. Henceforth, there is later for me, the crown of righteousness. And then he goes on to say, "Let no one bother me. For, I bear on my body the marks of Jesus."

Everyone will bear them because everyone has them. The marks are there, but they're not driven in with any little nails. They are twirling vortices. A vortex binds me here, a vortex binds me here, one here, one to my right, and two, my two soles. The six-pointed Star of David. That's the Christ Star. He is the Son of the Lord's handmaid.

So, you can safely say, and mean it when you say it, you have not yet brought forth the Christ Child, but *I am Mary and birth the Christ must give, if I, in blessedness for now and evermore would live.* In my own case, I have brought forth the Christ Child. But I can say to those who have not yet had the experience, you can put it in that test that I've just quoted because everyone's going to have the experience and not one will fail. And then you will see the mystery. The whole thing is a mystery. So tonight, you take your ideals, you take your dreams, and dare to assume that you have already realized them, knowing on the surface, you cannot do it. You do not know where to turn, but believe me, the depth of your own being knows: all things are possible to him.

Before Mary said, "Behold, a handmaid of the Lord." The angel said, "With God, all things are possible." The same thing said prior to the first Child promised in Genesis. "Is anything too hard for God?"—it's the same; it's simply a different translation of the same meaning. *Is anything too hard for God?* And so, the Child was named

Isaac because Isaac means, *he laughs*, and the Christ Child laughs. The minute you hold him, the face bursts into the most heavenly smile and the whole thing dissolves as you are holding him in your arms. You brought forth the Christ Child. When you dwell upon this, it may not seem practical. It's more practical than anything in the world. Far, far more practical than telling you how to go out and get a million dollars.

Here, this morning's paper, I opened up the paper, and here is one that I have seen and listened to at times, William Lawrence. A year before our ex-president said he would not run, he said in his column and his TV show that President Johnson will not run for office for a second term. The first was by the accident of assassination. This one is now his own by election, but he will not run for another term. They all laughed at him. Well, he was right. He did not run, but he kept it secret for one solid year. Well, he went off to New Hampshire to cover this election, coming up on Tuesday, the primary; went to bed seemingly all right, had all his friends that day, the maid goes in to clean the room. And there he is, he's gone from the world, fifty-five years of age. Went to sleep, thinking he would awake the next morning to write the column, coming up on Tuesday, to tell what actually is taking place in our election year and Lawrence didn't awake in this world.* A man, eighty years old, and still knowing that tomorrow he's going to be called and still is interested only in another billion. Well, to me, it's the height of insanity. But let him have it. Let him have all that he wants. I don't want it. With it goes a tremendous responsibility and I don't want that responsibility. If he wants it, let him have it. But tonight, on this level, you formulated in your mind's eye the one you would like to be, man or woman.

And then having formed it, if, perchance tomorrow, like my friend, you wander, don't waste one precious moment in condemning

* Neville is referring to journalist William H. Lawrence (1916–1972), widely known as Bill Lawrence. He died at age fifty-six.

yourself. Forgive, forgive, forgive, and forgiveness means testing one's ability to enter into and partake of the nature of the opposite. So, you find yourself in this state now, which is one wandering away, go back to that state that you have chosen; go back, how often? Seventy times seven. As often as it takes to keep the vision fixed. So that that mold will always be before the depth of your own being, for he works from the mold that you supply.

So, you supply him a glorious mold but don't condemn yourself when you depart from it. Don't. Condemn no one. Leave them alone. So, the Christ of the Bible, one day, he stands before you and calls you Father. And remember, Christ is the Son of God, the Jesus of the Bible. One day you'll know who you are and you are he. Jesus is the Lord. The Lord God, Jehovah, and Christ is his Son. We put them together like one name, like Neville Goddard. It isn't Neville Goddard in this world. Yes, I'm Neville Goddard. But Jesus Christ are two separate states, I would call them. One is the Son, that's Christ, and Jesus is the Father. Listen to the words: "He who sees me, sees the Father. How then can you say to me, Philip, show us the Father? Have I been so long with you and yet you do not know the Father? If you knew me, you know the Father."

So, he is telling you, he is the Father. And David in the spirit calls him, "my Lord." So, is he not now the Father? For my Lord is the Father. And David called him, "my Lord." So, David is calling his own father. And he's telling you now who he is. It's the greatest mystery in the world, eternally taking place, eternally true. So, take it to heart and if you have it down on tape, play it over and over; these ideas that are so different from what man has been taught to believe.

Lecture VI

God's Son

day unknown, 1972

I thought I would gather all of the pieces together that I've been trying to tell you over the years. Tonight, we will take the opening passage of the epistle to the Hebrews. "In many and various ways, God spoke of old to our fathers by the prophet. But in these last days, he has spoken to us by his son." This son reflects the glory of God and bears the expressed image of his person. This is the heart of the Christian message. This is the gospel spoken in the universal language that all would understand. Whether you are living here in our marvelous land of America or living in any part of the world, we all know the relationship of father-son.

So, he spoke in many and various ways. As we're told in the 19th Psalm, "The Heavens declare the glory of God, and the firmament shows his handiwork and man has done marvelous things in the study of the heavens and the study of things of earth." You and I are now benefiting from the things that we've discovered in this search right here on earth. And with the great telescope, we've discovered a number of beauties of the heavens, and we've gone so far as to actually walk on the moon.

But all of these things will fade into nothing compared to the final revelation of God. In the last days, he reveals himself by his son, you will not find God, no matter how you find the things in the wonders of the earth, and we find them day after day. You will not find him if you go to all the heavens of the world, you aren't going to find him there. But you will find him, and everyone in the world will find him in the relationship of father-son. This is God's final revelation of himself to man. And so, whether you be living now in Africa, living here in America, living in China, everyone knows this relationship. You could be today without a child, never married in your life, but you know the relationship.

You could be female, and still, you know the relationship of a father-son. I will tell you that in this state when you are above it all, you're neither male nor female. As we are told, "Male-female made he them, and called their name, man."

So, in Christ, there is no Greek, there is no Jew, there is no male, no female, no bond, nor creed. We are above it all. But we all know this relationship. And it will not shock a woman to know that she is God the Father when the time comes for it to be revealed in her. Revealed in a man, revealed in anyone in this world. So, this is God's final revelation to man, and he reveals it by his son.

Now, let me share it with you. In this same book—what is the source, I do not know—he tells us that Moses was told to see clearly and make everything according to the pattern that was shown you on the mountain. Make it according to the pattern. So, we are living in a world that is only a copy. This is a copy. The reality is not here at all. This is all a copy. Why the author of the letter to the Hebrews stated that the urn, the golden urn that contained the manna and that the rod that budded, Aaron's rod that budded, was in the Holy of Holies, I do not know because I know from experience *it is himself.*

Now we are told by our historians and our archaeologists that when the temple was destroyed in the year 70 A.D., and Jerusalem was destroyed, when they opened the Holy of Holies, it was empty. There was nothing there when they opened the Holy of Holies. Why he incorporated this into his story, I do not know. What was his source, I do not know. It is not in the Old Testament. There is not one line in the Old Testament where the rod that budded, Aaron's rod that budded, and the urn that contained manna, the golden urn, was found in any Holy of Holies. And I know from my own experience that the Holy of Holies is right here, and God sleeps in it, and when God awakes without the help of anyone, he doesn't need anyone's help, God emerges from the Holy of Holies, which is called the Holy Sepulcher. And when you awake within that Holy Sepulcher, it is empty, may I tell you. You are the only presence in it, and you come out by your innate wisdom as to what to do and you push yourself out of it. You push and something gives and you come out. And so, the story is true. It is empty.

And so, if our archaeologists found the temple, the temple that was destroyed, and the Holy of Holies lay open, was found to be completely empty, so not a thing is in it but the sleeper and the sleeper in man is God and his name forever and forever is *I am.* That's God. There is no other God. But he is a father, and then in the not distant future, after he comes out leaving the empty sepulcher, he will know who he is. He still doesn't know who he is when he comes out. It takes his son to reveal him. And the son doesn't even call him. He calls him father, but he doesn't have to call him father. The minute he appears, memory returns, for the thing that God gave up to become man was memory. That was his great sacrifice. He completely gave up all the wisdom of the world, all the power of the world, and the knowledge of who he is. He gave up his memory. Having predetermined exactly what he would do in becoming humanity, in becoming human, God revealed who he is. He is made up of his sons. *Elohim* is a plural word and God descended and became fragmented, divided into the unnumbered son, he is God, buried in the skull of man. He awakens in the skull of man, you awaken individually. We do not awaken collectively. You are unique. No one can take your place. Salvation external to man is of no avail whatsoever. You can be the Holiest of Holies in the eyes of yourself and your friends—that hasn't a thing to do with it. You could be so good that you can't believe for one moment you could get better—that hasn't a thing to do with it. You can go on diets, go to holy places, do all these things—that's nothing. The final revelation is when the son stands before you. And the son is the resultant state of your journey to this world of death. This is a world of death.

And God came down into death, buried in the skull of man, and overcomes death, and the result of his journey stands personified as a son, the eternal son. So, in many and various ways, God spoke of old to our fathers by the prophet. But in these last days, he spoke to us by his son. That son reveals exactly who you are. You could be now the lady of ladies, unwed, and never known a man, makes no difference. In the resurrection, you are above the organization of sex. But you're not above fatherhood.

And this son is not begotten of sex, he is the resultant state of your journey through the experiences of this world of death. But when Blake wrote in *Jerusalem* how they come forth from the furnaces, these are the furnaces—and how long, how vast, how severe the anguish. Here, they find their father, were long to tell. This is the anguish. This is the hell, for heaven is nothing more than the presence of the awakened God and hell is his absence. While we sleep, we dream nightmares and God is the dreamer in man—and this world that we think is the waking world, this is a dream, too. And here, this is God asleep. When God awakes in man, it's heaven.

As he awakes, everything within his presence is made perfect. That I know from my own experience, that Heaven is not a realm, it is a character, it is a body, and clothed in that body, no matter where you are, everything is made perfect. If you went through the Petrified Forest, it would suddenly bloom because you are present. If you were in the desert, it would bloom. Nothing can stand in your presence that is imperfect. I know that from an experience at sea in 1946. When I was risen from within, and where they all sang, my praise, "Neville is risen." I'm clothed in this glorious, luminous body. I walked by and thousands waited for me to come and they were all imperfect, blind, lame, withered, shrunken, you name it, there they were. I did not raise a finger to transform them.

I had no compassion to transform them. I did not stop to do anything or talk to one of them. I made no effort whatsoever. But clothed in the perfect body, as I glided by, everyone was made perfect. Eyes that were missing came out of the nowhere and fill the empty socket. Hands that were missing came out of the nowhere and fill the empty shoulder. People who could not rise, jumped for joy. And everyone was made perfect and I didn't raise a finger to make it so. What made it so? I was in my body that is perfect. And everything has to be perfect in my presence. So, I know heaven is nothing more than the presence of the risen God. And hell would be the other. When he has not risen, he dreams these strange dreams of death and decay. And whenever you are risen, and you will be, because he in you must awake. And when you awake you are clothed in your immortal body, and that is perfect. And you cannot be any place where it isn't perfect. If you wake through hell, you will be easily transformed into heaven. And heaven means harmony. Everything is made perfect, made right, in your presence. So, the final revelation is not going to be going to the sun or to the outside planets or finding more of the earth, marvelous as it is. For you and I enjoy the comforts tonight, we have light. We've found that right here on earth, how to do it. It was always there, but not discovered. You aren't going to discover anything that it wasn't, it was always there. We have just unlocked the energy in the atom. It was always there.

We had not discovered the means by which it could be unlocked. We never even believed it contained this power. All of a sudden, man discovered it can be unlocked and devised the means to unlock it. And you and I enjoy all the marvelous things that man today is discovering on earth, as told us in that 19th Psalm: "Not only do the wonders of the heavens declare the glory of God, but his firmament shows forth his handiwork." And here is his handiwork. And day after day to come forward to something entirely different, something new, making it an easier world in which to live, as far as the burdens go. But the final revelation of God is in his son, and that is the universal language that everyone can understand. Because if tonight I lived in Africa, but I knew the story and I read the story, so I picked only the Old Testament, but that's the story. And in the Old Testament, I read of a man. But as I read it, I think, well, if he lived a thousand years ago, as I read it in the first century, or he is supposed to have lived a thousand B.C., living today. I would say, well, he lived 3,000 years ago. So, I don't associate myself with him at all. I was born and raised in the Christian faith. I call myself a Christian. I knew no other religions. I simply knew only what my mother taught me, what I learned in school, and I call myself a Christian. So, I read the story and my mother would read me these stories. But they belong to a world that was thousands of years ago.

And these men died, as far as I'm concerned, that was secular history and they were of the past. If all of a sudden, one night here in Beverly Hills, sound asleep, my skull explodes. And standing before me as it explodes, and I am sitting at a table, and before me is David—and there is no uncertainty as to who he is. He is not *a* David. He is *the* David. He is *the* David of biblical faith. And he stands before me, and I know exactly who he is and he knows who I am. And before is the severed head of the giant Goliath, right on a table before me. And there he is, leaning against the side of an open door, and I am looking at him, and I know I am his father. And he knows that he is my son. And here is this perfectly marvelous thing, 3,000 years went by, did it? And here it is, contemporary. Then what happened? My memory returned.

Memory returned, all that I read in Scripture was all about me, and I didn't know it. I was told it in the 40th Psalm. In the volume of the book, it is all about me. Well, when you read it, don't think a man called David or one called Jesus is reading that book. Think of yourself, for Jesus is the *I am* of man. That's God. Jesus is the Lord. He is buried in every man. And in the story, David calls him, *my Lord*, which is a name referred to as the Father. Every son spoke of his Father as *my Lord*. So, you read the 40th Psalm and because it was written a thousand B.C., you think, well now, I'm not related. How could I be related to these characters of the Old Testament, and they were all Jews? And I call myself a Christian. And here is the only reality. I am the Father of this great Jew called David.

Therefore, I must be Jesse, and yet I had no change of identity. Then I look up the word Jesse, and it means Jehovah. It means the Lord. It means a self-existent being. That's what the word Jesse means. And Jesse is the Father of David. And suddenly I am aware, memory has returned. So, the only thing that you gave up in your descent into this world was a memory, and completely forgot who you are, that you may experience death and not pretend that you are man. You could not actually accomplish the adventure if you pretended. An actor steps up on the stage, and he plays his part. But he knows after that curtain comes down, and the final curtain comes down, he is going to go home to his lovely home, if he has a lovely home.

If he's a great star who's made money, he goes home to a fabulous home. But that's not the story. You have to completely forget that you are God to become man. And you have completely forgotten that you are God in becoming man. But all day long you call upon his name, and his name is your name. You say, *I am*. Who are you? And before you answer anything, you say that *I am*, and then you'd say, John so-and-so, I am Doctor so-and-so, but you precede it with *I am*—and that's God's name. But you don't know who you are until the very last of the journey, and that last is when his son comes into your world. And his son is your son, and then memory returns. And now you know that every child born of woman is the same being, is God buried there. And everyone is going to have the identical son, not another David. And therefore, *we are one*, as told us in the Scripture.

I dwell in them and they dwell in me. And we are one. So, you are now different, and you call yourself by another name. You will not lose your identity. And yet you and I are one because we have the same son. Together, collectively, we all form the Father. And therefore, I only had the son. And that son is David. So, you will not lose your identity, but you and I are one. Having the same son, we are the same Father. So, the Father is a compound unity. The word is *Elohim*, one made up of others. And the others, we are the others. And the others are called in the Scripture, the sons of God. So, the sons came down, but the sons formed the Father. Now we are awakening individually as God the Father, just raising us to a higher level than we were when we descended. That is the adventure. And God is in this adventure. He is not on the outside of it. He is *in it*. And he's in it where he is buried. He's buried in his holy sepulcher. The Holy of Holies—and that is your skull, that's where God is buried, buried in his tomb.

And so naturally it is empty when they find it. So, this world is a copy. It's a shadow world. Make everything according to the pattern, which was shown you on the mountain, and so it has to be perfect. So, here at the very end, you see the son, and the son reveals the Father. Everyone in this world is going to have that experience. I promise you because I know it happened to me so suddenly, so unexpectedly. It's going to happen to everyone. Not one can fail.

So, here in these closing nights, I thought I would tie it all together and show you the important things of Scripture—that the Old Testament is a recorded shadowland. I call it an *adumbration*, a foreshadowing. In a not altogether conclusive or immediately evident way, but when it happens, then the whole thing unfolds within you. As we are told, "This is the God who said let light shine out of darkness, who has shone into our hearts and given us the very light of the knowledge of the glory of God in the face of Christ." Christ is David. Here is the glory in the face of Christ. So, when Browning brings it out in his beautiful poem, he has Christ speak to the sleeping God called in the Scripture, Saul.*

And Saul is simply God, sound asleep and he is called a mad person, because if he is sound asleep, he has strange dreams. And David stands before Saul, and he said, "Oh, Saul, a face like my face shall receive it. A man like unto me, thou shalt love and be loved by forever. A hand like this hand shall throw open the gates of new life to thee." Then he stands before him and his face sees the Christ stand. This is Browning's poem. When David, and it was all inspired by the 16th and 17th chapters of the first book of Samuel, and David came before the demented king and revealed who he is, but the king could not see it. When he stands before you, you'll know it. You'll be completely awake and you'll know that you are God the Father. You could have all the children in the world. A world of death, makes no difference. You could be barren or you could have many. Marvelous, if you are a father or a mother but you are destined to have *the son*, and the son is only the resultant state. When you have played all the parts, you too will say, "I have finished the work thou gavest me to do. Now return unto me the glory that was mine. The glory that I had received before that the world was." You're not asking for anything else other than the return of that glory—and glory and God are synonymous terms in Scripture.

Return my Godhead. I gave it up. I gave up my memory to become man, and now return it all unto me. And then you will say, "I have finished the race. I have fought the good fight. I have kept the faith. Henceforth, there's laid out for me the crown of righteousness." And everyone may be crowned with righteousness. And what is righteous-

---

* Neville is referencing and shortly paraphrasing the 1855 poem *Saul* by English poet Robert Browning (1812–1889).

ness? In the Scripture, when man completes the condition imposed upon him by a relationship, he is accounted righteous. And that relationship is called the Son. The minute it happens to you, you are the righteous being and therefore you wear the crown of righteousness. No mortal eye can see it, but it is seen. It is only *the crown*, it is not *a crown*. And Paul used these words in his letter to Timothy, he spoke of *the crown*, not an indefinite article, but the definite one. "I have fought the good fight, I have finished the race, I have kept the faith. Henceforth, there is laid out for me, the crown of righteousness." He finished it, where he said, "Now I bear on my body the mark of Jesus." And one thinks it means, the great mark that the world will paint on a picture. No. The marks you have done are the stories I've told you concerning how it unfolds within you.

First, you awaken. Then you come out and you are born from above. Then you discover the son who reveals you as God, the Father. Then your body is split in two from top to bottom. And then you take the blood, that golden liquid light at the base of your spine, and then you fuse with it, and like a fiery serpent, you ascend into your skull, and taking with you the blood through the curtain, for you are the temple of the living God. And the only curtain that is split isn't some little thing made by human hands. But your own body is split in two. That's the curtain. And so now you make a new and living way into the Holy of Holies. And that Holy of Holies, it was empty when you came out. And you go back now and you're the only living reality in it. And all of those who preceded you and those who will come, together you'll form one being, one infinite being, which is God, the father. And then your final state is when the Holy Spirit descends upon you in bodily form as a dove. That is the seal of approval of the work being completed. And then you'll tell the story that I'm telling to you now. You'll tell it to anyone who will listen in the hope that they will listen and believe it; for it is destined that they will experience it. But no one can really understand and appreciate Scripture until he has experienced Scripture.

You have no idea how altogether wonderful it is until you've experienced it. The thrill that was mine when this thing happened with David. I jumped out of my bed and I wrote it down. It was early in the morning. My wife was sound asleep and I didn't want to wake her. And the next morning when I told her, I said, "You may not believe this, but do you know I am the Father of David?" Well, she likes all the things that I have in my vision, and she never ridicules or makes little of anything I tell her, and it struck her forcibly. But I said, "Yes, honestly, I am David's Father." But at that moment, believing it to be of secular history, my wife would think of me, is this now a memory of the past? Going back 3,000 years ago, you lived and you were the man called in Scripture, Jesse? Then in time, it all unfolded. The meaning of Jesse. Jesse means Jehovah. And yet here I am, limited in this world, restricted by the body that I wear, imprisoned by this body, and continue to be imprisoned to the very end when I take it off for the last time. This time when I take it off, I am not reimprisoned, as all who have not had the experience will be, for all who have not had the experience will be restored to life in a body just like this, only young and healthy and nothing missing; perfect about twenty years of age to continue the journey until that last revelation.

All the revelations in the world, marvelous as they are, they must wait to the end. And the end is when he reveals himself in the son. So, we are told, set our hope fully upon the grace that is coming to you at the revelation of Jesus Christ in you. The unveiling of Jesus Christ in you is the unveiling of the Father and the Son. Jesus is the Father. He who has seen me, said Jesus, has seen the Father. And the son is David, who calls him, my Lord. And so, when that whole thing is unveiled within man then he knows who he is. And everyone came here for that one purpose—to give up completely and overcome death. For the last enemy to be overcome is death. Really nothing dies anyway, we all are restored, everything is restored by these eternal images that are forever in heaven. And they are restored by contemplating the image. But that doesn't mean the end, that's only restoration. Resurrection is something entirely different, death comes at the end. And after the resurrection, which is the awakening within the skull, comes the birth from above. Then the discovery of David, then the stripping of the temple, and then the descent of the dove. And these are the marks of Jesus upon the body that Paul says, "I buried upon my body, the marks of Jesus."

He did not spell them out. I am making every effort to spell them out and to give you the actual interval of time between these marks that you may check it. It took me 1,260 days or you can say three-and-a-half months, or three-and-a-half years, pardon me, or forty-two months. These things are all in Scripture. Forty-two months, three-and-a-half years, or "time, times, and half a time," or 1,260 days. It takes exactly 1,260 days. From the 20th day of July of 1959 to the first day of January 1963, comes to 1,260 days. And that was the interval in which the whole thing happened. Our visions came after that but they are not considered the mark. These are the marks that took 1,260 days. Now here because we are at almost the end of the journey, let us go into the silence and give you a longer time tonight to ask questions. If you feel like it. Now let us go.

Neville: Are there any questions, please? Yes, ma'am.
Questioner: [inaudible]
Neville: Did you all hear that question? Why when we have a dream—I wouldn't say all dreams are of that nature, most of them are symbolic, granted—but the lady wants to know why is it that if they are supposed to be instructive, why are they so difficult for the individual who had the dream to understand them?

Well, I must confess that man is a taskmaster at misinterpreting his dreams. He tries to read everything into it and it only has one central jet of truth. But he tries to give every little piece of the dream significance, and it doesn't have that. But we are told in the book of

Numbers, the twelfth chapter of Numbers, "I will speak to man in a dream and make myself known in a vision." He reveals himself in visions but he speaks in a dream. And some dreams are so simple they need no interpretation. Others need interpretation, as we are told in the 41st chapter of Genesis when Pharaoh could not interpret his own dream and the wise men could not interpret it for him. Then he called Joseph. And Joseph came and interpreted the dream, and as he said, so it came to pass. He understood the universal language of symbolism. And so, all I can say to you is, well, make an effort, try your best or ask someone that you trust who can interpret the dream. But don't try to read everything into a dream. Some are very simple; others that seem simple, may have tremendous significance using the symbolism of the dream.

If you want help in a book, don't buy these dream books, they are no earthly good. But there is a book put out today in one volume. I have it in two when it first came out. It's called *The Lost Language of Symbolism* by [Harold] Bayley (1912). And he shows you through the centuries, going back to pre-Christian days, the imagery that the Egyptians used and all civilizations prior. And it's a universal language. The animal world and what it means when encountered in a dream. And it's called *The Lost Language of Symbolism* because it's universal. A man in China could dream of a dog, they have dogs. We dream of a dog. We have dogs. So, it's not necessarily a dog, an animal. It has certain significance. And the actions of the dog. We all have horses. Everybody has a horse in the world. That is, all nations have horses. And if we do not have tigers in our land, we know what a tiger is like. And all these things are part of this one-volume today, and it's a perfectly wonderful volume. It might help you in interpreting your dream.

But he does speak to men in dreams, and he makes himself known in a vision. A vision is just like this, you know, just as real as this, where man is in control, although he's automatically doing all the things, he seems to be in control of what is happening. And yet it's unfolding rapidly but just like this.

Questioner: [inaudible]

Neville: Well, let me, did you hear that question? If you were here last lecture night, you would understand the question better. For we spoke on a different level altogether. We spoke of the impregnation and using the story of a lady, who is present tonight, where she saw me standing at the foot of her bed with my back to her. And then I was sitting on her bed and then I leaned backwards and my entire body sank into her body. And there she is, alone, and yet I am within her. And then I came up by the side of her and then I took my left hand and covered her body with my left hand and felt the body. And then instantly I am on her. And then she had a climax. An ecstatic orgasm, and then I disappeared. She got off the bed, hoping to stand and she fell to her knees. And she wondered, "What was that experience?" Well, I explained it last lecture night that that was an impregnation. That the remnant spoken of in Scripture is not a remnant of a certain race of people but the elect of God. They are the apostles. The apostles are called. They are elected. They are chosen. But the word apostle means *to be sent*. And so, when you are called, you are also sent. Then you are sent in the capacity of one to sow the seeds. Not everyone sows the seed, any more than when you have racehorses, if you want to breed horses, you don't take every stud because he's a stud and use him as a stud. We have chosen one that we use as a stud. And you'll bring your mare to be courted by a certain stud.

Well, the same holds true in this copy world. That same world takes place above. And the apostle is simply the called, the chosen. They are the chosen stallions who will plant the seed. They are totally unaware because they also have their own moral-ethical code in this world by which they live. And if they were called upon to perform such acts in the knowledge of what they're doing, they couldn't do it, and would not do it because it would be in conflict with their ethical-moral code. So, they are relieved of the memory of it. For it is said of them, "He came to do the Father's will. And then the Father speaks, 'That I have found in him one after my own heart who will do all my will.'" So, it is the Father's will that that seed is planted at this moment. Now, there, there, there. And the chosen ones called the apostles, they've planted the seed. Not everyone is going to be chosen to plant the seed. There are eight ranks in the heavenly structure. The apostle comes first, then the prophet, then the teacher. So, you have a complete rank as you have in the army. And what comes down from the supreme general goes on to the next and the next and the next, and finally, you get to the soldier without stripes. But it's all in writing. So, the apostles in all of the divisions, no matter where you read it in Scripture, they come first. But not everyone is . . . [recording cutoff].

Lecture VII

*Know What You Want**

March 6, 1972

Tonight, the subject is our real belief. And I really want this series to be the most productive that we've ever had. And by that, I mean I want everyone present to really have a goal, a noble goal, and realize it, realize it before we close in May.

May I tell you, you can realize it. I mean that seriously. So, what do I mean by our *real beliefs*? Our real beliefs are what we live by. Real belief and knowing are one. What a man really believes is just as though he knows it. It's tantamount to knowing. So, when I tell you *believe*, I call it faith, I call it belief, it is not complete until it becomes experience. One must experience it and then they know it. Now you will hear the same thing tonight. Everyone present will hear exactly the same thing, but no two will hear it in the same depth. Some will hear it on the surface, others will hear it below the surface, and others will hear it down in the very depths of their being. It's where you hear it.

* This lecture is also known as "Our Real Belief."

As we are told, "The Word came to them as it did to us, but it did not profit them because it was not mixed with faith in those who heard it." They heard it and rejected it, but they heard it. It came in and went out. It did not receive acceptance by those who heard it and so they instantly rejected it. Tonight, I hope you will not reject what I'm here to tell you, but that's your choice, you're free. You will accept it or reject it. But I tell you if I get through tonight and you apply it because you are the operant power. I can tell you that it doesn't operate itself.

If this very moment I ask you to think of a friend, just think of a friend. And now hear him tell you something lovely, something lovely about himself, about a mutual friend or about you, just hear it. Do you believe that that actually took place? You may say, "Well, I imagined it, but it didn't really take place." I will tell you the day will come, and I hope now, that when you imagine a state before you have external confirmation of that state, to you it is as though you heard it externally. You know it. That this internal act is equal to the external confirmation of that act. You get to that point because the difference between God and man is measured only in terms of this imaginative power.

If I were to speak of the power that is God, as we are told in Scripture, is revealed constantly as power, sheer, third chapter, fourth, fifth, and sixth verses of the book of Exodus, sheer power. Moses stands in the presence of power, but it's creative power. And the distance between God and man are measured by simply power. On this level, if I'm in the service of my being, only this is real and what my senses allow. But if I go deeper into my own being, moving ever towards the core of my being who is God, then my imaginative act becomes externalized. Quickly externalized as I go deeper and deeper. On the surface, it seems to take an interval of time, if I believe. If I don't believe it, it never comes into some external form at all, never. Yet I'm living in a world, not understanding it, not knowing what it's all about.

So, really the story that I want to tell you is trying to ask you, and plead with you to buy your religion wholesale, go to the maker, go to the source. Don't buy it in retail from some man in between. No one in between you and the source. You go right into the depth and buy your religion wholesale. By going to the source, which is your own wonderful human imagination, your own *Iamness*, that's God.

The story we told you last Tuesday of one whose name was Eddie. Eddie had the identical experience to the one recorded in the book of Exodus. When he heard, "do not come up here"; read the words, the words are, "do not come here." Read it in the book of Exodus, the fourth, fifth, and sixth verses of the third chapter of Exodus. And the Lord said unto Moses, "Do not come here." And then Moses hid his face, not in shame, but in fear; he was afraid to look at God. So, Eddie saw the symbol of God and he ran, he was scared too. The identical story. What did he hear? The revelation of God's name, *I am*. He first heard it, *I am*, no one in sight. Then it repeated itself so loudly, he thought it came from above. He looked up thinking it was some machine, maybe some helicopter with a PA system is broadcasting the name, *I am*. There was not a thing in sight. And then the third, *don't come up here*. Being curious, he did go up there to the hill to confront a rattlesnake. Fortunately, it was not coiled to spring. It was simply a four-foot-long snake, all stretched out: the symbol of the creative power of God. But it scared him, it scares man. That man actually sees what really is in himself, that he's solely responsible for everything that's taking place in his will, solely responsible.

It scares him. It's too much. Until he goes deeper and deeper and hears the same word of truth but hears it in depth and then he assumes full responsibility for all that is taking place within him. So tonight, let me share with you a few stories. Seven years ago, a lady, she's not here tonight, she's now on a new job and is taken away for a while. But when she heard it, that imagining creates reality, she said to herself, "Well, if that is so, I would like to go to Egypt." She had no money. She's never been a lady of means, always working, small sums of money, could never accumulate what it would take to make the trip. And so, the usual story, she told her dream, she didn't keep it to herself, she told it, nothing wrong in it. If you really believe it, you can tell it. As you're told in the Scripture, "Go, tell no man, but show John, show the world."

Well, that's if you don't tell man before—will man believe you after the event? He may question your honesty. But if you tell him before the event, then he is assured because actually, you have a witness to the fact, that you did tell him before the event. So that is also in Scripture. And now I will tell you before it takes place that when it does take place, you may believe; but that is courage in the depth of the soul, where one knows the imaginal act is in effect at the very moment of the act, though not yet seen by the outer man. But not everyone has that courage and that faith in the imaginal act. So, she told it and naturally her friends criticized her. It is stupid to go to that man, you waste your money. It's not religion. What is it? He's telling you that an assumption, though false, if persisted in will harden into fact—but that's stupid. It doesn't make sense.

To them, a true judgment must conform to the external fact to which it relates. So, if I say, well, isn't this a lovely dog, and there is no dog to bear witness to my judgment, my judgment is false. So that's what they gathered from what she told them that I am teaching. And so, the whole thing is insane; it's stupid. Well, the years went on, it's been seven years now, and this is what happened this past week. She got a job, she's a nurse. And so, the job moves around. She goes from home to home where the need is there. And so, she found herself in the environment or the neighborhood of a friend she had not seen or contacted in a year. She had exchanged a birthday card and a Christmas greeting with a little note on the card, but no telephone call and no other contact.

Finding herself in the neighborhood, she calls her. When this friend heard her voice on the wire, she said, "Oh Jen, you can have it, you can have it." She said, "All right, all right, I'll take it. What is it?"

And then this is the story. There was a party, a pre-Lenten party at the hotel, Hilton, some Mardi Gras by a Catholic society, the Joseph and Mary society. There were door prizes. The major prize was a thirty-day trip, first-class, all expenses paid, and stopping along the way at the Hilton hotels in the Near East. And Egypt is part of the setup. The lady and her family had spent several months last year abroad and had no desire this year to go abroad again. In fact, they've already arranged to go to New York City for the World's Fair, which opens in April. So, a trip abroad is out. Furthermore, this ticket, this door ticket only accepts one person, not a group, not a family.

So that was what her friend said to her, she would give her. Jen said, "All right, I'll take it." And then called me up to tell me the story. Delayed seemingly seven years, she still now has her ticket, if she wants it, to the Near East where Egypt is included. And she goes, first-class, all expenses paid, everything paid—because she believed. Maybe in the interval, her faith wavered, maybe she justified it by saying, "Maybe I don't want it." Or in some strange way, try to explain it away. But it still, in its own good time, came to the surface. I'll ask you not to throw your dreams away and feel that they are impossible, a realization in this strange drab world of external facts. Every dream can come true if I can get through to you that your imagination is God, and that your imaginable act when you think of a friend carrying on the conversation, that is Jesus Christ in action.

Examine yourselves to see whether you are holding to your faith. Test yourself. Do you not realize that Jesus Christ is in you? If he is in you, then who is he? He is your own imagining. God is your imagination. God in action is imagining. And God in action is Christ. Christ as defined in Scripture is the power and the wisdom of God. So, I tell you, everyone can realize if you really believe in Jesus Christ. One billion will say they believe in Jesus Christ and cross themselves before a piece of wood or a piece of marble or clay or something other than a living God. And they've been kneeling before these external icons.

Here is the king of Greece, who just died. And they brought what they considered a holy icon for the man who has died. In the eyes of God, a king is just like a servant. They do not differ. One's love for one is not greater than his love for another. To what extent have they heard the word of God and believed; so, he's dying, they'll bring a holy icon. It didn't work, just saw the little icon, and so he makes his exit like any other person in the world. I hope that everyone here will find the *real Jesus Christ. The real Jesus Christ* is your own wonderful human imagining. That's God in action. *The real God* is your own wonderful, lovely imagination. When you say *I am*, that's God.

Now let me share with you that which was given to me this past week by a gentleman who is here tonight. He's written the most glorious stories. I hope he keeps it up because they're exciting. I share them with those who came home since I received his letters and I will share them with you tonight. He's a writer. He writes for TV. He started three years ago on this show that has been running for three years and he writes every third of four scripts. He said when I started my price was $2,500 a script. And in two years, my agent got it up to $3,000 a script. Then a year ago, last Christmas, my mother came west, came from the east to visit us, and I told her what I receive for a script, $3,000 a script. And she said, well, I always assumed that you got $3,500 a script. She wasn't all impressed with $3,000. And then he tried to explain to her that as far as he knew, there was no writer in the field, solo writer, who got more than he did. He was getting $3,000 a script. She was not impressed. Didn't disturb her at all. She still said that as far as she was concerned, it was worth $3,500 a script. Well, two months later, the agent was called by the studio for a contract, a renewal of the contract for the next year of writing.

Before that thing, he would go over to the studio, he would have to discuss it with the writer. And so, he explained to the writer, he didn't think that they should ask for more. They moved it from $2,500 a script to $3,000 a script, and you shouldn't price yourself out of the business by asking for more. And so, the writer agreed. It was a nice, friendly relationship between himself and the producer. So why ask for more and get out of the business? So, it was agreed. The very next day after this agreement, a conference was held to discuss stories, a story conference. And so, the producer said to the writer, "Have you come to an agreement with the contract for the next year?" And he said, "Yes, I'm going to sign." He said, "Have you asked for more money?" He said, "No." "Did you ask for more?" He said, "But you are always complaining about the budget, it isn't big enough, and now you are telling me to ask for more." He said, "You ask for more money." Again, he said, "I don't want to price myself out of the business." He said, "You tell your agent to ask for more."

So, when he went back, he called his agent. And when he told the agent to ask for more money, the agent thought he had too many cocktails for lunch. So, he said, "No, I will give you the source." And he told him what had been told to him that very day at the conference. So, the agent now armed with this information that the very producer had recommended an increase. So, he called up the business office of the studio and asked for more. And they simply blew their top, they screamed. And then very generously, they said, forget it as though you didn't even ask for it, so that the nice relationship between the producer and the writer can go on as it has for the past three years.

But the agent knowing the source was adamant. And so, when he came out of that office, he came out with a contract for $3,500 a script. So said the writer in his letter to me, "My mother merely assumed that I was getting $3,500 a script. And so, her assumption went behind the backs of all of us, producers, everyone, and bore fruit." So, then he said, "I called her up and I told her what I was getting a script now. And then she started to seriously study your books." And he said, "A problem, a very great burden had been with her for twenty-five years, a most distressing problem, which I will tell you about at some future date. But may I tell you, last Friday, it was completely swept out of her life. And now a confession is in order. When I first heard you, I couldn't understand you. And then I began to be afraid that I was going mad because I *could* understand you." Then he said, "I will explain that later."

So, I am waiting equally for that explanation. But we are told in the book of John, "He has a devil. He is mad. Why listen to him?" You have your Bibles. That's the 10th chapter, the 20th verse of the book of John. That is the chapter where he said, "I and my father are one." He had just gotten through in the previous or the eighth chapter by saying, "I know my father, my father is he whom you called God, but I know my father and you know not your God." And for this, they stoned him, stoned him with the little facts of life. That's the stone of Scripture. When you throw the facts at a man, when the man dares to assume what reason denies, what his senses deny, then you who will not go along with his depth, you'll throw the stones or the facts of life at it to deny the reality of what he's claiming by a more imaginal act.

And so, he had just gotten through making these bold assertions—"That I and my father are one. And my father is he whom you call God, but I know my father and he knows not your God." And so, this story, he said, "I didn't understand you. And then I began to fear a form of madness because I *could* understand you"—for this is, it takes you into an entirely different world for reason on this surface, over the mind, doesn't really prevail, that you really believe in the reality of what inwardly you are doing. And then it comes to the surface if you don't tell it before, and you tell it afterwards, they will question your honesty. If you take them into your confidence and tell it before, if you have enough faith, go about your business, if you don't, they will plague you and throw the stones at you.

And every time they meet you, they'll say, "Well, where is it? You said you're going to have a certain home, a certain job, a certain sum of money. Where is it?" And so, they are always throwing the stones at you or the facts of life. Now, here is something and you listen to it carefully. It's a long letter, and he's bringing out certain points that might have escaped you, for here what we are trying to do is to find out all the little facets of the greatest secret in the world: the secret of imagining. For as Fawcett said, the secret of imagining is the greatest of all problems to the solution of which all should aspire for supreme power, supreme wisdom, and supreme delight lie in the solution of this far-off problem.* This great mystery. And he has found some light on it. So, if I can recall, it's a long letter, typewritten four pages, but I will give you some of the highlights of it:

So, when I met my producer three years ago, he was a very subdued and reserved sort of a gentleman. Reserved, he says, would be the right word to use to describe him, very reserved. So, unlike the volatile enthusiasm of whom I formerly worked, he was very reserved. In fact, he couldn't express the superlative in any way. In fact, his greatest praise was the word, *good.* So, you brought in the script and he would accept the script and his highest praise was *good.* Well, I thought I'm going to change this. So, I lay on the bed and I heard him say to me, *great, just great.* Now I hadn't started on the script. I had just given him a script and he pronounced the script, *good.* I am now doing this about the next script. And I heard him distinctly. I went over and over in my study or set up as it were. So, I heard him inwardly pronounce the new script as *great, just great.* And while I am lying there, the phone rings, I haven't started the script. The phone is ringing and it's the producer. And he is telling me that the script that he had formerly pronounced *good* was *great, just great.* Well, he said, he threw me a curve because that's not what I was expecting, it was about the new script, which I hadn't even started. So, he not only threw me this curve, but someone had their lines crossed. So, right there, I kept on now working on the new, I would say, line for him to

* Neville is referencing and paraphrasing English author and philosopher Edward Douglas Fawcett (1866–1960), an exponent of philosophical Idealism.

use, and I change it from *great, just great* to *terrific*. And so here I am. I only heard one word, it is *terrific*. Well, I submitted a script and that's exactly the word he used when he said to me, it's *terrific*. And with the same enthusiasm that matched my imagining. Now I said to myself, two months later, every script I presented within two months, it was either *great, just great*, or *terrific*. It didn't go back to *good* anymore. So, I said, now, I'm going to experiment again. So, this time I'm going to make him say *absolutely sensational*.

So, I heard him say *absolutely sensational*. Then he says to me, what the hell if you're praising yourself why not get the best? So, I am doing it to myself anyway. So, why be modest about it? I am doing the whole thing because he's only echoing it. So, I said, *absolutely sensational*. So, I finished the script, took the script into him and he pronounced it *good*. He said, I almost fell out of the chair. It was not the role that I had written for him. And he said, do you know how authors hate ad-libbing? You know what that means in the theatrical world when the author writes a play and some actor thinks he knows more than the author and he changes the script and he ad-libs, or maybe he forgets his lines. And if he's smart enough, he can throw a few words in, and he ad-libs. But no matter how smart he thinks he is, he doesn't flatter the author. The author feels, he knows better than any actor, what should be there at that moment. And so, he said in his letter, you know how authors hate ad-libbing. So, what could I do? The script had to be cut. So, he gave me back the script to cut a certain portion of it. I took the script home, did all the cutting, and then mailed it to him. And I mailed it as a petulant child. I didn't even revise what he had said. But the very next day he calls and he said to me on the wire, it's *absolutely sensational*.

Now this is the point I want you to pay strict attention to. He said, you know, my experience with the producer disturbed me, greatly disturbed me; to hear or to occasionally think about this, isn't so bad. By that, he meant you hear that all that you behold, though, it appears without, it is within, in your imagination of which this world of mortality is but a shadow. Well, to hear that and to occasionally think about it, isn't too bad, but when it seeps in, and takes hold of you, and goes deeper, you realize that it's true, that that producer who is so important in the production of this great series, who is spending its fortunes, he has it to spend, that is, he allows it. He knows what he's doing. He's been successful for thirty-three years. And yet he had to actually utter the word that this writer is writing for him.

And when he met him, he was so reserved, he never used any superlatives, and could never bring himself to praise a thing beyond the word, *good.* And he raised him from *good* to *great, just great, terrific, absolutely sensational.* That's an enormous accomplishment in anyone's vocabulary when he began as a most reserved party. So, when the individual writer now sees what he did with a man, he said, you know, it distressed me. It distressed me for the simple reason, I had to remake my world only as I remake myself. Only as I could remake myself, could I in any way remake the world, and what an undertaking. But if I found a solution. I will not now think of myself X number of years into the future. I am painting a portrait of myself and portraits are not painted by one stroke with a brush. And so, I am taking it easily. I start with the little things in my life, the little things, and I change them to make them conform to the portrait of the being I am painting of myself.

I started with a simple thing. We have a cat, or we had a cat, and it simply clawed up the entire rug. All the rugs were simply pieces of felt, all torn up. And so, we delayed buying a new rug. Really, said he, we were hoping that she would die. After all, she was fifteen years old and she seemed determined to outlive Methuselah. But because she still was very healthy and she didn't die, we bought the new rug and right away, she started all over again to tear up the rug. And for two days, I said something must be done in my imagination. I had proved it with the producer. So, I went to work in my imagination and saw this cat in the backyard tearing up a mat that we had in the backyard for just such a purpose.

On the third day, she was out in that backyard, clawing the mat until the day she died, she never once tore up our rug. Here is the destructive power in the world, saved in the imagination of man. If someone heard that story and didn't believe it, they could this night have a cat in their house and they will say, oh, that was just coincidence, in his case, it wouldn't work here, so I'm not even going to try it, that borders on madness, and no one wants to be mad. In fact, to say that you were once put away is like leprosy. They don't want that. That you were once committed to some asylum, to go to a hospital because you had a pain and you needed an operation, that's allowed today because everyone has them. But not everyone is put away for some mental, I would say, side issue.

And so, in his case, he did it. The average person would've heard it and who would believe that in their own home, they too, could make the dog or the cat or the bird or anything else conform to an imaginable act. Well, having done this, now he sees the power within him. He's not going to go all out, he knows he's done it. He has tangible proof that he's done it. And from now on, he said, he's going to actually be faithful to what he has found within himself. He's found, Christ. The day is coming, he will actually stand in the presence of infinite love. But before he stands in the presence of infinite love, he presents himself first as infinite might. And throughout the Bible, you can't find any basis to deny it, it is might, it's power and authority. From beginning to end, when he presents himself, it's sheer might, sheer power, until one day, man will see that this power on this level and in many levels below resolves itself into infinite love, and it's man. And it's the being that you're moving toward, and it's God the Father. So here, in his own case, it scared him or rather it depressed him to think that such power was in man, and yet it's no other place. It's only in man because the power of which we speak, the greatest power in the world, really the only power, is your own wonderful human imagination.

Now, the lady whose story I told first, Jen. Jen said that this present job of hers, this little boy came home from school, and the high winds we've been having took the aerial down and flattened it. It's still on the ground, she said. And so, she tried the TV and there was no TV. She tried it and tried it and there was no TV. The little boy came home and she said, oh Lord, he's going to be so disappointed because he's back from school, and he wants to see the TV. So, he goes straight to the TV. He turns it on. He saw the aerial flattened. Then he put his two hands on the top of the machine and just put them there. And she said to him, you know, there's going to be no picture; he said, oh yes, there will be. That does it. And she said, what does it? He said my imagination. I just imagined it, it'll do it. He came back, got in front of the picture with Jen, and here comes this beautiful picture.

Now, Jen couldn't do it. And yet she knows this principle, but she's an adult now. We become adulterated as we grow in this world. The little child could actually believe that that power in his hand was all his imagination. It'll do it. And Jen told me over the telephone because she's working, she can't come here now, that the little boy only put his hands on it and swore that there would come a picture, and the picture came to Jen's amazement, but not to the boy's. He sat and looked at it and Jen sat there bewildered. The one who has the thing now to go to Egypt.

Now to come back to the gentleman's story, He said, I saw an ad of a Swiss record changer, and so I went over to my electronics dealer and I told him that I would like one. He said they aren't in the country and they will be possibly a few weeks before they get here. But we have eleven orders so far, would you like to order one? He said, yes, I'd like to order one. So, he ordered one. So, he said at the end of the month, he received a bill for $375 for the changer, while he hadn't received the instrument, so he called up the office and they apologized. They said that the girl mistook the order for a sale. And so, we have bad news for you, said the girl, it will not be here for three or four months, but they corrected their mistake, it was not a bill. It was simply an order that they had misinterpreted. He then said to himself, I will now look around the house and spent three days instead of writing to see where he is going to put the outlet for this machine.

And when he decided where he'd put it, he called the electricians and had them bore a hole through the wall to put in the cable for this changer. Now he said, I will need a stand for it. So, he went out, looking for a stand, went to all the places, and one salesman said, what kind of a machine have you? Because you don't like these stands. So, he told the nature of the machine. And the man said, if you have one, it's a miracle because there aren't any in the country. And there won't be here for three or four months, which was only confirmed in what the agency said. He said, oh, I can't find the stand, I will design one. So, he designed the stand and had it made. When the stand came, and he placed it where he intended to place the machine, he said to himself, I will now see the machine in there, which he did. Now, he said, now that I have the machine it is the only fair to pay the bill. So, he sat down and wrote the check out and sent the check off to the electronic firm for $375 in full for his machine.

Two days after this, they called him to say, we have your record changer. He wondered why there were twelve of them on the list. The man only received four in his shipment of an order of twelve. And this friend who wrote me the letter said, well, it could be that I sent my check in advance because I paid for what to me was before me in my imagination. It could be that, on the other hand I'm not asking questions, why he gave me the first one in and why he jumped me from twelve to number one. However, I have the machine, and now my next problem is this: It's a very delicate, complicated, sly, tricky thing. And so, I am now trying to imagine myself smart enough to operate it.

So that is the story of using your imagination. I say *faith,* as we are told, we understand that by faith, the world was framed by the word of God, but you know who God is now, your own wonderful *Iamness,* that's God. He's framing his world but it takes faith to hear it. Without faith, it won't work. To hear it mixed with faith, it will work. If you sit down as he did, he said, I lay on the bed, you can sit right here and carry on this inner, mental conversation from premises of fulfilled desire, for thinking follows the tracks laid down in one's own inner conversations. You control the nature of the conversation and see to it that it's not an argument, it's simply from *wishes fulfilled*, regardless of the nature of that wish, you carry it on the inside. Some are better at the video, they can see better, they can hear, but I find hearing so very, very easy, and I am not a musician. So, you don't have to be musically inclined to really hear.

I appreciate music, but I don't play. And I don't understand music in the true sense of the word, I simply appreciate it. Yet, I can hear it vividly, a man's voice as he speaks for one second, let me get the tone, then put upon that tone any word I want to hear, and I hear it as though he were here. Now how long it takes for what I have heard him say to come to pass, I don't know. As we tell you in that story of the book of Habakkuk: "The vision has its own appointed hour."

"It ripens, it will flower. If it be long, then wait, for it is sure, and it will not be late." So, one seed grows overnight. Another seed takes a month. Another seed takes a year as in birth, a boy, a child comes to this world nine months, but a chicken comes out in twenty-one days. And so, everything has a different interval of time between conception and birth in this world. So, what determines the nature of an interval, I don't know. But have faith that it is sure and it will not for its own sake be late, not for its own nature will it be late. So, if a child comes out in nine months, it isn't late for a child. If a chicken comes out in twenty-one days, it's not late or early for a chicken. That's the interval of time between that moment when it was fertilized and properly nested and then the moment of breaking the shell and hatching.

So here in our case apply it. And you will, in the next few months, I'm only here for three months, not yet three months. And you'll be able to tell me the most fantastic stories in the world because you couldn't start from anything more behind the eight ball. You meet a conservative gentleman who would never beyond, well, the wildest dream, go outside and exclaim something is really, absolutely sensational. It's all against his nature. A thing is good, that's good enough. You're being well paid for it. You've got $2,500 and you've got $3,000 for a script. And every three weeks you're bringing one in because it's a half-hour's show. It runs weekly. So, every three weeks, you're getting a check for $3,000. Now you're getting $3,500. And yet the man I'm quite sure like all writers, he is not contracted to write only and only for that, if he has time outside of writing these scripts, there are other outlets for his talents as a writer. He's not confined to that. And therefore, the man who is not given to exploding, he made him explode and raised him gradually to *great*, *just great*, *terrific*, and then the final explosion. And he said in this letter is the warmest and the friend is the relationship between us.

So, I ask you to do the same thing. I don't care what it is in this world, know what you want, conceive a scene implying the fulfillment of that dream, and then inwardly carry on these mental conversations from the premise of the fulfilled desire. If you can see at the same time that you hear like a TV set, all right, put them together, it's better. But if you can really visualize, and not many can visualize, you will find the audio very, very simple. But when you begin to visualize, may I tell you, it's the most thrilling thing in the world, to be able to actually see just like this, to be in a dream awake. It's like being in a dream, only awake. And so, then you take it and return to this level where it hasn't taken place, you have no fears, you have no doubts. The whole world could collapse. You know you saw it. You're still seeing it in your mind's eye now. But you actually saw it and you heard it. And so, it must come to pass. You saw it and you heard it. And so, you meet someone who is passing through sheer hell and they ask of you anything, still in your world, sing them out and hear them tell you that they have what they sought, just as though they have it. And then let it go. Don't raise a finger to make it so. Don't get in the phone and call a friend to ask the friend to intercede, to help you out. Don't do a thing. Just simply believe in the reality of your imaginal act.

Because if you go to the end, then you can't concern yourself with the means to that end. That will deny the end by any means that you would even entertain to aid the growth of it because you went beyond the pregnancy right into birth. And so, you saw it and you heard it. Now leave it alone and let it work. And may I tell you, it will work. And then you will find God, and when you come to the final grand, I would say the last stretch, the final stretch, when you're going home now, really going home, leaving behind you, this world, this age altogether. They will come one after the other, the most fantastic mystical experiences where everything said of Jesus Christ you will experience and you will know beyond all doubt who Jesus Christ really is. That he truly is supernaturally born. Born out of a skull of a man. How he discovers the fatherhood of God. And how he ascends into Heaven and everything said of him happens to you. And so, you know how true the story is, how altogether fantastically wonderful Scripture is when one experiences it. And so, I ask you to join with me in testing this greatest of all mysteries. Put it to the test. Start with something simple. The average person would have a destructive animal like the cat wouldn't consider that a simple problem. And yet in 48 hours, it was resolved.

But one point he made when the man told him, he used the words, he expressed himself when he said to me, *terrific*. He expressed it with the enthusiasm that matched my imagining. The world is the only response, infinite response, it's an echo. And the whole vast world only echoes. And so, what echoed in this case, when he said, *terrific*, you can see what the writer's imaginal act was. He actually caught a mood that was really forceful. So, then the word *terrific* came through, it wasn't simply, "Oh, I think it's terrific." He exploded with *terrific* to equal the emotional state of the man who made him say terrific. So, catch it and feel it and use your imagination as a great actor would. He has to put himself into the part and play it. And to the degree that he feels it, he gets beyond the footlights. If he doesn't identify himself with the character that he's trying to depict, he never gets over. He has to become the character. And so, this one became the character of hearing the actor whose lines he wrote. And the actor was given a line to say, you said, *terrific*, and I'll listen carefully because you've got to say it and I am directing it. I don't want any little terrific. I want you to really *give it*. And so, I will now give you the mood that I want you to adopt.

And so, he gives them to him and the word comes through exactly to match his imaginal act. And his use of words fascinates me because not everyone understands the baseball language. When he said he threw me a curve, something entirely different. It wasn't what I expected. That was less the script that you read, he said and pronounced, good. I don't want that. I want you to pronounce this new statement and say that it is really great. *Great. Just great.* Of the new script, I haven't even started the new script. I used my word, but you sort of predated it. You went back in time and called it the other script, and then the man comes back and actually calls it. But after he changed the word from that to *terrific*. That's really discovering how you use your imagination. But if you don't and you think, "well, it's just on this level," you will never get off. But I want everyone here to really believe it and try it. If I take from you this night, if you're here for the first time and I've taken off, shaken your belief in a personal God outside of yourself, a personal savior outside of yourself, I don't apologize because I know it is true what I've told you. I am not theorizing. I'm speaking from experience. And so, when I take this platform and tell you that I know the reality that is God.

I wouldn't care what the whole world would say about it. When they say, "You don't mean that God truly stood before you or you stood before him and you looked into the face of man." I say, yes, I did, and it is man. *I am* is spirit but it needs man its perfect form to really express anything in this world. So, it assumes the form of man. So, when you see *I am* in form, the form is man. Just like the little girl who told her grandma, "You know what? I went up last night in my dream, right up to the sun. And you know what? He has a face. And you know what? He has hands and he has feet. And you know what? The ocean, the big ocean talked to the sun. And you know what? The sun came down to the earth. And you know what? He has legs and he can walk. And he walked right over to me and kissed me on the cheek, and it was hot. Now, isn't that a silly, silly dream, Grandma?" But it's true. There is nothing but God and God is man.

And so, when Blake was asked, when you see the sun, do you see a big round guinea?* He said, no. A host of angels claimed holy, holy, holy. He drew him as man. It's nothing but man because man and God are one. God is man. So, I ask you to take what I've given you this night, take it home and you try it. It costs you nothing, only the effort and the little time that you will spend in doing it. But bear in mind, when you do it, believe it. Because the words are, "The word was spoken to them just as it was to us. But it did not profit them because they did not receive it with faith, those who heard it." And so, when you do it tonight, do it knowing that that in itself is a creative act, that imaginal act, and be faithful to it. Though faith does not give substance to that imaginal act, that unseen reality. *Faith is loyalty to unseen reality.* You simply are loyal to it. You made a pledge, all right, now you're loyal to the unseen reality.

Questions, please. Yes, sir?

* A guinea was an English gold coin issued during William Blake's (1757–1827) lifetime.

Questioner: [inaudible]

Neville: No. The three tests are quotes from the book of Deuteronomy. And man in this world, the only devil in this world are the facts of life, the doubts of man. If you could take it, personify doubt, and give doubt a voice to speak, it would throw at you all the facts of life that would be in conflict with your dream, that the dream in itself was the reality before wearing a form. And so, doubt is telling you, "Well, if you think you can do all these things, then cast yourself down. For he has given the angels power to lift you up . . ." [recording cutoff]

Lecture VIII

Feel Chosen

day unknown, 1972

I want to ask you to feel that you are wanted, that you are chosen, that you are the elect. As we are told, he chose us in him, before the foundation of the world. But man will not believe it, he will not believe that he is that important. So, we are speaking now of the Lord, the creator of the universe who chose us in him before the foundation of the world. So, tonight I will try to convince you that you are the chosen.

The most controversial verse in Ecclesiastes, the most disputed, is the 11th verse of the third chapter: "And God has put eternity into the mind of man. Yet so, that man cannot find out what God has done from beginning to the end." This is the only time in the Scripture that the word is translated *eternity*. In the King James version, it is translated *the world*. The other books, say, Moffatt, James Moffatt.* And he translates the word as *mysteries*. "To the mind of man, he appointed mysteries. Yet so that man cannot fathom God's own purpose from beginning to end." Paul comes on and he tells us he waited for the

* Neville is referencing Scottish theologian and translator James Moffatt (1870–1944).

fullness of time. "And when the fullness of time came, God sent forth the spirit of his Son into our heart crying, Father."

And that he is made known unto us the mystery of his will, according to his purpose, which he set forth in Christ as a plan for the fullness of time to unite all things in him both in Heaven and on earth. Now, the word translated *eternity* or *world* or *mystery* is the Hebrew word *olam.* Now this is the only place in the entire book where it is translated the *world* or *eternity* or *mystery.* And yet, it is used hundreds of times in the Bible. The word is *olam.* Here is one. "And when you go to the people of Israel and they ask you, who sent you, simply say, *I am* has sent me unto you. This is my name forever." The word forever is *olam.* When you read the word everlasting in scripture, in the Old Testament, it is *olam.* And you read all of these, it is *olam.* Here in the 136th Psalm, there are twenty-six verses and each verse ends with the same statement: "Thy steadfast love endures forever." And that forever is *olam.* Now, he put *olam* into the mind of man. Remember his name endures forever, "which is my name forever."

What did he put into the mind of man? His name is himself. His name forever is *I am.* That is the immortal being who created the universe. His steadfast love endures forever. So, into the mind of man came God himself, which is *I am.* That's the Lord. There is no other God. If you could only believe for one moment, as you are seated here, you are aware of being, awareness of being is actually saying without the use of words, *I am.* And that is God. If you could only believe that you are that altogether wonderful being that he chose to give himself to, your entire world would change. You will see everything differently. To feel that I am wanted. The average person in the world feels that he is unwanted, he's unknown. And yet you are known and loved by the only presence in the world that matters. That's who you really are. You are the being that God so loved, he actually became you that you may become God. So, when you say *I am* that's God, and there is no other God. Now, in Hebrew thought history consists of all the generations of men and their experiences fused into a single whole, and that *concentrated time* into which all the generations of men and experiences are fused and from which they all spring is called *eternity*. The predominant sense of the word *olam* is *permanent*. It means the *continuous* as against or in contrast to the fragmentary time that quickly passes away. That's something that is forever. So, he put *forever*, which is himself, in you. So, Blake could quite honestly say all things exist in the human imagination. So, when you sleep tonight, though you may not be able to pay rent, though you may think you are unknown and unwanted, dwell upon this thought: you're not only known but you are known by the only being that really matters. And that only being so cared that he became you. He dwells *in you* as your own wonderful human imagination. When you say, *I am*, that's God, there is no other God. And that is God forever and forever. That's the immortal you that cannot die. I could chop off your head right now and see the body turn into dust by putting it into the flames. Yet you cannot die.

That's only a mask that you wore when I saw you. But you, the real you cannot die, it is eternal because it is God, the real you. If you could only catch this feeling, your whole world would change, you'll feel important, you'll feel wanted. Wanted by what? The government? No, that's nothing. That's transitory. All things pass. But this one that so loved you passes not. He simply so loved you, he actually became you. And he is the eternal being in the world. You dwell on that and your whole feeling changes concerning your value in this world, who you really are, and what you amount to; you are the chosen one, you are the elect.

Let me share with you a few letters that came this week. I see a few of them here who wrote them. One lady wrote saying that she found herself in her swimming pool and she was floating on her back. And she decided to make the entire swim on her back from one end to the other. And she said I felt that I had had too much wine. And I felt really to the point of capacity. And I shouted out, "I have had too much *swine*." And then I got embarrassed that I had so much wine that even my words would not take the proper course. And I corrected myself and said *wine*. I said, I do enjoy a drink, but it's not wine. I like something stronger. I am not given to excessive drinking, but when I do have a drink, I like something stronger, but here it was wine. And I am floating on water in my own pool. Then she said, I felt your presence. I didn't see you. I couldn't say to anyone, I saw you. And now I cannot actually say that you were another. Yet here, I know you were present and you and I are one. We are one. So, I could no more use the word, "we." I will have to say "I." Yet, I know that you and I are one and I cannot divide it and say, "we," it is simply "I." And then I awoke. Well, she caught it perfectly. Where do you think I am going when I depart this section of time? If heaven is within you, and that's where I am headed, all of my experiences have completed the journey in this world of tears.

Where can I go but within heaven and heaven is within you. Read the 17th chapter of the book of John: "I dwell in them, in everyone, and we are one as thou and I are one." And I mean that seriously, we are one because there's only one God. So, when you awake and you are the Father of God's only begotten Son, you are God. So where are you going to go? But back to your source, which is God. And so, she felt my presence and yet you were not another I could see, I couldn't refer to you as something, as another. I could not even use the plural and say *we*, and yet I knew we were one. I felt your presence. And yet it is my very being. So, in the end, God played all the parts. There is nothing in the world but God, he conceives the entire play. He played all the parts for his name forever is *I am*. You say, *I am*, don't you? Well, that's God. I say, *I am*. It's the same God, it's not another God.

So here in this marvelous story but concealed for the word *olam* means to hide self. It means to conceal. It means to hide from. It also means the lad, the youth, the stripling, the young man, and he put *olam* into the mind of man. What did he put into the mind of man?

There's only Jesus Christ but divide the word. Jesus is the Lord, that's *I am*. Christ is his Son, is the Son of the Lord. And that Christ is David. He is the man. So, when he stands before the King, the demented King Saul, and Saul said to him, "Whose son are you young, man?" He first inquired of his lieutenant, Abner. He said Abner whose son is that? "As your soul liveth, O King, I cannot tell." *Inquire whose son this stripling is*. And then when you could not find out, he brings him before the King with the head of the giant, in his hand. And then the King addresses David. He said, whose son are you, young man? He said I am the son of Jesse. The son of Jesse. Well, Jesse means *I am*. I am telling you, I am the Son of God. The word Jesse means *I am*, in any form of the verb to be. It means Jehovah exists and Jehovah is *Yod Hey Vav Hey*, which really means *I am*.

He is telling you, *I am* the Son of the one whose name forever and forever is *I am*. Who stands before you? Well, who did he put into the mind of man? He put himself and his Son into the mind of man. So, Paul, making the discovery could say, "Do you not realize that Jesus Christ, which is the Lord and his anointed one, his Son, is in you?" And at the end of time, his purpose is revealed. God's purpose is to give himself to us literally. So, in the end, you awake and his Son calls you Father. You tell the story to those that he gave you, out of all that he has, that you may bring them to a certain level of awareness. And then you depart—and where are you going to go? Into heaven? For where is heaven, but within? So, when she said, "I cannot say we, I can only use the personal pronoun in its singular form, *I*, and yet I felt your presence, I knew that we were one, but I can't use the word, we, I am so much you, I can't say we." That's what I'm trying to tell you. So, we come to the end—and the journey is over. I am just simply your own wonderful, *I am*. So, in the end, when the curtain comes down on the entire drama, God who conceived the entire thing, played it all, and forgave all. Forgave everyone because he played every part in the world.

Now, another letter and he is here tonight, it says through my years, I have used imagination to achieve my goals in this world. And yet I have found myself having used my imagination and I've completely forgotten the incident. Then it came to pass and I reap the results. And I can't get over that belief that I, intellectually, did it. And so, I completely forget that imagination did it. I imagined it to be done and then dropped it. And then in the interval of time, it happened. I'm confronted with the evidence, and yet here I am stuck because I cannot get over that belief that I intellectually did it. And yet I do remember having done it in my imagination. Then he quotes several lovely passages of Scripture. He quoted the 20th chapter of Numbers. He quoted the 8th of Deuteronomy, He quoted the 10th of Isaiah. And the 7th of Judges. If you read these stories, the Lord is trying to convince Israel that Israel didn't do it, that the Lord did it.

So, in the book of Judges, he said, I am now stuck. I can't understand this test that the Lord gave to Israel in the book of Judges. You'll read it in the 7th chapter. He is about to conquer Midian for Israel. And so, the call goes out and 32,000 responded. Now he gave them two tests. The first test was one based upon fear. And 22,000 of them confessed that they were afraid. So, they were released from duty and sent back to their home. He still had 10,000. He thought that's too many for Israel would say, "We did it." But if I can reduce that number from 10,000 to just a skeleton against the mighty hordes of Midian, they can't say that my mighty army did it but the Lord must have done it.

So, then he gave them a second test. Anyone who could lap water as the dog laps water. And so, then they all had to make the test at a running brook, and those who went down on their knees were disqualified. Those who cupped their hands and drank it from their hands, being alert constantly, they were drinking water, bear in mind, that the lady said she was floating on water, and she was filled with wine. The first sign in John is to turn the stone and fill it with water and then turn the water into wine. There are three levels of awareness:

there's solid, objective fact, the reality; then the water is the psychological meaning of Scripture; and then comes the wine, the spiritual understanding of it. So here only 300 cupped their hands and drank from it.

And they are put aside, that they were the only ones who would be taken to conquer all the hordes of Midian, that Israel could not say by my own strong hands, I did it. What does it mean? That's a parable. All these are parables. It's a parable of life for all of us. Spiritual nourishment. He's obtained by those who, while they move along the normal, natural paths of experience, feed themselves as it comes. And there are those who think there must be a special occasion, a retreat for my meditation, a withdrawal from the world. I must actually put myself apart and be something entirely different for the spirit of God to come upon me. May I tell you, they will wait and wait and wait for unnumbered of years and it will not come that way. Go about your Father's business, going to the marketplace, and whatever you were doing, do it, but always remember the Lord. So, they cupped their hands but they were alert. They didn't get down on their knees and bury their head in the running stream. They cupped their hands and they were alert for they were on a journey. Three hundred. So, he reduced it from 32,000 to 300.

So, I say to him, you feel that you take credit for your intellectual accomplishment and you know from experience that you did receive that with an imaginal act, and then you forgot the imaginal act. But the imaginal act didn't forget itself. It came to pass and you reaped the harvest of what you had done, imaginably, knowing you did not really accomplish it with your own intellectual powers. Well, go back to seeing now, you do not need any withdrawal from this world for spiritual nourishment. None whatsoever. You think you need some special occasion. If you need some little retreat where you can go and meditate, you have the wrong concept of God, for he is in you. Where are you going to find him more than where you can find him wherever you are? If you're standing at a bar, he's present. No matter where you are this night, he is present in you. He is not in any holy place in the world, wherever you are that's the holy place. There is no cathedral in the world. No so-called holy place, call it a sanctified cemetery. Cemetery of what? He is buried in you, you are the sepulcher where God is buried. He is not buried in any cemetery in this world. He never was. He's buried in the skull of man. That's where he is buried.

So, a lady now writes from San Francisco and she said, you know, I had the strangest dream and I can't understand it. I met you and here you are expounding Scripture. And then you came over to me and you embraced me and I pushed you away. And I said, no, Neville. What I did, I do not know. She doesn't say that in her letter. And then she said, I said to her, you know, I would've married you. And she said, but I am married. And I said, yes, I know, but the day will come when you will know that Jerry, that's her husband, and I are one. It is not a union of sex. It's a union of my teaching. Take my yoke upon me and learn from me for my yoke is the teaching.

So, she loves it. She has the records because she made them herself at the last meeting in San Francisco. So, she made ten, and she tells me she plays them over and over and he made others before that. So, they must have maybe thirty or forty of these recordings. But she hasn't quite absorbed it for she could not have said no. There would be no sex in this. It's a union with God. For I am telling you, I became one with him when he embraced me. So, we are no longer two, just as my friend said, I can't use the pronoun, *we*; I will use now the singular, *I*; and yet I feel your presence and I am you. And yet I haven't lost my identity. And I can tell you from my own experience, we're all the sameness of identity; when this thing happens, there is a radical change in form. It's not this form at all. It's spirit.

Now take these words and see if you aren't shocked by them. In the book of Proverbs, the 8th chapter, the 22nd verse: "The Lord created me at the beginning of his way. The first of his acts of old." Look at the word beginning, "at the beginning of his way." And this is the definition given in *Strong's Concordance*: "To shake the head, the top." The beginning is when that head of yours vibrates, so you think this is the end, and it's only then the beginning. When your head so vibrates that you think this is it, meaning to yourself, never having experienced anything comparable to this, that this is the end of what the world would call, now, you're dying. Far from dying, the Lord shook the head. He vibrated the head. And that vibration woke you. Who did he wake? If you would be asked, who heard it? And who actually was wakened when he heard it and felt it? You would answer, *I*. I am wakened. And who found himself within the tomb and knew it to be his own skull? You would answer *I*. And who then knew how to come out? You would say *I*. And who came out? You would say, *I*. And who found the child and knew it to be his own? *I*.

So, the *I* is buried in there and it's God. And it comes with the vibration of the head when the whole head begins to shake. It is the shaking of the head. *Rosh*, we have a New Year. We speak of *Rosh Hashanah*. *Rosh* is the shaking of the head. It's not another year pass by and I mark it off the calendar and go to another year. This is an entirely new age when that head shakes. You can mark off year after year, we call this now the year 1972. And the Jews speak of their year, going back over five centuries, meaning 5,000 years, but that's not the *rosh* of the Rosh Hashanah that Scripture speaks of. It speaks of the shaking of the head, of the top. And then it goes on to say *the first born, the first fruit,* all these are the definitions given to *rosh*. When the head begins to shake, then you come out, and you are born from the top. You are born from God. And all ends run through the origins. So, if the origin is God, the end is God. It is God that is born.

So, then you are in this world. You are now only an extension of the Lord, for he extends himself in those that are born, born from above, but all will be born from above. And that's how God expands and expands and expands himself. So, "He has put eternity into the minds of men. Yet so that man cannot find out what God has done from the beginning to the end." Nevertheless, at that end, he does make known his purpose. As Paul said, in his letter to the Ephesians, "He's made known unto us the mystery of his will, according to his purpose, which he sent forth in Christ as a plan for the fullness of time." So, when the fullness of time came, God sent forth his Son who is Christ, which is David crying in our heart, Father. And we look up and he is your Son. And he has called you Father. Who did he call Father? He's calling you God, Father, and God is your own wonderful, *I am*. Who is he calling? He is calling me, Father. *I am* his Father and everyone is going to have that experience.

So, in the end, as my friend had the experience, we are one. We are not two. I dwell in them and they dwell in me, and we are one. "Keep them in my name oh Holy Father. And the love that thou gavest me is the love you give them that they may be one as we are one." So, I am not a God of far-off, said he. I am a brother and a friend. But many will not believe it. And he turns down, tired and weary, he turns down that that is God. He won't believe it. He can't believe that the one he dislikes is himself. He can't believe it, that the man who stole from him this day is himself. He can't believe that the man who gave him good this day is himself. They're all separate. And I'm not saying that you're going to be absorbed. As her words are beautifully told in her letter, I felt your presence. The identity was there. No question about it, but for all the sameness of identity, we are one, I didn't lose my identity and yet I am, and I am you. And your presence is an identity. And yet I cannot use the plural in speaking of *we are floating on the water.*

So, she was filled with wine. Are we not told in Paul's letters to Timothy, "Drink no more water, use a little wine for your stomach's sake and your many infirmities?" Do not constantly absorb the Law and apply only the Law toward the getting of things in this world. From now on, let it become wine, let it become spirit, so it becomes a part of you. So, you drink wine, not the little bottle of wine, although

I'm very fond of wine. I love it. I had my full bottle of wine today with some cheese for my lunch, and thoroughly enjoyed a bit of wine and, oh, a section of Edam. Thoroughly enjoyed it, but that's not the wine spoken of in Scripture. The wine is the transforming of the water into wine. That psychological law is forever. Apply it towards becoming the man, becoming the woman that you want to be. But it's enough, after a while, to become this, become that, become the other, set your hope fully upon the grace that is coming to you at the unveiling of Jesus Christ within me. When the Father is unveiled and he can only be unveiled to his Son who reveals you as his Father. And that is the story. So, he has put, yes, I would use the word eternity. I use the word world. For he has put everything within you.

You don't have to go outside of self to find anything. You find it within. And by applying the principle, you rest having done what you are supposed to do and let it come to pass. But do not forget what my friend so wisely said, in quoting these passages from Scripture, that he finds it so difficult, trained as he is. He's a college graduate. He's a professional psychiatrist, teaching psychiatry to many, and he finds it difficult not to claim that his own intellectual powers brought these to pass. Even though he remembers that there was a moment in time when he, not intellectually, but when he imagined the state by denying the evidence of the senses, by denying reason or reason did not come into it, because he denied what he is now doing in imagination and having done it, he forgot it. And then, in good time, it happened in this world and he reaped the harvest of what he did in imagination. But he said, I find it so difficult, trained as I am, not to take the credit. And that's exactly what these passages that he quoted in the Scripture are against. They will not give the credit where it belongs. They have taken it to themselves, their own puffed-up intellectual state. And this whole vast scene is so unlike what the world believes it to be.

The whole vast world. I haven't time tonight to develop it—I will on Monday—to show you that everything in this world on this level is so unlike what it is on the next higher level, and man can't believe it until he's had that experience, he can't believe that this is not what it appears to be, but I'll show it to you on Monday. But hear that most disputed verse in the book of Ecclesiastes, the 11th verse of the third chapter: "And God has put eternity into the mind of man. Yet so that men cannot find out what God has done, from the beginning to the end." But in the fullness of time, shows it to those to whom he now comes at the end of time. He does not consign them to silence. They may go and tell it to the best of their ability exactly how it happened. So, when Ecclesiastes tell us that we will never find out, now in the end, you do find out God's own purpose. You find his mystery, and his mystery is to actually, literally give himself to us. That's his steadfast love forever. And that is forever.

"And thy name will endure forever." That is *olam*. The word *everlasting*, he has made an everlasting covenant with me. That word is *olam*. David's last words in the second book of Samuel, the 23rd chapter: "And he has made with me an everlasting covenant." And that word is *olam*. It is forever and forever. And so, he will now be a witness for all generations. He will always come at that appointed moment when I need to be revealed as to who I am. And then he will rise and here, I look into the face of my Son, but I know that Scripture told me he was God's Son, but I have no feeling of God as another. He has so become me that I am his Father. So, he was perfectly right in saying, I can't use the plural. I can't say *we are his Father*. He has so become me that *I am his Father*.

And so, she in the floating filled with wine, and may I tell her, don't be embarrassed because you said you are *filled with swine*. The pig has been the symbol of the Savior throughout all the generations. And so, you've eaten of it. You've eaten his blood. You drank his blood and you ate his flesh, which means you actually absorb the teaching. That's how you eat it. You eat it by absorbing the teaching.

Now, another friend of mine, she's here tonight, and she writes, but here I had this vision. I am in a cathedral and there is an enormous choir. And there are two persons present writing out announcements of my death. And I say it, but I am not dead, look, I am alive, but they're all writing out announcements, announcing my death. Then the choral group bursts forth into this most glorious *hallelujah*. This song of praise, *hallelujah, praise Jehovah*. That's what the word would mean. And I joined in with the chorus singing of my own death. Death of what? It is death to his level. Death to this level. She is joined with the choral group in singing her own departure from this level, moving into another level. So, I'm telling you, you are all awakening. My letters are now becoming more and more along this line. This week, I must have received at least two dozen. I had to give one today to a friend of mine to answer, please answer this for me because I don't have the time. And yet I hunger for the letters.

But if it demands an answer, and this one did, an interpretation because they're not here, they are a thousand miles away. And naturally that has to be answered. But you who are here, I can answer your letters from the platform. But those would come, like my friend from San Francisco, I haven't answered that yet. It's been there for ten days, but I may get to it this weekend, but I have so much to do at home with my wife, that I do not have the time to answer letters. If I could answer them from the platform, it's a tremendous help. So here, I hope I have convinced you this night, how wonderful you are that you were chosen. Not by some head of government. What would it matter tonight if you had the Stalin medal? And so many were given this Stalin medal and the Hitler medal. Well, you should melt it. But to be chosen by the Creator of the universe. He so loved you that he became you. And his name is forever and forever. And his name is I am, and it's buried in you. That's God in you.

Sleep in the feeling of being so wanted, being so chosen, being the elect, and you cannot rise feeling unwanted and feeling shunted in this world.

Now let us go into the silence.

Lecture IX

John the Crown of Scripture

March 6, 1972

Truth which man knows from experience, he knows more clearly than he knows anything else in this world. For then he can know that same truth in any other way. If what I tell you is true and you believe it, a benediction is pronounced upon you, as we're told in the very end of the book of John.

But the day will come, if it is true, that you yourself will know it from experience, and then you really know it. Then you can be called as a witness. So, we are told the truth, grace and truth came through Jesus Christ. Is that true? And what is this mystery called, Jesus Christ?

Well, tonight, let me share with you what I know from experience. The gospel of John, is in many ways, the crown of the Scriptures. It is the simplest and yet the most profound book in the New Testament. It starts off with these stories and the stories never come to an end. They pass off into conversations and the conversations fade from into a dialogue to a monologue. We find subtle use of words with double meaning. And in each case, those who hear it take the obvious meaning in its context, which is not the meaning intended. There is another meaning, a meaning that is related to the history of redemption. We find this especially in the conversation between Nicodemus and the Lord. Nicodemus came by night. He was a ruler of the Jews, a member of the Sanhedrin, a Pharisee, a brilliant mind, the interpreter of the law. But he recognized in this teaching that which, well, all were expecting; they couldn't quite understand how it could come embodied in a man for the man was simply a man, like all other men, how could it possibly be embodied in a man?

So, he came by night, and as a teacher, "I know that you are sent from God. For no one could do these signs," and in John, they're not called miracles, they're all called signs, there are seven signs. And these signs are not done out of compassion, but simply to reveal the divine power. So, "I've seen these signs and only one sent by God could manifest such signs"—and then starts the conversation and it breaks completely from this. And he turns to Nicodemus and he says, "Unless you be born anew"—or the word could be *again*; another meaning is *from above*—the word is *anothen*.* Nicodemus takes it in its first and obvious form: "Unless you are born again, you cannot enter the Kingdom of God." He replied, "Can a man that is old once again enter his mother's womb and be born?" And the Lord said to him, "You, a teacher of Israel, and you do not know? Unless you are born"—and he uses the word *anothen*, which again, Nicodemus takes to be *again*—"you cannot enter the Kingdom of God." But as you read it, you can see that the word *from above* is intended. Not *again*, as the world teaches reincarnation, it hasn't a thing to do with that. There are two modes, one is *from below* and one is *from above*. We are all born in this world *from below*. From the mother's womb in these garments of flesh and blood. But there is another birth and it comes *from above*. And that birth is out of the skull of the individual, which no one heard of such a birth before. And when that one comes out, it's the same

* This is a New Testament Greek term. With thanks to Richard Smoley.

being who is now clothed in this garment of flesh and blood, but it's an entirely different being that's coming out. It is God himself that is being born.

It was God who entered death's door, the human skull. It is God who laid down in that grave to share with the individual these visions called the dream of life. It is that God, in the end, who will actually bring together the one who is called John, called Stan, called by any name. And so even within himself, he will actually be that being and that being will be God. That is the being that is being born from above. Nicodemus could not understand it. There is another word with a subtle double meaning. And the word is translated *wind* or it could be *spirit*. He said, "As the wind blows where it will, and you hear the sound of it, but you cannot tell whence it comes or whither it goes, and so it is with everyone who is born of the spirit." Nicodemus cannot understand that. And yet it is from actual experience a wind and it is the spirit. When it happens to you, you hear the wind. It is an unearthly wind, fantastic wind, you'll think it is a storm, a frightful hurricane, if you've ever gone through one. I've gone through many at sea and maybe one or two on the earth, on the land, but I've gone through quite a few hurricanes at sea and they are disturbing, but you can't compare it to this sort of wind. It's a wind that takes place within you and yet at the same time, it is taking place seemingly coming from without. You hear it and your whole head is vibrating. And yet, you feel that the source of it is in the corner. The wind awakens you. That's when you'll be born. When this peculiar wind takes place. He sends his spirit and the spirit awakens you and the spirit is the wind. And when you awake, you awake within your own skull and you know it is a grave, it is a sepulcher. That's where someone, at some moment in time, placed you. And they place only the dead there. Therefore, you must have been dead or they thought you dead. And so here, death is turned into sleep, and the dreamer of this sleep is God, who entered death's door with you.

Now, he tells you that this is a gift. What gift? The gift of God is Christ. The gift of Christ is the return of memory, for Christ gives the Holy Spirit, and the Holy Spirit will come upon you and when he comes upon you, he will bring to your remembrance all that I have said to you. So, the gift of God is his Son, Christ is the Son of God. The gift of the Son is to bring to your remembrance. What remembrance? That you are God, that you are the Father. That's the gift of the Son. It takes the Son to bring to your remembrance who you really are. It takes the gift of the Father to give you his Son. For if he doesn't give you his Son, you'll never know that you are God the Father.

So, the conversation goes on and these are subtle double meanings between the uses of words, the obvious meanings, because we always take that first, and that's not what it intended. Now he tells us, the Son of man—and here every scholar misinterprets it—he said, "As Moses lifted up the serpent in the wilderness, so must the Son of man be lifted up." And they said that he's foreshadowing the nature of his death on the cross. There's no statement in the five books of Moses that there was a cross on which the serpent was nailed. He was lifted up, a fiery serpent lifted up on a rod, a single rod. The obvious meaning is, all right, that's how he's going to die, on a cross. I tell you from experience that's not what it means. It's actually being lifted up, a fiery serpent and you are that fiery serpent, lifted up on the cross of your own spine. And lifted up where? Listen to the words. "As Moses, lifted up the serpent in the wilderness, so must the Son of man be lifted up." On a cross? No. On the rod. Well, lifted up where? Lifted up into Heaven. For no one will ascend into Heaven but he who first descends from Heaven, the Son of man. So, the Son of man descended from Heaven, and only the Son of man can ascend into Heaven. But who is the Son of man? The question is asked, who is the Son of man? They mentioned all kinds of names, John the Baptist, Elijah, Jeremiah, some other prophet, but who do you say that *I am*? He equates the Son of man with *I am*.

And when you are lifted up, who is lifted up? *I am*. And you go up like some fiery serpent into your own wonderful skull and it vibrates like thunder. So, all these truths are so subtly stated that man completely misunderstands it and takes the outer or first meaning and it isn't the first meaning at all. That's the book of John written by the most profound teacher that we have in Scripture. If you mention another one, yes, you could mention Paul and the unnamed one who wrote the epistle to the Hebrews. These are the three giants in the New Testament. They're the ones who experienced it and then told it in their own wonderful way. But John so poetically told. Every verse is like poetry when you read it. And having had the experience, you stand amazed that someone could tell it so beautifully as the unknown author called John wrote it. That grace and truth came through Jesus Christ. Grace is love in action. And John said, "God is love." So, it's God in action. And grace is an unmerited, unearned gift. If you had earned it, it would be your wages, it could not then be a gift, it's a gift, an unearned gift. And what is the gift? He gave his only Son. He gave me his only Son to bring to my remembrance the being who I am, for I am God, your God, everyone is God, but not until the gift comes.

Now, in Scripture you read, "He who has seen me has seen the Father." This is all in John. The word *to see* and *to know* are the same word in Greek. So, he who has seen me knows the Father. If you do not see me, you do not know the Father. But if you encounter me, you cannot help but know the Father. "So, you have been with me so long, Philip, and you do not know the Father?" He who has seen me has seen the Father. If you see me, you instantly know the Father, for you're going to see your own Son. And he is the Son of God the Father. And the minute you see him, you know, he's your Son. And that was God's gift to you. He gave himself to you. That is the purpose of Scripture to reveal to man God's infinite gift, which is himself. But he can't persuade you that he actually has become you unless his Son appears whose Son is your Son. So, he gave his only begotten Son that you may know his gift to you. For he gave you his Son but in giving you his son, not as a companion, but as your Son, then you are God the Father. There is no other way in eternity that you'll ever know that you are God unless his Son appears. And that Son, is David. Yes, the sweet Psalmist.

The great David of Scripture that is the Son of God. He is the Christ. And so, God gives you his Son that you may know you are God. So, the gift is only to reveal to you who you really are. That's why I say it's the crown of the Scriptures. It is the most profound book in the Scriptures, and yet so simply told. But the subtle use of a word, with double meaning, and it's always misunderstood. The wisest of men, the Sanhedrin, they were considered the wisest men of Israel. They were the rulers of Israel. There were the great Pharisees, they knew the law backwards. They were the brilliant minds. "He sensed in this one, what he was not expecting." What no one of the members of the Sanhedrin could grasp. "He came to the defense of Christ," as you read it in the 7th chapter of John. He said, "Does our law judge a man before he is heard?" And then they say to him, his own members of the Sanhedrin, "Are you too a Galilean? Is there any prophecy in Scripture that he comes out of Galilee or a prophet comes out of Galilee?" Yes, there is, but they didn't know it. Jonah came out of Galilee. And you're told as Jonah spoke and then they believed him and Jonah's prophecy came true; by the word Jonah in Scripture, again, a double meaning, it's called by a name of a man, yet the word Jonah means *dove*. So here again a subtle use of the word, all through the book of John.

So, I tell you from my own personal experience this is what is going to happen to you. It's going to come suddenly, without warning. You'll go to bed, maybe this night, as you did last night, and suddenly without any warning, you would feel a vibration that you will interpret as the end of your earthly days because you'll feel, how can I really endure this? How can I possibly remain in this world? This means death, it's like, I have never had any stroke that I know of, but having seen people who are crippled because of a stroke, and there was a cerebral hemorrhage, you think, well this must be a hemorrhage, and how can I survive this vibration? But instead of dying, as you think you are going to die, you don't die. You awake and you awake as you have never awakened before. There's a clarity of mind that you've never known before, only to find yourself in a grave, in a sepulcher, and the sepulcher is your own skull and you are all alone. Not only all alone, you're sealed. The skull is completely sealed. No, there aren't any two eyes, so you can look through; no ears, no nostrils, no mouth. It's a completely sealed tomb, yet you know it is your skull, and you have an innate wisdom what to do, and so you act upon that impulse and push the base of your skull. After you awake, you stand up in your skull, the same being fully grown, you matured, and you know who you are and you push the base of the skull and something gives, as has been told you in John, "And the stone was rolled away and he was on the inside now comes out." Now in John, not in the synoptic gospel, in John alone, the birth again is told in a symbolic form. Matthew and Luke tell of a birth of a child. John doesn't mention the birth, but he tells it for those who have eyes to see or who have experienced it.

So, when they came into the tomb and found it empty, they found the linen clothes, then they found the napkin removed from the linen clothes. The napkin that had covered his head. And here it was removed from the linen clothes. The linen symbolizes the body. This is the linen clothes. Removed from the body, but it was covering his head, is a napkin. Well, the ancient word *napkin*, which we translate napkin, meant more than simply what you and I use today, where you speak of a napkin, a dinner napkin, a cocktail napkin, or a cemetery napkin. That seems the limit of a napkin in this twentieth century or when our Bible was translated. But in the ancient days, it meant more than that. The napkin was simply that which is the afterbirth. An afterbirth, if you see the afterbirth, then something was born. So, he tells you something was born by removing the napkin from the linen clothes. As in birth, you always remove the afterbirth. And that was what they found.

That's all symbolism proving that something was born—and what was born? God was born. For unless you are born from above, you cannot enter the Kingdom of God. Only God can enter. And so here is the symbol of birth, as told in John, and not told in any gospel and not told in any of the letters of Paul or any other part of the New Testament. So, I say, it is the most profound and yet so simple, as you read it. But always double meanings throughout the entire 21 chapters. So, when you come out, the tomb is empty. You look at the body, yes, out of which you emerged and you see exactly what it was. It was your body, you came out of that ghastly veil, turning its head from side to side, just as though someone was suffering. Someone in recovery; then comes the wind. As you're told in the book of Acts, that Pentecostal choir that came when they all heard the wind like a mighty storm wind. And that's when the spirit descended upon them and the word *spirit* and the word wind are the same in Scripture.

Here comes now the spirit, but you interpret it as wind. And then comes the evidence of a birth, which is only a sign, for the child is not a little child that you formed within you and gave birth to—the child is a sign of *your birth*. You are the only one spoken of in Scripture. And you are born and here comes the infant that symbolizes your birth. Then comes the next gift, and that's when now he gives that graceful gift of his Son. "And God so loved the world, he gave his only begotten son." That's what will happen to you 139 days after this first experience. Well, the first thing that happens is you're awake. Awakening in Scripture is the same as rising, the same as resurrection, the same word. To awake is to rise, to *resurrect*.

You awake within your own skull and you stand up, you are resurrected. Therefore, you must have been dead or you are in a tomb. Then comes the evidence of a birth, following that. So, there are two sides of the same coin. Resurrection begins the drama and the same night is the birth of you out of your own skull. Then 139 days later comes your wonderful discovery of who you are. So, John puts it in the most marvelous way, in the 18th verse of the very first chapter. The first 18 verses are the prologue, then comes the narrative, and then comes the epilogue. But here in the 18th, the very last verse of the prologue, for it is stating the entire picture. No one has ever seen God but the only begotten son who is dearest to his heart, he has made him known. That's the gift of his Son when David appears. He makes the Father known and the minute you look at him, you know exactly who you are. Till that moment you didn't know who you are. Hadn't the slightest idea that you are God the Father, until his Son appeared and you know he is your Son and he knows you are his Father. Now all in that concentrated third chapter, 126 days later, there comes or 123 days later, you can check me on it; here you are split in two from top to bottom. And then like a fiery serpent you go up like one twist and that twist is simply a spiral and you enter your head and it vibrates like thunder. So as Moses lifted up the serpent in the wilderness, so must the Son of man be lifted up. Do you think he's lifted up on a cross? No. The whole drama is taking place in you. It has nothing to do with anything on the outside. And you are lifted up—that fiery being that you are.

And I'll tell you, your face is human, your hands are human, your voice is human, but ask no more. You are a fiery being. A being that you cannot use any images here outside of the human face, the human voice, and the human hand, but you are transcendently beautiful beyond your wildest dreams, and a power that no one on earth who has not experienced it, can be deemed to imagine it, they can't imagine it. It is something entirely different, the power that you will exercise. You'll exercise it only because of the gift of love. Not until love touches you, because with this power, without the guidance of love, you could wreck the world. You will not wreck the world. You will exercise it only in love.

It's a fantastic power that you will possess. It's all there now, all completely wrapped within you awaiting the appointed hour when you will awaken you. And then comes the seal of approval, as recorded again, and the dove descends upon you. The dove is the seal of approval. The holding is perfect. You are as perfect now as your Father is perfect because you become your Father. A man matures when he becomes his own Father. And so, you actually become God the Father and the seal of approval is the descent of the dove upon you and to smother you with love. And then the drama, as far as that section goes, that section is over. So, when you read the book of John, you find all these double meanings. Unless you eat my body, my flesh, and drink my blood, you have no life in you. He tells you, you search the Scriptures because you think in them, you have life. And yet they're all about me. They bear witness to me, yet you will not come to me that you will have life. Now in the fourth verse of the first chapter, it is simply stated, "In him was life." What is his mission in the world? To give life. You do not have life until it is given; you're an animated soul but not a life-giving spirit, not as yet. So, "In him was life." And the purpose of his mission is to give life, so, he said, "Unless you eat my flesh and drink my blood you have no life in you."

You absorb, you assimilate his body which is Scripture, for you search the Scriptures as something external to yourself. And I tell you, absorb them because you're going to experience Scripture. Everything in that entire book you are going to fulfill. And the whole thing is going to unfold within you, casting you in the central star character. And when the whole thing unfolds within you, you've assimilated it. And this is the truth of which I speak. The truth that a man knows from experience, he knows more thoroughly than he knows any other thing in this world, or than can know that same truth in any other way. I can tell you in the hope that you believe it but the day you experience it, you'll have confirmation of it, and you are a witness in your own right. Although a benediction is pronounced upon you if you can hear it without experiencing it and still believe it, but the majority will not believe it. Only one of the Sanhedrin believes it: Nicodemus, which means, victor of the people. He was victorious, he believed it without having experienced it. The others condemned, because they were looking for it in the letter and here comes one who brought life. He made the letter become alive. The entire Scripture became a living thing within him because he experienced Scripture. And then he talked about it. I am told that no one put him on any cross. You are wearing the cross right now, the body that you wear is the cross, the only cross that the Lord was nailed upon. And may I tell you, the nailing is not, I would say, painful. In fact, it's ecstatic. These hands, my feet, my head and my right side are nailed with vortices. Each has a vortex, a six-pointed star. And when I experienced it, I'm telling you it was a sheer ecstasy. And then you feel yourself cramped once more in this little garment into which you've been placed. You gave up the beauty and the glory of your being to take this cross upon yourself. After having fulfilled Scripture, you will take off this garment and take it off for the last time.

But you will ascend before you take it off. You'll be born before you take it off. You'll discover the power of your own being before you take it off. You'll have the dove descend upon you before you take it off. But when you close your eyes, whether it be this or the next night, you will do it in joy because you're exactly where you are headed. You're headed into heaven and bear in mind, heaven is within you.

So, when I go, I am not going into some square, I am going within. And if you seek me, seek me within. That's where you're going to find me. Heaven is not a realm. Heaven is a character. It's a body, a body that has been made perfect as the Father is perfect. And wherever you are clothed in that body, everything is perfect. So, seek him, seek him within. Don't seek him without, you will not find him without. So, this is the truth that I would share with you. I've experienced Scripture. I've experienced it from beginning to end. And I know the entire Old Testament is the prophetic blueprint. It's all there. It took one who knew his Old Testament backwards to experience it, for he was of the Jewish faith, in whom it happened. And the whole story unfolded within him and they knew his background and it wasn't what they were looking for, any more than they are for you as something that could actually, you don't save anyone. He's not a savior. You are the Savior. There's no intermediary between yourself and God. The whole drama is unfolding within you. There's only God and his Son. That's the whole story. You need no priest, no rabbi, no teacher between yourself and self. The depth of your own being is God, the Father, and before the world was, he had a son, which is the resulting state of the experiences of being a man. That was all done. Then you and I were chosen in him before that the world was, we were the brothers, we are the *Elohim*. We are the Gods that together are called the God, the Lord. And we were chosen in him before that the world was. And then one man containing his choice, fell deliberately, for the experience of man, which is death. To become man, and man is death, and then to actually redeem man, individualized completely, and then raise man as God.

So, God became as we are that we may be as he is. And before he became as I am, he was the Father. And in becoming what I am, he is subjected to all that I must experience. But he experiences it with me in the end, because he was before the beginning, a Father, when he actually gives himself to me, in his fullness, I am that Father, not *a* father, *that* Father. There's only one Son and that Son is David. And so, I look upon David and here is this glorious radiant being, the eternal youth, the image of his Father.

And so, I know from experience that God is love. Therefore, his gift of grace, is love in action, which is God in action. I stood in the presence of infinite love and it is man. And when I was embraced and infused with him, I felt myself to be that body, to be that spirit without loss of identity. When I met David and memory returned as the fatherhood, he was the image of the being that embraced me. And I felt myself that being that embraced me. So, there's only one body, one spirit, one hope, one Lord, one faith, one baptism, one God and Father of all, who is above all, through all, and in all. So, in the end, not one will be lost, not one will be discarded, all will be redeemed. So that's what the story of John is about. You hear it, no matter how wise you are, as Nicodemus was, he was very wise, and he heard it and took the obvious meaning, which was not the meaning intended. Born again, an old man, and I enter once more into my mother's womb and be born with the whole vast world of, most of them, believe in reincarnation, as he implied by his question to enter again, a mother's womb and be born. And he said, you, a master, a teacher of Israel, and you do not know that unless you are born from above, that's what he intended to say, he used the word *anothen*, which means if you read the context properly, it means from above, you cannot then enter the Kingdom of God. He took it as *born again*. Born, as the world teaches reincarnation. It hasn't a thing to do with reincarnation, you're simply born from above.

Well, if I die tonight, they will say to me, and I haven't had these experiences, well, am I not going to be again? No, you are restored to life. Instantly restored in a body just like the one you're wearing, only it's young, nothing missing, and it's perfect. About twenty, not as a baby, just about twenty years of age, male, or female. And there you marry too, just as you marry here; there you grow old too, and there you die. And you're just as afraid of dying there as you're afraid of dying here, and you are instantly restored. But there is a vast difference between restoration to life and resurrection. Resurrection is the beginning of the new age, an entirely different world, when you awake within the skull. So, restoration is simply the continuance of the dream. This is a dream. You're dreaming what you are. You dream yourself into your present situation and you dream yourself out of it. So, you begin with a dream. What? A daydream. What's the daydream?

A wish, "*Oh I wish it were true.*" Isn't that a daydream? What would it be like if I were now the man that I would like to be? That's a daydream, but then dare to assume that you are it—that's the beginning of the dream of getting out the present dream into that dream, but it's still a dream. And the day will come, you'll have this experience that I'm speaking about, where you awaken from the dream. It is the most peculiar thing. When it happened to me, here I am, in a strange room, in a hotel in San Francisco. Room 725. Here I am a normal person sleeping, living a normal life, went to bed in the same normal manner that I've done year after year, night after night, to find myself waking. Well, I thought I'm going to awake, if I do awake, as I've always done. And I didn't. It was an entirely different waking. To awake within a sepulcher and to know that I'm sealed within my own skull. But what an alertness, you've never known such *awakeness*. So, to awaken is to resurrect. That is what resurrection means. Not some little cemetery. You are now buried in the only tomb that you will ever be buried in.

Put you in so-called holy ground? No, forget all that nonsense. Cremating the body is only simply quickening the pace that's going to take place if you put yourself into the ground, for there you slowly decay, while the furnace will make it a quick process, but it's the same dust. Only you awake in this world, just like this. And you are restored to life confronted with all the problems that you have there, and you fall in love and fall out of love, and you marry and you go through all the battles that you do here. There is no change whatsoever. There is no transforming power in what the world calls death. And you continue the dream as you have here, and then you awake in your own skull. And that is the resurrection. That's when you begin to enter the new age called the Kingdom of God. It takes an entirely new body, and that body is the body that you gave up, as told you in Philippians. He gave it up completely when he took upon himself the form of a slave and became obedient unto death, even death upon the cross. And finding himself in human form, he surrendered completely to the form in which he found himself. But he gave up all that was his. And what was his? He was God, you were God. And you still are God, but now you are fulfilling what you pledged yourself to do, to complete the dream and not to awaken before the end.

So, no one's going to awaken you before the end, because you are in control and no power in the world can awaken you before the end, because then your purpose would be void. And you are going to fulfill your purpose, go right through to the very end, and then return to the being from whom you came. And who is that being? Yourself. You are the sender and the sent. So, he who sees me, sees him who sent me. In the office of the sent, I am restricted; in the office of the sender, I am the Father. Unlimited power, unlimited wisdom. So, he who sees me, said he, sees the Father and because the same meaning of *seeing* and *knowing* is the same word, if you see me, really see me, then you know the Father, that's what he's telling you. The day you really see the Son, you know who you are and you'll see that you are God the Father,

This is the story of Scripture. The whole thing is completely given to us in the Old Testament. It's adumbrated. It's a foreshadowing in a not altogether conclusive or immediately evident way. But it's there. It's a blueprint, a prophetic blueprint. And when it comes into fulfillment in a living way, that's not what man expected. So, they rejected it. "He came unto his own and his own rejected him, they received him not." And the world has taken the story and made a peculiar story out of it. They said one little being called Jesus, 2,000 years ago. That's not it. Jesus Christ is the Father of the Son. And Jesus Christ is in you. The Father of the Son is in you or you couldn't even breathe for that breath is spirit. So, the Father is in man and by entering man, man became a living soul, but not yet a lifegiving spirit. When he awakens, he is now a lifegiving spirit. So, in him was life. And the purpose of the mission of the Son is that they have life and have it abundantly. So, the being in man will one day awaken as the man in whom now he is buried and he is that being.

Lecture X

You Must Experience God

March 10, 1972

God is known by experience or not at all. I have experienced God. I can no more deny it than I can the humblest evidence of my senses. And so, I feel qualified to tell you how you are going to experience God. There is only God in the world. When you say, "I am," that's God forever and forever.

Tonight, you will know why the term "Judeo-Christian" came to be hyphenated. The story as told in the Old Testament is a prophetic blueprint; that which is told in the New is its fulfillment. They are really two parts of one book: the prophecy and its fulfillment.

*God became as we are, that we may be as He is.** Every little child born of woman is aware that *it is*. Before it is aware of what it is, who it is, where it is, it is aware that *it is*. That's fundamental. That is God-in-that-child. It's the same God in the adult. It is the dreamer in man.

---

* Neville is paraphrasing from William Blake's *There Is No Natural Religion* (1788): "Therefore God becomes as we are, that we may be as he is."

It has to be awakened; and when it awakes, it is the being in whom it awakes, and then he knows who he is.

We are told in Scripture that: "The hour is coming when all of those who are in the tomb will hear His voice and come forth." They hear the voice of the Son: it's called the voice of the child. And the voice of the child, like a tuning fork, sets the tone; and then the dreamer awakes and knows that he is God. It's entirely up to the voice of the Son.

"When the time had fully come, God sent forth the Spirit of His Son into our hearts crying, Father." He is crying *Father*, but we do not hear it—not until "the fullness of time has come." So, we are told in the 44th Psalm: "Rouse Thyself. Why sleepest Thou, O Lord?" It is God who sleeps in man. It is God-in-man who does everything that man does—good, bad or indifferent. He actually became as *I am*—that's His name—that I may be as He is. And He is Father.

The day is coming; everyone will know the experience that I have had, for there is no other experience in eternity that can convince you that you are God the Father, other than this experience. His Son must call you, and you must respond; and when you actually hear it and then look and see what is calling, and it is your son, David, then everything returns. Memory returns, and you know exactly who you are: that you are God the Father, and your son is David.

This secret is told us in Scripture in the words *Jesus Christ*, and you take it as one being—one being only if you know that "I and my Father are one;" but if you do not know that, here you find two beings. Jesus is *I Am*. That's the Lord. "No one can say that Jesus is Lord, except by the Holy Spirit." The Holy Spirit is called the "Remembrancer."

"I will go and I will send the Holy Spirit who will bring to your understanding all that you have heard from me." So, he brings back the memory that you lost. So, no one can say that "Jesus is Lord" except by the Holy Spirit. So, when the Spirit comes and memory returns—but you will never know that you really are until you hear the voice of your own son, for you're suffering from complete and total amnesia. You do not know that you are God the Father. And you will never know it until you hear the son's voice; he is calling and calling, but only when the moment is ripe will you hear it. And just as we have told you, like the tuning fork it sets the tone, and it wakes you, and you hear it. When you awake, standing before you is your son; and memory returns—the Remembrancer, the Holy Spirit. And then you know exactly who you are, and you are God the Father.

It is going to happen to every child born of woman. And therefore, every child born of woman is one with the speaker who has had that experience, because it is the identical Son who is calling him Father. And there is only one God, one Father of all, and only one Son. So, when he calls you Father, and you know it because memory returns, and he has called me Father, and I know it—then you and I are one.

So, there is only one body, one spirit, one hope, one lord, one faith, one baptism, one God and Father of all, who is above all, through all, and in all. That's the mystery of Scripture. It hasn't a thing to do with secular history. It is all salvation history. Not a thing to do with history as the world teaches it. You and I are experiencing history—secular history; and my history is known to anyone who wants to investigate it. I wouldn't say that it is anything to write about. I was born in a simple little environment without any educational, social, financial background whatsoever. I am making a struggle like all people make a struggle in the world—to pay rent and to buy food, and then to put the garments on the body. That's a struggle for everyone. They seem to have no time for the Spirit. But the day is coming, all will have this experience, regardless of the struggle; and no one will be greater than the other, because everyone is the same God the Father—the Father of the one and only Son, who is David.

So, you know why we hyphenate the name "Judeo-Christian." Judaism is the foundation and Christianity is its fulfillment. That is the fruit on the tree; that's the flower. Without that tree, it couldn't bear the fruit; so, the whole thing is contained in that Old Testament, but it is adumbrated; it's a foreshadowing in a not altogether conclusive or immediately evident way. When it happens, it's not what the world thought should happen. They are expecting some being to come from without and save them, and He doesn't come that way. He comes to us as "one unknown," yet one who in the most ineffable mystery lets the individual to whom He comes experience who He is, and you will never experience who He is until He awakes by the voice of His Son who is calling: "Rouse Thyself. Why sleepest Thou, O Lord? Awake! Do not cast us off forever"—as you read it in the 44th Psalm, the 23rd verse.

So, as we are told in the 5th chapter of John: "And the hour is coming when all those who are in the tomb will hear His voice"—the Son's voice—"and come forth." And the tomb is your own wonderful skull. You are not buried in any cemetery in this world. Let them build all the great mausoleums they want. That's man. It is big business. Let them do it; let them build it. But you are buried in your skull. That's where God is buried. And out of that Golgotha, He will rise. And He will rise while you walk the earth. You will sleep this night without knowing you will be awakened by the call of that voice. The voice is a vibration. It is a sound. And so, David will sound the call. It will be in tune with you if the hour is right; and then you will awake to find yourself completely entombed within your own skull. And without any assistance from without, you will push the base of your skull and come out, just like a child being born from the womb of woman, only this is now being "born from above," not from below.

And when you come out, all the symbolism of Scripture will surround you. The witnesses will be there. There are three—and the infant wrapped in swaddling clothes, which is only the sign of your exit from that heavenly "womb." You are born from above. And from then, you go to another scene, another scene, over a period of three and a half years, and your journey is then completed. You'll remain in this world long enough to tell of your experience—to tell of your own experience of God. And until God is experienced, you do not know Him.

Let all the preachers do what they want; it's perfectly all right. They are sound asleep because God-in-them is sound asleep, and they are speculating. They are theorizing, based upon what they believe God ought to do. He should punish this one and punish that one; and they do not know everyone punished is God being punished for His dream. He is dreaming the dream of life. And many dreams are like nightmares; whether they be waking dreams or the dreams of sleep, they are nightmares. But nevertheless, it's still God dreaming.

Who is dreaming when he wakes in the morning? We will say, "Well, I had a dream," and you had a dream. "A horrible dream! I was"—and then he begins to describe it: but what is he saying? He is calling Him by the name of God. It was God who had the dream. When he wakes, "I am going to do so-and-so." Who is that saying, "I am going to do so-and-so?" That is God. There is nothing but God in the world. There is no room for anyone in the world but God and His only begotten Son. And His Son is David. That's His Son. Jesus is the Lord God Jehovah, and "David in the spirit called him 'my lord.'" That's the son calling him "my lord." Here is Jesus of Scripture—the awakened God. He's not asleep. Here is the one who first awoke in the world. But then he calls us "brothers." He said, "Go unto my brothers and tell them I am ascending unto my Father," but he said, "I and my Father are one"—"unto my God," and he also said, "My Father is your Father. My God is your God;" and "I and my Father are one;" and my Father is He Whom you call "God."

Here the mystery begins to unfold. Until you actually experience it, you do not know how wonderful Scripture is. Man must experience Scripture before he can begin to understand how altogether wonderful it is. It's eternally true. From beginning to end, the whole thing is true, and it is not secular history. It's divine history.

So, I share with you what I know from experience. I am not theorizing. I am not speculating. It happened to me—a simple man, as you are simple; and I did not for one moment suspect this was the mystery until it actually unfolded within me and I experienced it. When someone who supposedly lived three thousand years ago calls me "Father," I know exactly that I am his father; there was no uncertainty as to this relationship. I am looking into the face of the most heavenly youth, and he was the one who called me from my profound sleep; and when I awoke, it was God awoke, for he is calling upon the Lord to awake: "Rouse Thyself. Why sleepest Thou, O Lord? Awake!" And then you awake as though you had never been awake. It's a peculiar, strange awaking that takes place in you. And now you see this heavenly, eternal being who is the Son of God; and because he is going to wake you, you will know that he is your son, and he will know that you are God.

So, in the end, everyone will awake, and everyone will be God. So, it takes all of us to make the Lord. It's a compound unity—the word "Elohim." It is a plural word. "In the beginning God"—that word is Elohim. And "God said, let us make man in our image." That word is Elohim—a compound unity: one made up of others. It takes all of us to make the one God. "Hear O Israel, the Lord our God, the Lord is one"—not two.

So here, the only one who could ever rouse you and actually bring you from your profound sleep is your son, whose name is David. "I will tell of the decree of the Lord," said David. "He said unto me, Thou art my son. Today I have begotten thee." And so, we have confused it with Jesus, and Jesus is the Lord. He is the Lord speaking. He is the Lord who inspired the prophets to write what they did. And finding no one to fulfill it, He Himself came into the world and became man. He became you. His name is *I Am*. That's the Lord God Jehovah that we call "Jesus" in Scripture. That's *I Am*.

"Do you not realize," said Paul, "that Jesus Christ is in you?" Don't you know that He is in you? Are you looking for Him to come from without when He is within you? Well, He is within. You cannot say, "I am" and point elsewhere. Whether you are in a frightful dream, you are aware. To be aware is saying, "I am." And you can't point on the outside of self when you say, "I am;" and "that is my name forever and forever." And that is the Lord Jesus in every being in the world.

But his Son plays such an important part—that Son called David. You say he is the son of Jesse and Jesse means "I Am." The word Jesse means "Jehovah exists." It is any form of the verb *to be*. In other words, *I am*. That is the Father of David.

And what I tell you I am telling you from experience. I am not the scholar who simply went through Scripture and combed it to bring forward this theory. It's not theory with me. I am not qualified to go through the Scriptures—knowing Greek and knowing Latin and knowing Aramaic—to do that. It has happened to me. It was all *revelation*. So let the scholars go on and try to find it. Let them go on. Until it's revealed to them, they do not know it. Revealed truth cannot be actually, legally or—I would say—logically proven. It's all revealed. If it isn't revealed, well then speculate. And I am not speculating. I am telling you exactly who God is. And until you experience God, you do not know Him. And I am telling you from my own experience, you will experience God; and then you will know Him. And you'll know why we hyphenate the words Judeo-Christian. It's one tree. The tree is Judaism; the fruit is Christianity. Christianity is simply the fulfillment of Judaism.

So here, he tells you: "I will not leave you desolate. I will come again." And then He becomes invisible. The story is told us in the pre-existence before that the world was. And here, He becomes invisible, because He takes up His residence in us; and the darkest hour in the world, symbolized in Scripture as the three hours of darkness that descended—no; the darkest hour is when God became invisible. As He became invisible, he took up His residence in us; and man is looking for Him to come from without, and He cannot come from without. He will rise from within, but only at the call of His Son's voice.

So, in the fullness of time, He sent forth the Spirit of His Son into our hearts, crying what? "Father." And if you hear it, then you respond. Responding is waking. And you begin to awake within yourself to find yourself entombed within your own skull—completely sealed; but you have an innate wisdom. You know exactly what to do, for He prepared the way before He set forth. You know exactly what to do: you push the base of your skull, and it gives; and then you come out. And the symbolism surrounds you. You know exactly who you are—but not quite until the Son appears. At first, only the infant wrapped in swaddling clothes; and you are told in Scripture that's only a sign, like the sign on the top of the White House. I ask the guard, "Is the President in residence?" And he looks. If his insignia is flying, he will say, "Yes, he is in residence." If it's not flying, the President is not in residence. If the little child is found wrapped in swaddling clothes, then I ask, "Is God born?" "Yes, here is His sign." This shall be a sign unto you. You shall find a child wrapped in swaddling clothes and lying on the floor. When that sign is found, the question is asked, "Is God born?" Yes, here is the sign of His birth. But when the child comes—not the little infant—when the Son comes, then you hear his voice. And the voice is the voice of God's Son, who is Christ.

Christ is the Son of God. And the "Anointed" means Christ and Christ means the Anointed. And did he not say in the 89th Psalm: "I have anointed you with my holy oil." Well, who is He speaking to? He is speaking to David. Did He not say in the 89th Psalm: "I have found David, and David has cried unto me, Thou art my Father, my God, and the Rock of my Salvation." Did He not say in the Second Psalm, "Thou art my son. Today I have begotten thee." All these words were inspired by the One Being whom we call Jesus, the Lord. He inspired it through his prophets, and then Himself came down and took upon himself humanity. I am speaking of the Cosmic God—of the Cosmic

Son. So, He is buried in every child born of woman, but this is so unique: He comes to us individually. He calls us, one by one, in season.

So tonight, could be your call. It may be tomorrow night. I hope it is not in the distant future. But He will call all; and when you take off this garment, having been called and having seen the Son, you have taken it off for the last time. Until it actually happens to you, death is not death. Death is nothing more than simply leaving a room and entering another room, simply like the room you left—the same terrestrial world. With all the struggles you left behind you. You'll find them there. You are restored to life, not as a baby; no reincarnation. You are restored—a young man, a young woman, with not a thing missing. No need of anything to be added because nothing is missing; only you are young—about twenty years of age—to continue your journey in this world, to be confronted with all the problems that are here. Yes, and you marry there, too. You marry, and you grow old, and you die there, too. And if it hasn't yet happened, you are restored again to continue the journey until it happens. But it's going to happen to every being in the world. Not one can fail, because then God would fail, and that's impossible.

So, everyone will awaken from the dream of life. And it doesn't end at that moment in time that your senses cease to register that being and we speak of him as dead. He is not dead. He's in a world just like this—restored to life in a world that is terrestrial, in a young, wholesome, healthy body, with all the problems that faced Him; because in the Resurrection of which I speak, there is no marriage, no male, no female—a completely transformed being, who is God. But until then there is still sex—very much so in that world. But I am telling you what I know. I see them—my father, my mother, my brother—so many friends who are gone. I see them. They are not gone at all. They are in a world just like this, with all their struggles.

Therefore, I ask you to live so that your mind can store a past worthy of recall, for you are taking that with you. Spend all of your time entertaining noble thoughts, for you are taking that with you into the world where you are headed, unless this thing happens before you make your departure from this world. If it does not happen before that, you are taking with you what you have actually entertained in this world. So, live so that your mind can store a past worthy of recall, because you are going to actually take it right into your world to resolve it. And that is a part of your struggle.

But the day is coming; everyone is going to have the experience that I have just told you. No one can avoid it. If others have other ideas, let them have it. I wouldn't raise a finger to change it. They have all these "isms" in the world; let them have it—all kinds of concepts of what God ought to have done. What God ought to have done, He has already done. The drama is over. The Resurrection is taking place. It didn't take place once and forever two thousand years ago. It is taking place at every moment of time. But not everyone is articulate. Not everyone is sent to tell it after it takes place. So, they will go through their little exit from this world, not having told it to anyone. On the other hand, I was not restrained. I had to tell it, like Jeremiah: "If I say I will not mention it, or speak anymore in His name, then there is in me, as it were, a burning fire, all shut up in my bones, and I am tired of holding it in, and I cannot." So, I cannot restrain the impulse to talk about it. Others can. They are embarrassed even to bring it up; but I am not. It is part of my way of being, of thinking.

So, I tell you, the voice spoken of is a real voice, but like all voices, you are now interpreting the vibration that is coming from my mouth. It is all vibration; and then you actually translate it within yourself because it is simply impinging upon you. Well, this is the same voice. It's just like the tuning fork. And then it sets a tone, and the tone rouses you if you are in tune with that tone; and then you are actually hearing Him call you. He is calling you "Father." And you awake to find standing before you this heavenly youth. And then, at that very moment, you know exactly who he is, and he is David, the sweet

Psalmist David; and he is your "son," and you know he is your son. Memory has returned. So, "God became as we are, that we may be as He is." Don't for one moment forget that. That is the great sacrifice. It was God who "died."

"Unless I die, thou canst not live/ But if I die, I shall arise again & thou with me."* So, it is God who is crucified on these garments. And the God in you—His name is *I Am*. And when you hear the voice and you awake, who awakes? I awake. Who is waking? I am waking. And who is His Son's name? I am telling you, His Son's name is David; but because he has been anointed with the holy oil, he is the Christ. "Thou art the Christ, the Son of the Living God." In the Old Testament, the word Christ is not used, but the word Messiah is. He is the Messiah, for the Messiah simply means the "anointed one." And the Messiah is used only in the Book of John in the New Testament. He does speak of the Christ as the Messiah, and it is not Jesus. Jesus is the Lord. Yet the Son could say, "I and my Father are one." So, "When you see me, you see the Father." He is the image of the Father.

You are told, "It does not yet appear what we shall be, but we know that when he appears, we shall be like Him." I am telling you that is exactly what is going to happen. Forget the mask that you are now wearing. Behind that mask is the Ancient of Days, the Eternal One who is the Lord God Jehovah. And David is the image of the Lord God Jehovah. He is the Eternal Youth, and the Lord is the Ancient of Days, without beginning, without end.

So, when you dwell tonight on it, treat it seriously. What I have told you this night is true. I haven't speculated. I haven't turned to anyone for support. I was never taught it. It's in the Bible, but I never saw it in the Bible until I experienced it. That is why I can tell you, until God is experienced, you do not know God. One must experience God

---

* Neville is quoting from chapter four of William Blake's *Jerusalem: The Emanation of the Giant Albion* (1804–1820).

to know Him. He is not deaf; you don't have to scream to have Him hear you. You need not utter anything. Your simple thought is heard because who is hearing it? *I am.* That's God. The way they have all these prayers—"let us pray." They put on all these microphones and just blast the whole thing out calling upon God to hear them. That's not God. God is within you. And the God—the only Living God—is your own wonderful human imagination. When you say, *I am*, that is God!

"By Him all things were made, and without Him was not anything made that was made." In His dream, naturally, He makes mistakes. God makes mistakes? There is only one that can make a mistake, and that is God. There is only one that can make anything, and that's God. For in a nightmare, well, can you blame the man if he has the most horrible nightmare? You would console him in the morning if he told you of some horrible dream. You wouldn't condemn him. Well now, this is a waking dream; but it is still a dream.

So, in the end, everything is forgiven. Every being in the world is forgiven, for there is only God who did it all! So, the story is the Father and His Son, and there is no other being in the world. And you are the Father and His Son is your son. And if he can say, "I and my Father are one," then he can say of you, "I and my Father are one." When you look into the face and you see that beauty—you cannot describe the beauty of David. No artist could paint it. He is the image of you. But no one knows it, only the mask that you wear, for He is the image of the invisible you, and He bears the express image of your person. But your person is not the thing that you wear as a mask. You are the Immortal Being. You are the Eternal Being. When you hear it and you really believe it, you will see why this book of sixty-six books is really a library. When you have a Bible of both the Old and the New under one cover, you have a library. Very few homes have sixty-six books in them. If they have a Bible, they have sixty-six books, and they have the greatest library in the world in having the Bible. And one is the Old; the other is the New. One foreshadows, and the other tells you how it is fulfilled. But even though it is fulfilled, it still remains a mystery to those who have not experienced it. So, I tell you He comes to us as One Unknown, yet one who in the most wonderful manner lets you experience who he is. And when you experience who he is, it's your Self. That is God.

What a sacrifice. He literally became as I am that I may be as He is. And that is true of every child born of woman. Now, if you enjoy other things, enjoy them; but you will not in Eternity undo what I have told you. Not in Eternity will you disprove it, may I tell you? All the wisdom of the world cannot disprove what I have told you tonight. You may rise in opposition, and I wouldn't bat an eye to argue with you, for I know what I have experienced. So let them argue. I will not argue. They said he was silent. "You will not speak to me." Why argue the point? "So, you were a king. The world says so." "It's the Father's good pleasure to give me the Kingdom." Well, if He is going to give me the Kingdom, He is going to give me Himself, for He is the Kingdom. Read it in the 12th Chapter of Luke, the 32nd verse: "It is your father's good pleasure to give"—you don't earn it, it's unmerited, it's grace—"to give you the Kingdom." And when He succeeds in giving me the Kingdom, He succeeded in giving me Himself, for He is the Kingdom. The Kingdom is not a realm, as the world teaches. It is God. The character that is God, that is perfect; so, wherever you are, clothed in that perfect character, everything is perfect. Everything is alive. Nothing is dead and nothing is imperfect. Wherever you are after you have received the gift. You could walk through the Petrified Forest, and it would all suddenly burst into blossom. Walk through the desert, and the desert will bloom. Come into any place where they are imperfectly formed—eyes that are missing out of their sockets will come out of the nowhere and fill the empty sockets, and they will be perfect. Arms missing? No, not in your presence when you receive the Kingdom. In the presence of You, the Perfect Man, nothing can remain imperfect; but you don't do it out of compassion. You don't even do anything. Your very presence does it! So, no matter where you are—go down into hell, hell is transformed into heaven. Wherever you are is perfect, because you are now the King. You have received the Kingdom. I am telling you from my own experience. You walk into a world, and the world is instantly transformed to be in harmony with the perfection that is springing within you.

So, I tell you, "It is your Father's good pleasure to give you the Kingdom." That is a wonderful way of telling you it is your Father's good pleasure to give you Himself! That's how the evangelist told it in the Book of Luke: "It is your Father's good pleasure to give you Himself." And your Father is God. And God is Jesus. Jesus is the Lord. There is no other God! But He's a father, and because He's a father, He has a son. And I am telling you, in spite of the whole vast world, that Son is David, our sweet Psalmist of Biblical fame. And he will stand before you, and he too will call you "my Lord, my Father, the Rock of my Salvation."

Now let us go into the silence.

Good, now are there any questions please? Any questions?

Questioner: Can I have two for the price of one?

Neville: Yes.

Questioner: In any of Blake's writings can you tell whether or not he had received the Promise?

Neville: As far as I am concerned meeting Blake, as I have met him in this wonderful risen world, Blake had everything described in Scripture. When you meet him, he is one of the most majestic creatures that you could meet. Let me quote speaking of tonight's lecture, it's taken from his [1794] book *Urizen*, I think it's the seventh chapter and, "The dead heard the voice of the child and began to awake from sleep. All things heard the voice of the child and began to awake to life."

So, when God became man, he transformed death into sleep. God is infinite mercy and man is dead. God, in becoming man, made man a living soul. He transformed death into sleep and then in the dream he transformed the dream of himself into Himself and raises him as Himself.

Oh know, Blake had it. But you've got to read like all things, when Blake, read between the lines because as he said to the Reverend that criticized him.* The Reverend said to him, "You know, you need someone to elucidate your ideas." Blake said is that so?—"But you ought to know that what is grand is necessarily obscure to weak men. That which can be made explicit to the idiot is not worth my care. The wisest of the ancients considered what is not too explicit as the fittest for instruction because it rouses the faculties to act." Something that anyone can see, even the idiot, well then it isn't worth my care. So, he told in the way he did, causing you to dig for it. You have to dig for it. But Blake to me is one of the giants, spiritual giants of the world.

I've had people say to me, "Why didn't he have money?" Who wants money when you had what Blake had? All the money in the world today couldn't buy one single copy that is at Yale. He left behind him five copies of *Jerusalem,* only one he colored. It is now in Yale University under lock and key. When Blake sold it, I think he sold it for one hundred guineas. That would be equivalent to $500 when Blake sold it. You couldn't buy that copy today no matter what sort of money you brought for it. You couldn't buy it, it's the only copy in the world. He left five copies, four were not colored. This is the only colored copy that Blake left behind him. It's priceless.

* Neville is again referring to the Rev. John Trusler (1735–1820). Blake's quotes that follow are once more from the poet's letter to Trusler of August 23, 1799.

Lecture XI

Ends, Ultimate and Temporary

March 17, 1972

I think you'll find tonight an interesting night, for we are taking ends, the ultimate end and then the temporary ends. For it is the end that gives meaning to all that goes before. The Psalmist said, "Lord, let me know my end and the number of my days." We read, "Fear not, for it is your Father's good pleasure to give you the Kingdom of Heaven." That's the ultimate end. In giving you the Kingdom of Heaven, he gives you himself, for you can equate heaven with God. God is able to give himself to all of us, to each of us.

And the gift comes suddenly and without warning, after the tribulation of human experience. He said, "I have tried you in the furnaces of affliction for my own sake; for my own sake, I do it. For how should my name be profaned? My glory, I will not give to another." And when we read the story in the book of Exodus, we see that glory and God are equated: "I'll make my glory to pass before you. And when *I* pass by, so the *I* and glory are synonymous." He cannot give himself to another. So, the furnaces are simply to change man into himself. He became as *I am*, that I may be as he is. And so, I pass through the tribulation of human experience and then the end comes suddenly. The event comes in unique and unpredictable ways. Man thinks you can discover the way without having experienced it; you can't do it. For when you experience it, listen to the words carefully now, taken from the 48th chapter of Isaiah, the third verse: "The former things I declared, although they went forth from my mouth, I made them known. Then suddenly I did them and they came to pass."

Now here, the one proclaiming what is going to be done, his intention; but no one could fulfill it. He had to fulfill it himself. So, if he would give me himself, he has to fulfill it in me. So, when this unpredictable, unique event takes place, it takes place in the first person, single tense, in me. And it comes suddenly without warning. So, when I actually experience the gift of God to me, it isn't someone on the outside giving me something; he rises within me, and rising within me, he gives himself to me. Then I know who I am. And he set the entire thing out for us in his word. If I have heard, undoubtedly you have heard too. You've heard preachers claim that they met Jesus and they're waiting for him to return. I know I have heard them. I dare say you have; if you haven't actually heard them as I did, then you read their words, claiming that they actually met him in spirit. And then you ask them, and they are going to tell me who is Jesus and they'll reply, well, Jesus is the Son of God.

Then you can say to them, if you know Scripture, if you met him and you saw him and you say he is the Son of God, well, then you must be God. They'll be startled, shocked, and think that you are blaspheming. And yet we are told that no one knows the Son except the Father, for if they know him and they met him, they must be the Father. If they met him, and they claimed they met him, well, then they must be God the Father. I can tell you, you can say right into their face, you are a liar; some grand hallucination, because you cannot meet him from without. When you know God, you know him through his Son and you want me to know him through Jesus.

Jesus is the Father and David is the Son. When you meet David, you know that he is your Son and because he is God's Son, then you know who you are. And there's no other way to know God, it's the only way; it comes in unique and unpredictable ways, the entire story of Scripture. So, "The former things I declared are old, they went forth from my mouth and I made them known when suddenly I acted and they came to pass." Read it in the 40th chapter of Isaiah and the word Isaiah simply means, *Jehovah says*. It's the same meaning as the word Jesus. The same meaning as the word Jehovah. Jehovah is salvation. Jesus means Jehovah is salvation. The word Jesus and Jehovah are interchangeable terms. No one can say Jesus is Lord, except by the Holy Spirit.

And who is the Holy Spirit? The remembrancer. He will bring to your remembrance all that I have said unto you. So, when it comes, then all of a sudden it awakens within you. He told you what he will do. He's going to give himself to you. It is his purpose in life. His intention is to give himself to all of us, but to *each of us*, not collectively, but to *each of us*, he comes to us individually. And when he comes, he isn't coming from without he is coming from within for he is buried within and he rises within. So here now we are facing a day, two weeks from today, I think it is, when they all celebrate. I shouldn't use the word "celebrate" because it would be very sad about the day, because they do not know the day. It's called crucifixion and they will simply remember the day. What day? 2,000 years ago? No, he chose us in him before the foundation of the world. And one man fell and became fragmented into unnumbered beings, all sons, and then comes the great affliction, the great tribulation of human experience. And then he calls us back one by one. But when we return, we are the one who fell, who is God the Father. You're raised from the level of the fragmented being called the Son into the level of God the Father, and he's personified in Scripture as Jesus.

So, when someone tells you, I met him, I've gone on TV panels with ministers; they've brought on all kinds of pictures to show me, these ancient things concerning Jesus. Well, about thirty-five years ago, an artist friend of mine took me to the Metropolitan Museum, rather the Metropolitan Library on 42nd and 5th, the New York [Public] Library. He was a member and he took out forty-six pictures of Jesus, no two looked alike. They were simply personifications of the artists who painted them. There was the American Jesus, an open shirt, radiant blonde youth. Here came the Germanic Jesus, who would've enjoyed a lovely stein of beer. And here came the Italian with a sad face. Then the French, he could have winked his eyes at any passing girl. All these were Jesus personified by the artist who painted them. Yet, there were forty-six and he threw them on the screen and I looked at them for quite a long while. Forty-six, each claiming to be the Jesus as he appeared to them.

And there are those who put them on the wall and think there is a picture of Jesus. I saw in yesterday's paper, a coming TV show in the not-distant future, where the sculptor is going to actually show you how he sculpted the face of Jesus. And there'll be millions, if they have that vast an audience, who will believe it and possibly buy one of these things and stick it on the wall, too. That's not Jesus. You will never know him unless he reveals himself through the Son and the Son is David. And when David comes into your world, you instantly know, it instantly comes to pass; listen to the words, "I made it known to man, suddenly I acted and it came to pass." It's a sudden act all within you. No preparation whatsoever. It comes without preparation, without any warning whatsoever.

And suddenly when he appears, you know who you are, that you are the Lord Jesus. But no loss of identity. If your name is John, It's John, but you know, you are God, the Father of that Son. If he is God's Son, then you must be God, because he is your Son and you know that you are his Father and he knows that you are his Father. And there's no other way of discovering God in this world. You can do all the holy things in the world if you think holy. Someone came the other night for the first time; he asked me after the meeting if I knew a certain esoteric society and I told him, I'm not a joiner, I don't join any kind of society. I'm not a member of any club. So, he told me about this esoteric society, where if you are a member and then you'll be born from above and the seed must remain in you. I said you can sit on that seed from now to the end of time. And if you are not born literally from above you are going to have night explosions and you'll think you are doing God a favor. No, until that is turned around, suddenly without any warning on your part, you can have all the diets in the world, take all the saltpeter in the world, take all these things and you aren't going to stop the normal flow of that energy going down into generation. And when it's reversed into regeneration, you do nothing about it. You lose all interest in that impulse, the impulse is gone, and you've lost nothing. In the world of generation, it is part of living, but in the world of regeneration, you are above the organization of sense. It means nothing to you. You love them all equally, but you have no urge whatsoever to indulge in that which you wanted so badly when you were turned down into generations.

Well, I don't think I persuaded him one iota. He is going to actually become a holy man by restraining the impulse. Well, after all, the man's my age, he should. I mean nature should have outlawed it by now. However, it doesn't work that way. All these wonderful things that you read in Scripture, and these are the word of God, but they're only shadows. These are the shadows of reality. And when reality takes place, it is so unlike what the shadow appears to be. When you read the story of the serpent being lifted up on the tree or the trunk of the tree or the staff, and you think that someone called Moses took a serpent, a fiery serpent or a brazen serpent, and lifted it up with a staff, and all who looked upon it were cured, were healed. No, that was the shadow when it actually happens to you.

Now listen to the words. We are told that on this day when he rose, when they crucified him and then he rose, that the curtain of the temple was torn from top to bottom, the curtain of the temple. And you think of some temple, some cathedral, some synagogue. Now listen to these words: "You are the temple of the living God, and the spirit of God dwells in you." If you are the temple, well then, the curtain of the temple must be you or at least a part of you. So, if the curtain of the temple is going to be split in two from top to bottom, when that event becomes alive within you, it has to be you. And I'm telling from my own experience, it is you. And it comes suddenly and without warning and your body is split in two from top to bottom. And at the base of your spine is a golden liquid, pulsing living light. And as you contemplate it, you know, it's your very self and you fuse with it. And then like a fiery serpent, you rise. The entire thing is reversed. The fire that went down into generation is now reversed into regeneration. And who did it? Well, you said, but I experienced it. So, it's all now in the first person singular. So, listen to the statement again from 48th Isaiah: "The former things I declared arose. They went forth from my mouth. I made them known." It's all in the first person, *I, I, I.* "Then I acted and they came to pass." Well, who is acting? Who actually did the feeling? Well, I did. Who ascended? Well, I ascended. Who fused with the light? Well, I did. Who was split in two? Well, I was split in two. It's all in the first person. That's how God actually gives himself to man. For God is the "I" of man. When you say, "I am" that's God. There is no other God. But he sleeps in man and man is totally unaware of the true God.

When you hear the word, God, or you hear the word Jesus or the word Jehovah, the word Lord, and in some strange way, the mind jumps out to something other than the "I" of yourself, you have a false god. If you ever hear the word Lord and you think of something external to self, you don't have the right Lord. If it in any way conjures some feeling, something that exists external to you, then get back to Scripture and try to find out who he is, for he is buried in you. You are the spirit of God and the spirit of God dwells in you. You are the temple of the Lord and the spirit of the Lord dwells in you. Do you not realize that Jesus Christ is in you?

Unless of course, you fail to meet the test. If he is in me, then what am I doing looking on the outside? When I hear the word, Jesus, am I going to think of someone on the outside to come today, tomorrow, or maybe a thousand years from now? I've got the wrong Jesus. Then who is the Christ? His Son, Christ, is the Son of God. Well, then who is he, if Jesus is not? He is David. He's the Lord's anointed. Did David not call him in the spirit, my Lord, my God, my Father? So, when you hear any priest or any minister or any rabbi speaking of the Lord on the outside, bear in mind, they do not know the Lord. They do not know him. If you knew him, you would only think in terms of the *I am within you*. That's where he is buried. Now we promise you to take it to a practical level also.

The ultimate end is God is giving himself to you individually. And when you are awake, you are God. And there is no other God. But now we are told to imitate God as dear children until that gift is given. It comes at the end of human tribulations. But until I'm finished with the furnaces, and how long and how vast and how severe the furnaces, here I find the Father. And how long to tell, but he will try me by the furnaces for his own sake because he cannot give his glory to another. But when he gives it, it's going to happen suddenly and without warning. And then suddenly you'll know because the Holy Spirit returns and the Holy Spirit is simply memory returning. For he told the entire thing to us before the foundation of the world. When we came down, we were told in the beginning, but when we came down into the world of complete forgetfulness, we forgot it. But when it returns, memory returns after complete and total amnesia and then we know exactly who we are.

But we know individually because you are unique. Although we are one, still you are individualized, and not in eternity will you be other than the individualized being. Yet, we are one, have the same

Son and we are the same Father, but you are individualized as John, I am individualized as Neville. And this individuality tends toward greater and greater individualization, forever and forever. That's the story. But if I must imitate him as a dear child, and that's how he does it, now, let me now know my end, now. I do not mean the end of which he just spoke; I mean, a temporary end. I want to be successful, a man will say, or the girl will say, well, I want to be happily, happily married. And I want him to be successful and I want to live graciously in my world. Well, that's an end. Go to the end. View the world from that end. Don't think of it. If you think of it, you are not in it. I must actually occupy the end. Go to the end and view the world from that end. Now act in it. How would it be if it were true? What would the feeling be like if it were true? For this is simply taking the end and drenching it in feeling. I assume the feeling of the wish fulfilled and I drench myself with that feeling; then I open my eyes and the world denies it. It doesn't really matter. Let me remain faithful to that end. And then it will come just as suddenly. But strangely enough, I'm going to pass through, it may be not severe tribulations, but I will pass through certain trials, certain heartbreaks, and certain delays that I can't quite understand; but when I reach the end, and the end comes suddenly upon me and the whole thing is fulfilled, I will see it was all in order. Everything was in order.

My own disappointments in my world led up to whatever I am doing today. When the teacher in my school, I could ill afford the $500 that my father gave me to go to this small school in New York City, and she made me the goat. She called me out before an audience of about forty students. And she said, "Now listen to him speak. He will never earn a living using his voice." She should not have done that, but she did it—but she didn't know the kind of person that she was talking about. Instead of going down into the grave and burying my head in shame, I was determined that I would actually disprove her. It did something to me when she said to me, "you will never earn"—to the class, using me as the guinea pig to show them what not to do—and so, she said, I spoke with a guttural voice and I spoke with this very heavy accent, and I will never use my voice to earn a living. But I do not know what the others are doing. I haven't heard of them. And there is not a thing wrong with selling shirts for Macy's, you can use your voice there, too. And I dare say most of them wound up selling groceries or something. I met one of them and he was selling groceries at Macy's. And he said, "Neville, what do you do?" So, I said, "I talk on the Bible." "You talk on the Bible—are you a minister?" I said, "No, I'm not a minister. I simply talk on the Bible from having experienced the Bible." Well, I do not know what they do, if they're still in this world, but I don't think one of them ever earned a living using his voice unless he was selling groceries as this one chap I know, he sold groceries.

We all went to this school and this teacher simply singled me out to make some little, well, exhibition of what I should not be doing in class. But I went home and I was so annoyed that I had lost my father's $500 or $600 that he gave me for the six-months course, but I was determined that she was false, that she was wrong. So, I went to the end. I went to the end and actually felt that I was facing an audience and unembarrassed that I could talk and talk and talk forever without notes, no notes.

And so, class came to an end and I left. She was convinced, and maybe they were convinced, it doesn't matter what they do. It's what I do. So, others may be convinced. It doesn't really matter. The whole vast world is yourself pushed out. Maybe I needed that joke at that moment in time. And so, I went through the different tribulations and finally, I found myself doing what I always wanted to do, to tell the story as it happened to me in my vision. I was having all these visions and they were related—and yet how to do it?

So, the first night I started, I think six people came. I paid three dollars for the hall and they all came. I sat down, I wore a tux for the occasion and I sat down and spoke for ten minutes and dried up. And I asked them to ask me questions. So, they did, very graciously, they were all friends. I sent out fifty penny postcards—in those days, you could send a card for a penny—sent out fifty and six came. And out of, well, sympathy each gave a dollar bill. So at least I paid $3 for the room and I made $3. And that was my beginning. And then it grew from three to ten to twenty. And one night when I had about fifty a man in the building saw me growing and growing and growing. And he thought he would put a stop to it. And he was going to one of these New Thought conventions in Washington, D.C. And so, he asked me to take his platform and he had a very large audience of about 500. He thought that would throw me. And so, I accepted his generous offer. I learned afterward his purpose was to simply get me out of the place. He thought I would simply make a monkey of myself before a vast audience who were trained differently. Unfortunately for him, and fortunately for me, the next time I spoke, my room couldn't take them. I had to move several times in six months. And then I moved to an old church, attracted 1,100. So, you see, he thought he was going to hurt me. As Scripture teaches, "You meant evil, you meant evil against me, but God meant it for good." So, I got his audience. And then about three years later, for some little infraction of the laws of New York City, they put him away for a couple of years.

And when he came out, he asked me if I would speak for him, and I said, yes, without one penny, I will willingly speak for you. Because no one else would speak for him. They cut him off completely and said no. You don't realize how good you were to me, and so, I will speak for you. And I went up and I spoke for him without taking one penny. And then he couldn't get going again. And then he and his secretary got into his car, turned on the ignition, closed up all things, and called it a day. But you see you go through these things and that moment they seem to be against you. And they're all for you. If you remain faithful to the end. So, let us be imitators of God, as their children. So, then we are told I was not ungrateful. I was not, I will say, forgetful of the divine image. I remained faithful to it. If I remain faithful to it, let anything happen, and then say within yourself, you meant evil against me but God meant it for good.

And I can go back in my own family. When people tried to take from my father the little equity that he had in the business, and we thought the world came to an end on that day, for he had a large family, and how to feed them? How to support them? Ten children, your wife, yourself, your mother-in-law, and the few servants that we had. And no one would come to see him because they weren't quite sure that the accusation might be true. And that, on reflection, was the turning point in the family's fortunes. So, from being a minor partner, having very small equity in the business, he turned around without partners and then transcended the wildest dream of the family. And that was the turning point. He kept his vision. He knew he hadn't done a thing that was wrong. He kept his vision concerning what he wanted in life and what he wanted for the family.

So, if you have a vision, and by vision, I mean, a daydream. What would you like to be in this world? Do you know it? Just what would you like to be? How would you like things to be in your world? Well, that's a vision. Well, now remain faithful to it. Tomorrow you may be given a severe blow and you may interpret that as being a setback. Time will prove it was a turning point in your fortune. Everything will add up towards the fulfillment of your dream if you remain faithful to that vision. It's all in your own wonderful human imagination. That's God. God actually became, as I am, as you are, that you may be as he is. And he takes upon himself all the weaknesses of man. But we say, well, God doesn't suffer, but now I ask you a question. If you are in pain, are you in pain? And you will say to me, yes, I am. But that's his name. God's name. He has no other name. That's who he is. So, you say, *I am in pain. I am embarrassed. I am unwanted.* That's God's name. He's doing all the suffering because he goes through life with you, as you, until one day, he reveals that he is you. It is God and God alone playing all the parts in the world. There's nothing but God. If God did not become as I am, I couldn't breathe. He's my breath. But he doesn't limit me to my wishes. He doesn't limit me to my outlook on life. He plays all the parts. He waits on me just as quickly and as indifferently when the will in me is evil as when it is good. And therefore, he subjects himself to all the things in my world.

God is like pure imagining in you, in me, in every being in the world. So, you imagine, all right, that's God. And he waits on us because we imagine this, that, and the other. Now, you know this—go to the end, a noble end, a successful end in your world. All right, having seen it clearly in your mind's eye what would the feeling be like if it were true? Drench yourself in that feeling. Now tomorrow, you may be disappointed; don't expect it tomorrow. It may come tomorrow. When it comes, it's going to come suddenly and unexpectedly. But remain faithful to the end. And all the little things will happen in your world that will seem to deny it, they're adding up to it. Everything will add up toward that.

I am telling you from my own experience. There's nothing but God in the world. He's playing all the parts. The most horrible part and the noblest part. He's playing all the parts. And no one is greater than you are because no one is greater than God. Let no one pull any rank on you. No one is greater than God. You have a background that goes back to God. It's not a physical background. You're not a horse. If I'm breeding horses, I want to know their background, but you are not a horse. You're not breeding pigs. You're not breeding sheep. You are simply the unfolding of God. And there is nothing but God. Let anyone challenge it. And if he wants me to go to the Bible to support my claims, I'll go with him to the Bible, and then I'll find the passage just suited or the argument he is trying to present. So, when they tell me, I met Jesus and I say, you met him? What did he look like? And they begin to paint a word picture of him.

Now tell me who is he? Well, he's the Son of God. He's the Son of God. Well, then you must be God. So, do you not know in the 11th chapter of the book of Matthew that no one knows the Son except the Father? And you say, you know the Son and you've seen him, but if you've seen the Son, well, then you must be the Father for no one knows him but the Father.

Now listen to these words: "No one has ever seen God but the only Son who is dearest to his heart, he has made him known." That's the first chapter, the 18th verse of John. So, if now you say you've seen him, well I tell you, if you have seen God, then you must have been named the Son for no one has ever seen God, except his only Son who is dearest to his heart. And he has made him known. You're either Christ the Son or you are Jesus the Lord. One or the other. Yet they are one. One reflects the other. The Son, not only radiates but reflects the glory of God and bears the express image of his person. So, when you look into the face of the Son, he is the eternal youth and you, the Ancient of Days, and you're one, he reflects your glory and your glory is simply, *I am*.

So, I tell you, the greatest book in the world is the most misunderstood book. When he said I've declared these things of old, but they were shadows. All these were shadows of the reality. And when he himself comes into the world and fulfills his own declaration, then his shadow world rejects him, it's not what they were expecting. So, we are told they rejected him. "He came unto his own and his own received him not." They could not accept it because they were looking for some man on the outside to be a savior. No one on the outside is going to save you. God and God alone is savior. Listen to the words of the 43rd and the 45th chapter of Isaiah: "I am the Lord, your God, the holy one of Israel, your savior. And beside me, there is no savior."

I am he—not a being on the outside, talking to you. I'm speaking from within you, your own wonderful, *I amness*. That is the Lord,

God Jehovah. That is your savior. And beside him, there is no savior. And when he reveals himself to you and completely unfolds himself within you, it's because he has brought the only one in the world that could reveal him as you. And that is his Son and his Son is your Son. If his Son is your Son, then you and he are one. So that is the story. So, the end gives meaning to all that goes before. If I only know the end, for the end is, it is God's purpose to give himself to me as though there were no others in the world, just God. Just self, and not two, just one. He broke down the barrier of partition between us and now we became one. So, he cleaved to me, his emanation, yet his life until the sleep of death was passed. And when the sleep of death was passed, then I awoke, and I awoke as the Father and that is God the Father, and there is no other.

Now, tonight you have your wonderful dreams, dream nobly. You want to be happily married. You want to be financially successful. You want to be known in your chosen work. All these things are but dreams. And if you know the Law you can dream them and make them come into this world. And when they come, they're going to come suddenly. Just without any warning whatsoever, they happen suddenly. Not even a little foreshadowing, just suddenly it will appear. I know in my own case, these events one after the other, I had no inkling, but I slept that night, that this night a great event would take place and casting me in the central role.

So, we are told, and I acted, and it came to pass. I acted and it came to pass. And so, I didn't see a being on the outside calling himself God. I awoke within my skull and found it to be a sepulcher. It was I who awoke, it was I who came out. It was I who found a little child wrapped in swaddling clothes. It was I who saw the three witnesses, bearing witness to the event that I had just experienced. It was I who heard the wind and the wind was like some storm. It was I who saw David, who revealed to me that I am his Father and he is my Son. It was I whose body was split in two from top to bottom. And it was

I who actually looked upon that liquid golden living light, fused with it, and then like a fiery serpent rose into my own skull. And it was I on whom the dove descended and smothered me in kisses. It was all I, as you are told in that passage. Read it carefully, the 48th chapter, the third verse of Isaiah. The whole thing is centered in the first person, singular, not we but *I*. It's unique. That's the being that you are. And all that has happened to me is going to happen to you, that you may know in the end that you and I are one. And we are the Father. Therefore, the Father is a compound unity, one made up of others. And that's what the word *Elohim*, which we translate God in Scripture, is. It is a plural word. It's a compound unity.

And so, the very first time it appears in Scripture is the very first verse of Genesis. "In the beginning God created the heavens and the earth." That word God translated, God is Elohim, plural. And God said, "Let us make man in our image"—after all like that word is plural, it's Elohim. So, the Elohim is a compound unity, one made up of others. And we are the fragmented *ones*. Now we are called back into that unity. But when we are called back, we become *the one*, the Father. And there's no way to reveal you as *the one* other than the Son, the only Son calling you Father. And you know it. So, the Holy Spirit comes, the remembrance returns. So, say what you want about the Father, say what you want about the Son, all that's forgiven, but the sin against the Holy Spirit is not forgiven.

When remembrance returns, you couldn't possibly deny it. So don't be concerned. You will never in eternity deny it because memory has returned. So, there's no possibility of sinning against the Holy Spirit. And you've heard all kinds of arguments. It means deviation in sex, all that nonsense. It hasn't a thing to do with it. When memory returns from the total amnesia that you suffered, you can't deny the being that you are. So, all the arguments about God and his Son, we're told, all that is forgiven, but the sin against the Holy Spirit and who is the Holy Spirit? I will send you the comforter, the

Holy Spirit, who is the spirit of truth. And he will bring to your remembrance, all that you have heard from me. So, everything you heard before the world was, then the whole thing comes back and you'll see who you really are.

So, I'm telling every person in the world who will listen, *you are God the Father.* And the day will come, and it will come suddenly and without warning, in the most unique, unpredictable way, and here you can't deny it. And then when a little thing called death takes place, you've taken it off for the last time. And then you and I in the eternal world will be one in the most intimate sense and yet separate because we are individualized—and yet one. It's something that only you can experience when you are in that state. How can two bodies fuse and actually literally become one body? I have had that experience. *Two fuse.* You can take the most intimate embrace in this world, and yet they're two. Now when I talk about, when you are embraced, you become one. He who is united to the Lord, becomes one spirit with him, you become one body with him, you become one with eternity—and yet you are individualized.

"So, Lord, show me my end, tell me my end and the number of my days." And he was told, it is not for you to know the day or the hour, only the Father knows. And when that moment in time comes, it will not be delayed, but you will not know the moment. It's going to come suddenly and unexpectedly, and then your entire world has changed. No matter what you believe prior to that moment, everything has been rearranged within your mind. And then you go about your Father's business and you are the Father. And what is your business? Trying to awaken everyone who is sleeping because that's the Father, he's buried in every child born of woman.

Tonight, if you know someone who is now up on trial for the most horrible crime, he still is the Father. And if you hear of some glorious person, he's still the Father, not any more than the one on trial for his life. So, it's all God and God is playing all the parts. And in the end when it comes down, you and I will understand why as the poet said, be patient, our playwright will show in some fifth act what this wild drama means. So, when you meet any person in this world, regardless of the pigment of the skin, regardless of their background, you are looking right at a mask behind which God hides his face.

Lecture XII

Rearrange the Mind

March 24, 1972

You should find tonight a very practical night, something that you can test—take it home tonight and prove it. You'll take it from Scripture, but something first, I think with which you're all familiar. If you took a piece of steel that's magnetized, it does not differ in substance from the demagnetized piece of steel, only in the arrangement of its molecules. The rich man, the poor man, the beggar man, the thief are not different minds, but simply different arrangements of the same mind. There is only God in this world. So, when you say *I am*, and I say *I am*, it's the same God, but we have arranged the structure of our minds differently. We have different concepts of self and that's all. But not one is better because he is richer than the one who is poor. These are only different arrangements of the structure of the mind.

Now Scripture tells this and I'm quoting now, the book of James, the Epistle of James.

James is really a letter from Jacob. The word James and Jacob are identical. In Hebrew, Greek, and in the Arabic tongue, the same word. So, when they begin, James, a servant of God and the Lord

Jesus Christ to the twelve tribes in the dispersion, you can see it once. It's simply a Christian revision of this Jewish letter; it's the letter of Jacob and if you read it carefully, only twice do they insert, say, Jesus Christ our Lord, all the others, there are eleven other times, it is simply God. The Lord is God, not Christ. So here it is really the servant of the Lord speaking. And he is giving us some fantastic instruction and very practical instruction. Now, listen to it carefully. I am now going to quote from the very first chapter of the book of James: "Be doers of the word and not hearers only, for he who is a hearer and not a doer is like a man who observes his natural face in the mirror then goes his way and at once forgets what he is like. But he who looks into the perfect law, the Law of Liberty, and perseveres, he will be blessed in his doing."

Now, how do I look into the Law, the perfect Law, which sets me free, the Law of Liberty? I look into my mind. I'm now imprisoned. I've heard the sentence. I know exactly how long I'm supposed to serve. Now, I look into the Law of Liberty in my mind, and I assume that I am free. I'm set free. How? I am not concerned. Who brought it about? I am not concerned. I simply look into the perfect law, the Law of Liberty, and I dare to assume that I am free. If I dare to assume that I am free, I rearrange the structure of my mind, the same mind that heard the sentence that I accepted when I heard it. Now, I do not accept it. I look into the perfect law, the Law of Liberty. And if, as I'm told in Scripture, I persevere, then I will actually receive that which I am doing. I must not forget what I have done and sleep this night as though I am in prison; for if I am now set free, where would I sleep? Let me know exactly where would I sleep? Well, dare to assume that I am sleeping there now.

If I sleep in the assumption that I am free, I am not in jail. Even though the bars are there, I don't see them, close my eyes against them. As Blake tells us, man's perceptions are not bounded by organs of perception: he perceives more than sense, however acute, can discover. And so, reason or the ratio of all that we already know is not the same that it shall be when we know more. If I take this tonight and test it, and it proves itself in the testing until I have added to my knowledge. And so, I know more than before I tested it, and so when I find myself up against something that seems beyond solution, I have found something that can solve it. All I have to do is to rearrange the structure of my mind. So, I dare to assume that I am the man that I would be and sleep as though I am. That's the rearrangement of that structure of the mind. I am the same being. I'm Neville. I know exactly those that I knew before, but now I know them differently. I know them now as a freed man, but I must not be a hearer of what I heard in Scripture. I must be a doer. I must do it.

So be not a doer, only, be a doer in the full sense of the word. So that I actually, I do it and persist, the word is *persevere* in Scripture: the first chapter, the 22nd to the 25th verses of the Epistle of James. So, I will simply do it. And though tomorrow, I am confronted with the obvious facts of life that I'm still in prison, it still doesn't matter. I did it. I am doing it and I will continue to do it until that which I have done is perfectly externalized within my world. I am telling you this from experience. I know it. If you go to jail and you say five to ten years. All right, you know, five years, and maybe you get off in six for good behavior. But when you are drafted into the army, there is no date that you are promised where they'll let you out. You are in for the duration. Well, I was drafted into the army with 17 million of us. Well, I didn't ask the permission of anyone. I only consulted myself. I looked around, I knew what the world knew. It was something that had to be done. But I must be honest with myself, I didn't want any part of it. But no part of it. Others would tell me, is that the act of a coward? I didn't care what they said. Is that being a good citizen? I didn't care what they said. As I just said earlier, what we now know, which is called reason—it's a reasonable thing to do, we are at war, and we're all Americans. And we should be going there because our country has declared war. Go in there and fight. And so, reason tells us that should be done. I was drafted. I did not oppose it. They drafted me. Took me down to Camp Polk, Louisiana, for my basic training. And while I was there, I didn't want any part of it. And I dare to assume that I am out of it and made my normal natural application, as you have to do in the world of Caesar. Within twenty-four hours, it came back and it was simply rejected. It was signed *disapproved* and signed by my colonel. A very nice gentleman. His name was Colonel Theodore Bilbo, Jr. His father was the senator from Mississippi. I said nothing. My captain said, "For your sake, Goddard, I am very, very sorry. I know exactly how you feel. You want to be with your wife and your little girl. Your son is in Guadalcanal with the Marines and you are now almost thirty-eight. And so, I know, but I would like to go through this war with a man just like you at the side. So, I can't say that I am sorry for myself. I'm sorry only for you." I didn't say one word to him, to the colonel. I didn't oppose it. That was the decision of Caesar. Now, I looked into the perfect law, the Law of Liberty, and I persevered in that law. And I slept that night as though I slept in my own home in New York City on Washington Square, where I lived on the 7th floor. I lived on that floor and it was a very large apartment, with two bedrooms, a lovely, big living room, a dining room, a huge kitchen, and a foyer.

And I slept in that place just as though I were there, not in the army. I fell asleep in that state, having done all the normal things that would make me feel this arrangement is perfect. I rearranged the structure of my mind. Instead of seeing twenty-five men around me, sleeping upstairs and knowing that twenty-five were down below in the next area, I slept in my own bed with my wife in her bed and my little girl in her crib in the corner. I felt everything in that place just as though it's taking place. And I rearranged the structure of my mind and fell sound asleep in that state. At four o'clock in the morning, here comes a sheet of paper before my eye and a hand from here down with a pen in its hand and the pen scratched out the word "disapproved" and it wrote in, in a bold script "approved." And then I heard the word: that which I have done. *I have done*. Do nothing. And then I woke. It was too early to disturb the twenty-five other fellows sleeping there. But I waited until the very first moment that I could leave that room and went down to the latrine and shaved and bathed early and came up, filled with the glow that the whole thing was done. I walked in that assumption for the next nine days. Nine days later, the same colonel that disapproved of my request called me in.

He said, "Close the door, Goddard." So, I closed the door. He said, "Take a seat." He never asked me to take a seat in his presence before. I was a private. You always stood in his presence. He said, "Take a seat." And then he gave me all the reasons in the world why I should still be in the army. He said, "Do you still want to get out?" I said, "Yes, sir." He gave me another reason. "Do you still want to get out?" I said, "Yes, sir." Another one. When he exhausted all the reasons why I should be in the army—and I'm still saying, "yes, sir"—he said, "all right, bring me another application and have your captain sign it," which I did that day. I was honorably discharged and out of the army. I didn't run away. I was honorably discharged.*

When vision breaks forth into speech, the presence of Deity is there and who can oppose God? "To that which I have done, I have done." Do nothing. So, he thought he initiated the urge to let me go free. I looked into the perfect law, the Law of Liberty, and I persevered in that law and he played his part, for I rearranged the structure of my mind.

I was convinced I wanted out and I didn't ask anyone's permission. I did not discuss it with anyone as to why I should want out when 17 million men are being drafted plus numberless girls to make

* Neville's surviving military records confirm that he was inducted into the army on November 12, 1942, and honorably discharged about four months later in March 1943.

a tremendous effort against this monstrous thing that was in Europe. I still wanted out. I did not take anyone into my confidence as to why I wanted out. I had my thirteen-week basic training. And then when I came out, they gave me my citizenship papers and became, I could have been back in 1922, I could have been an American, but I just didn't have the time or the urge to get around it, to become a citizen. So, I drifted on and drifted on and drifted on. And finally, after this little episode, that's why I went into the army. I would still be drifting through and being a citizen of Britain. But now I am an American by adoption and they gave it to me because I did fulfill a thirteen-week training course in the American army. So, I tell you, I know from experience how true this statement in James is, read it carefully: "Be doers of the word and not hearers only, deceiving yourself."

For he, who is a hearer of the word is not a doer, he is like one who looks into the mirror and sees his natural face. And then he goes away and at once forgets what he looks like. But he who is a doer, he looks into the perfect law, the Law of Liberty and perseverance, and when he does that, he is blessed in his doing. *That is acting*, making the thing become alive within you. Now he tells us in the same chapter, "Faith without works is dead. As the body, apart from the spirit is dead." So, faith without works is dead. He is not proposing that I substitute works for faith. Works are the evidence of whether the faith I profess is alive or dead. I say I believe the story of Scripture. Well then, if I believe it, then do it. He said, "Whatever you desire, believe you have received and you shall." Well, if I really believe that I can't say I believe by quoting the Apostles' Creed, that's not belief. Going to church and genuflecting before some manmade little cross, that's not Scripture. Do you really believe the doctrines, the teachings of Scripture, not the traditions of men, not the rituals, not the outer ceremonies, but the teachings of Scripture? "When you pray, believe that you have received and you will."

And "all things are possible to him who believes"—but do I believe that? Well, then believe it, if I really believe I am out of the army, what and where would I be? Well, I will be at home in my place a thousand miles away on Washington Square. If I look through the window, I will see the Holly Apartments. If I look to the left, I will see Washington Square. If I looked to the right, I will see Sixth Avenue. It's now called the Avenue of the Americas. But then, and still is to me raised as I was there, it's still Sixth Avenue to me. And there I will look at Sixth Avenue. Well, I did that that night. I saw Sixth Avenue. I saw Washington Square. And then I went through the entire apartment and touched these objects with my imaginary hands. Now, was that rational? The world will say that was the most irrational thing that one can do. Now, what is reason? The office of reason is simply, well, to extract conclusions from premises. Must my premises always be based upon the evidence of my senses? Must they always dictate what is rational to me? Well, having done this and proved it to be a fact, reason doesn't mean to me, what it means to the world. For they would sleep in the army. And I wrote a friend of mine who was a Freudian and he practiced psychiatry in New York City.* He was drafted. He was an Englishman, too. And he was drafted and he was off in Florida, a man my age. And so, when I got out, knowing exactly what I did, I wrote him a detailed letter telling him what I did and how to do it. No, he was a Freudian. And that was something that didn't make sense to him. To him, the whole thing was centered in sex, not on this use of the imagination. I said, all right. He didn't answer my letter. I got out in 1943 in the spring, in the month of April, or was it March?

---

* The friend to whom Neville refers is almost certainly occult philosopher Israel Regardie (1907–1985), another Englishman who entered the US Army during the war and who wrote extensively of Neville afterward in his 1946 book *The Romance of Metaphysics*. Neville further references these circumstances and Regardie by his first name in the November 19, 1971, lecture "Facts Overflow the World." Regarding Regardie's practice of "psychiatry," he was a chiropractor by profession and the field uses the term "chiropractic psychiatry," e.g., see "From the Occult to Chiropractic Psychiatry: Francis Israel Regardie" by Nicholas T. Papadiuk, B.A., et al., *Chiropractic History,* Volume 27, No. 2, 2007. I am grateful to Hugo Santos for this insight into the friend's identity and for his helpful consultations on other aspects of this book.

March or April of 1943. They drafted me November the 19th, 1942. And I got out in March 1943. When the war was over and all the other fellows were being discharged, he was discharged. And he said to me afterwards, "You know, Neville, I love to come to your lectures and to hear you because it's interesting, it's fairy. You turn my daily bread into the substance of fairy. But while I listen to you, you know, what I do, I put my feet right down on the carpet, and I hold onto the sides of the chair to keep my sense of the reality and the profundity of things."

Well, he kept on holding his little cot in the army for another three years, because he couldn't let go and put himself where he wanted to be. So, I am telling you how it's done. I am telling you how it's done from my own experience, that my perceptions are not necessarily bounded by organs of perception. I perceive more than sense, no matter how acute they are, could discover. My senses couldn't discover what I am seeing. Only in my imagination could it be done. I am seeing the Holly Apartments. I am seeing Sixth Avenue. I am seeing Union Square. I am seeing the bed, my wife, my child. I hadn't seen them in three months, but they are all there. I didn't bring sex into it. No, I didn't go to bed with her. There she was, the girl I love. She was in her own bed and I in my own bed, we have twin beds. And my little girl was then just over a year, not quite a year. She was born in June of 1942. And this was not yet June of 1943. So, she was not yet a year old. Here's my sweet little child, Vicky, in her bed. And I walked through the entire thing and touched all the objects and felt them, so normal and so natural, came back to my bed and slept in it. If anyone was sensitive in that room, they would have seen me sleeping there. I was so natural to myself that they would have seen me actually sleeping there. And then the next day he had a change of mind, but he couldn't act upon it. He was resisting that change, but that which I have done, I have done. Do nothing. So, he resisted it for nine days and then he called me in and told me to bring a new application, which I did. And that day I was out. So, I tell you how it works. This is the most practical law in the world. He looks into the perfect law, the Law of Liberty. Well, doesn't that liberate you?

If you look into the Law of Liberty, then what are you now? The man, the woman you really want to be, but then you are in prison though you're not behind bars. You are imprisoned by your present concept. You're not behind bars. You're going to go home tonight and sleep as the woman, as the man, you really want to be. So, you are in prison. Now look to the perfect law, the Law of Liberty, and persevere. Do not only be a hearer of what to do. *Do it* and you will be blessed in the doing. That's what the Scripture teaches. Go home and read it. I am not misquoting. I am quoting accurately from the Epistle of James in the New Testament. And this is the story that I'm trying to tell everyone in the world. He said I am not in prison. No, you're not in prison, not physically, but you are in prison. You may today, need money. And you say I'm still not like the fellows who are behind in Sing Sing. All right, you're not behind jail doors, but you are still behind, behind in rent, behind in this and the dunning notes from all the places where you charge, you are behind bars. You can't seem to find the necessary sum to pay them. All right. Look into the perfect Law of Liberty. That's the perfect law.

Well, how do I do it? Rearrange the structure of your mind. That demagnetized piece of steel does not differ in substance from the magnetized, only the arrangement of its molecules. And then one lifts up enormous weights when it's completely one-pointed; when all these molecules face one direction, it's a powerhouse. The other is scattered. So let not the double-minded man think that he will, in any way, receive from the Lord; you're told in the same first chapter, if the double-minded man comes, who is unstable in all his ways that he not think he'll receive anything from the Lord. What can you give a man who does know what he wants? I've gone into a restaurant just to prove this principle, sat down, and said to the waiter, what would you like for a tip? And he's embarrassed. I said to my friend, I'll give him what he wants, within reason, I'm not going to give him any hundred dollar bills, but I'll give him, if he said, give me a five dollar bill. I didn't order that which warranted a five dollar bill. And he was embarrassed and embarrassed and embarrassed. And all he expected was exactly what he got. He just didn't know. He just had no concept of putting something, of course, he didn't know it, so how could he put it to the test?

So, I am telling you, you rearrange the structure of your mind. That's all you do. It doesn't differ from Einstein's mind. It's only one mind. There's only one God. There's only one Lord. Listen to it. One body, one spirit, one hope, one Lord, one faith, one baptism, one God and Father of us all, who is above all, through all, and in all. If he's in you that's the same one with the one body, the one spirit. So, I'm not using a different mind. It's the same mind but differently arranged. Go into one room and you see that someone doesn't know what to do with their furniture. Bring someone in who knows how to set a room. Come back an hour later after she's through with it and you'll think you're in an entirely different home. My wife used to pull that on me all the time. I'll come home and think I just stepped into an entirely strange apartment and wondered if I'm really at home. And she was hiding some other place. She had completely rearranged the structure of the furniture. It looked like an entirely different home, but she has that sense of how to do it and so she did it.

So, with what you have, all you need is exactly what you have, for you have the mind of God. It's not a different mind, the same mind. And you simply rearrange the mind by a mere assumption. What would the feeling be like were it true that I am now the man that I want to be, now the woman that I want to be? It's added but persevere. You must persevere in it. If I call you now and you answer, one thing, well, will you respond an hour later to the same call? Then if you persevere, you will. If now, an hour later, you think of yourself as you now, when you dare to assume that you are now the man that you want to be. An hour later, are you still assuming that state? If you're not, you're not persevering. You are the hearer who looked into the mirror with his natural face, he saw it, then went his way and at once forgot what he looked like. So, if one hour from now you are not still assuming that you are the man that you want to be, you've forgotten. You are the hearer and not the doer. And he warns us of the vast difference between being a hearer and being a doer. The doer acts. God only acts and is in existing beings or men.

So, bear in mind that your wonderful world is not bounded by your senses. You perceive far, far more than your sense, no matter how acute it is, could discover. Your senses can't discover but now you are capable of assuming that you are. Your senses dictate what reason will allow and your reason, your senses are bound together. Go beyond it for what you now know from experience. What you know from the past will not be what you will know when you know more than you now know. But having done it and proven it, I know more than I did when I was bounded by my senses. When I couldn't get out of a certain island on time to meet a commitment in Milwaukee, I knew what I did in the army. I simply applied the identical thing and I got out.

There was a long, long waiting list. Thousands waiting for all the islands and only two little ships, not big ships, two small little ships, one carrying up more than sixty-odd passengers and one carrying one hundred and twenty and thousands waiting. And they only came once a month into the island. One, every thirty-two days, and one every three and a half weeks. How long would it take to get them all out? I didn't ask anyone a favor. Didn't ask my brother, who was a powerful businessman on the island. He criticized me for not arranging passage back to America when I left America. That's the place where you should have done it. That's the powerhouse of the world, New York City. That's where all these things are done. And you dare to leave New York City when you could arrange a round trip and you come here on a one-way ticket? Well, I didn't ask any favors from him or any favors from any member of the family.

I simply did exactly what I did in the army. And in twenty-four hours, I was called by the Alcoa Company and given my passage over thousands who were waiting. It isn't my concern why she did it or why someone else didn't get it in preference to me when my name was down at the very bottom. I wasn't at the top. I'm at the bottom of the list. It isn't my concern. I looked into the perfect law, the Law of Liberty, and I persevered. I sat in a chair in my hotel room and there I sat in the chair and assumed that I am next to the boat; I'm climbing up the gangplank. That's before we had a deep-water harbor. So, we had to go out to sea, maybe a half-mile or a mile to sea on a little tender, and then take the gangplank and go up to the ship. So, I felt myself bobbing as you would on the ocean. And then moving up the gangplank, I could smell the rawness of the sea, got up to the top, and my mind wandered, I brought it back again and did it all over again. It wandered, brought it back to them again, and kept on doing it over and over until finally, I did it. I fell sound asleep sitting in the chair, in the act of doing.

Next day, Alcoa calls me and gives me my passage for my wife and my little girl. So, I'm telling you from experience, it doesn't fail, but we must not simply be hearers of the word. We must be doers of the word. For if you are a hearer and not a doer, you deceive yourself, he tells you, for we are the operant power. This law doesn't operate itself. It doesn't care if you are good, bad, or indifferent. Look around the world, who would think that tonight someone serving a life sentence in our jail is the same mind that sits in the White House. Who would think the one who sits now in the Vatican, that mind of the Pope is the same mind of the one who is groveling on his belly, trying to kiss his hand?

So, on Sunday there'll be Palm Sunday and they'll do all these things on Palm Sunday; the holy palms, and then comes Good Friday, then comes Sunday and all this will go on and have all the show, fabulous show. And he who is being born on the backs of strong, strapping men does not differ from those who are his slaves, bearing him; the same mind, but they have rearranged their minds to be slaves. And he has arranged his mind to be the Father, to be papa, the great Pope, same mind. There is only one mind in the world. There aren't two minds. That's why I can tell you, I know that when he stands before you, he will know you as his Father and you'll know him as your Son. And because I know him as my Son, are we not one mind? Are we not one being when the same being who called me Father will one day call you Father, are we not the same Father? The same mind, the same spirit, the same body without loss of identity. So, I'm telling you tonight, try it, try it every moment of time. You know, tonight what you want to be. I don't care what you want to be, it's simply a rearrangement of the mind. And you rearrange the mind, not through any study or any effort. It's simply a mere assumption. What do I want to be?

Get it clear in my mind's eye. Well, then assume that I am it.

Listen to the words in the book of Joel: "Let the weak man say, I am strong." *Let the weak man say I am strong.* That's in the book of Joel. Jehovah God, that's what the word would mean, Joel. You're called upon when you are down to assume that you are exactly what you want to be, not down, because you don't want to be there. You want to be as free as the wind. Well, assume that you are. May I tell you in a way that no one knows you'll become it, but you must persevere. And the word perseverance is true. If I don't believe it, well then one second later, I've turned back to my former state and become once more Lot's wife, the pillar of salt. Salt is a preservative in the old days, the only way to preserve something is to salt it. Not so long ago when I was a little boy, we caught fish, an enormous quantity of fish because we didn't have these enormous fleets catching our fish. So, we had fish to burn, literally burn. If they didn't get in before, say three o'clock in the afternoon, what did they have? They could either put it onto the dung heap and make dung out of it or clean it up and salt it. So, they cleaned it up and salted it. It would keep indefinitely for we had no refrigeration. So, you salted the fish and we could have salt flying fish if you wanted it that way.

But fish that were not consumed by sundown were discarded. Use it for bait the next day or use it in the dung heap to fertilize the fields with it. So salt is a preservative. So, when Lot's wife was turned to salt, she turned back and went back to her former state. And that is all that it means. You looked back and became a pillar of salt. You turned back to the state you said you would leave behind you. And looking back, you were salted. You are preserved in it. So, turn away from what you really want to be. Turn back. You're going to be salted in it.

So, I ask you to leave what you are unless you like what you are. There are portions of what you are today that you like, all right, wonderful. There are other portions that you do not like. Well, you don't have to give up everything in your living room when rearrange the structure of it. Certain pieces you'll keep. You may change its location, but you'll keep it. The same thing is true with the structure of the mind. You'll keep certain things and you let other things go. Take friends in your world who are not doing well, rearrange them in your mind's eye and they're doing well. So put that part of the structure in your mind's eye. Rearrange the entire structure, and dare to assume that it's true, and walk in that assumption. And that assumption though at the moment is denied by reason and denied by your senses, if you persevere in it, it will harden into fact.

This is the law of Scripture. That I came not to abolish but to fulfill the Jewish law and the Jewish prophets, for there was no other Scripture in the first century but the Jewish Scriptures. So, the word Jew is not placed before it to qualify it but the only Scripture that he knew. He came to fulfill the Jewish law. He reinterpreted the law psychologically and showed them exactly how it's done. So go out and do not abolish anything, simply fulfill it, fulfill the law and fulfill the prophets. The prophets, when they're fulfilled, that's done by sheer grace. That comes, that comes by prophets. And no one's going to stop it, may I tell you. But you could go on living in a state that you do not wish in this world, but in spite of that, you will still receive the Promise because it isn't given to the one who is rich and denied the one who is poor, but why remain poor and bat your head out morning, noon, and night against the inevitable blows in this world. I hope you do not wish for money for the sake of money, but if you need money, well, then apply this law. What would the feeling be like if it were true that I was now free of this pressure, free of it? Dare to assume that you are and then persist in that assumption. And that assumption will harden into reality.

So, this is my lesson tonight. I think you found it a very practical one but I must remind you: you can either be the hearer of what you heard tonight and not the doer. It is my hope that you will be the doer of what you heard tonight. That when you leave here, you leave here in the assumption, not wait until you get home, leave here in the assumption that you are already the man, the woman that you want to be. And then between here and home, think of the man that you have assumed that you are and let that assumption spring in your mind constantly. You are that man. Go to bed in that assumption. Maybe this night, as it did with me in the army, something will come and a voice will speak. And when vision breaks forth into speech, the presence of Deity is assured. And maybe you will have confirmation that what you have dared to assume is. I know in my case it came that way. But it will come whether it breaks forth into speech or not. If you persist in the assumption.

Lecture XIII

Fulfillment of God's Promise

March 27, 1972

I think we're all aware that this is the most dramatic week in Christendom. And yet I dare say that not 1 percent of those who call themselves Christians really understand what it is all about. It's the story of the fulfillment of God's purpose. That's the week. The triumphant march into Jerusalem, the crucifixion, and then the resurrection. And it's told as though it took place on earth. That's how the story is told, or as Tennyson said, "truth embodied in a tale shall enter in at lowly doors."* So, men cannot think abstractly. So, it's told in the form of a story and man has mistaken the story for the reality. So let us now look to see who the one is spoken of in Scripture. They say his name is Jesus. You may not believe me, but I'll tell you who Jesus is. Say *I am.* That's Jesus. Don't say I am Nan or John or Peter, or anything just, *I am.* That's Jesus. That's God. That's the Lord, God, Jehovah. The crucifixion is already over. That was in the beginning of time, a deliberate act on the part of God. It's all over.

---

* Neville is quoting Alfred, Lord Tennyson's (1809–1892) 1850 poem, "In Memoriam A.H.H."

The resurrection took place and is taking place and will continue until everyone is awake. So, you say, *I am*, that's Jesus. Now it begins with the march. Mark tells us that he took the twelve and then he walked ahead of them. And the way Mark states it, it's as if he were one whom a dream had possessed and who went forward to fulfill all that the prophets had foretold. For he said, "I have come to fulfill Scripture." The only purpose. Now, not a man on the outside, fulfilling Scripture. This one, which is God, is buried in you when you say *I am*. You may not be aware of it, aside from dreaming the dream of life, which is this, he also is dreaming the fulfillment of his purpose. And the day will come, you are going to reproduce within yourself, all that is said in Scripture, concerning Jesus. Then you will know who Jesus is. It is said that when he told them, "We are going up to Jerusalem and all that was written of the Son of man by the prophets will be accomplished." And then the evangelist adds, "They understood none of these things."

This saying was hid from them and they did not grasp what was said. Only the risen Lord can interpret Scripture. Only his finger could trace the ambiguous phrases of Scripture and extract their heavenly meaning. It's a pattern in Scripture that only when he rises in you, as you, can you take the Old Testament and simply follow the pattern. You know what the pattern is because you've experienced it. And the whole thing unfolds, and the whole thing is told to you in the Old Testament. But it's a pattern. It's told you as though it's history. Ancient history is divine history. And that history, not page after page, but a pattern goes through the entire thing. And then that pattern unfolds within you. And when it unfolds within you, you know who you are. You gain the certainty as it unfolds within you, you actually gain that certainty, that *I am he*. There is no other way you'll ever know it until it unfolds within you. Now God came and comes into human history. And now we're going to give him a name in the person of Jesus, but the Jesus in you, in me, in every child born of woman. That's the only Jesus in eternity. *I am*—that's he.

But now he's the Father. When God is born within you, for that's the beginning of it all, you first awaken within you—and you do not know you are God. You only know that you have awakened from the most profound sleep ever. And it seemed like eternity. You did not awake on the bed where you fell asleep the night before. You awoke in a tomb. And the tomb is your skull. And you are awake within your skull. And you are all alone, there's no one present. But you have a built-in, innate knowledge of what to do. And you do it and you come out of your skull. As a child comes out of the womb of a woman. But you are coming out of your own skull and you pull yourself out of your own skull. And then the imagery of Scripture concerning the birth of God surrounds you, including the little babe wrapped in swaddling clothes and three witnesses to the event. So, you are told, "When they came, they saw the heavenly being, but him they did not see." It's the birth of God. God actually took about himself the limit of contraction, which is man.

Now he is born, the birth being an expansion. There is no limit to expansion. God is forever expanding. And then at a moment of expansion, he then has a new venture of contraction. Then he expands beyond what he was. Then he contracts. Then he expands beyond what he was. And that is God's play. There is no limit to expansion. He puts the limit to contraction. The limit here is man. So, when you break the tomb, you come out and you are God, therefore no one can see you. The heavenly hosts who are present to witness the event can't see you for you are spirit, you are God; but you see them and you see the babe and you see everything roundabout you just as described in Luke and Matthew.

But you do not know that you are God. That comes later. And you'll not in eternity know you are God until God's son calls you father. And God's son, the Christ of Scripture, is not Jesus. It's David. Jesus is the Lord. Jesus is the Lord God, Jehovah in you. When you say *I am*, that's Jesus. That's not David. Who then is the Christ? The son of God, David then comes and when David comes, there is no uncertainty as to who you are, for he calls you Father. And before he utters the word Father, you know you are his Father, and he knows he is your son. And this relationship is now what every heart is aching for. When this is established by an actual experience, the drama is over. Everything is over that you came to perform, to find the Son who in turn will reveal you as God the Father. For he is sound asleep in humanity and man doesn't know that he's God. And when he is born from above, he still doesn't know he's God. And not in eternity can he find out who he is until the son appears. So, we are told in Scripture, "No one knows who the son is except the father." And no one knows who the father is, except the son, and anyone to whom he chooses to reveal it.

So, people will say, "I know Jesus is the Son of God." And you ask them, "You really know that?" And I've had people say to me, "Oh yes, I've seen him. And he is the Son of God." Then you say to them quite honestly and simply, well, then you must be God. Well, no one has slapped me so far. The impulse was there to put me in my place. And yet here is Scripture. They say they have seen Jesus. And Jesus is the son of God. And Scripture teaches that no one has ever seen God but the son, and no one knows who the Father is but the son. Well, if you know the son, well, then you've seen the son. And if you saw the son, then you know, you are God. For only God sees the son. Only the Father knows the son. So don't tell me you know the son and do not know at the same time that you are God. For you cannot know the son and not know the father. So, when they kill you, you're told, and put you out of the synagogues, I think they do God a favor. They do it because they know neither my father nor me. Had they known my father, they would've known me also, but they know neither my father nor me.

So, you'll find you've got to actually feel between the words, for he is speaking in one moment as Father and then speaking in another moment as son. It's a mystery. And how are you going to tell it? Unless you tell it in the form of a story that it may enter in at lowly doors. That man hearing the story learns to feel behind the story and feel what it's trying to convey. But when you actually experience the story then you know the mystery. It's the mystery that everyone one day will unfold within himself and he'll know that he is God. So, this is what confronts man this week as it's dramatized, but not told, for they do not know it. They do not know the story.

So let me turn now to the 55th chapter of Isaiah: "I will make a covenant with you." Now, he is speaking to all of us. "I will make a covenant with you." And this is his covenant: "My steadfast, sure love for David, I have made him a witness to the peoples. That is my witness to the peoples." Now, what is he going to witness? The truth of God's word. For God's word is Scripture and the Scripture spoken of was the Old Testament. "And thy word is truth. I make him now a witness to the peoples and he has my steadfast and sure love forever. Now that is my covenant with you, said the Lord to us."

We turn now to the trial and here we find one called Jesus standing before Pilot. And he turns to Pilot and he said, "For this, I was born. And for this, I came into the world to bear witness to the truth." Now he tells you, he is not of this world. Unless you are born from above, you cannot enter the Kingdom of Heaven. He's not speaking of the birth from the womb of a woman, in spite of all the priesthoods of the world. He's speaking of an entirely different birth, born, not of blood, nor of the will of the flesh, nor of the will of man, but of God.

I am from above, you are from below. Now, he's not speaking to you, the being who is God. He is speaking to this body here. This is from below. This came out of the womb of my mother. But there's that in me, which is *I am*, that no woman can bear. That must be born from above. It is now entombed in my skull, entombed in your skull. But the skull of which I speak is a divine skull containing all of us. That is the skull. And it is said in the 87th Psalm, "And this one was born here and that one was born there and that one was born there all within the one grand skull that is called Zion, another name for Jerusalem." So, when Paul said, "The Jerusalem from above is our mother and she bears children into liberty. The Jerusalem from below bears them into slavery." Well, my physical mother bearing her ten children that she raised, she wove garments of flesh. And these garments of flesh came from below, from her womb, into slavery for we are all slaves of the bodies that we wear. But housed within that, from above, there is another Jerusalem and she is our mother who bears us into liberty, into freedom. You come out of your own skull, that divine skull, and you are set free. But then you come into this world to bear witness to what? To the truth. So, I made him a witness to all the peoples, for what is he going to witness now? The truth of Scripture: that God is a Father. And that he did say to me, "I will tell of the decree of the Lord," said David, in the second Psalm. He said unto me, "Thou art my Son. Today, I have begotten thee."

And now listen to the words in the 10th of John: "And Scripture cannot be broken." *Scripture cannot be broken*. "And the Lord said unto David, Thou art my son, my only son. Today, I have begotten thee." If Scripture cannot be broken, what other son are you holding up now before me that I may see? You may see all the hallucinations in the world. As artists have painted dozens and dozens of different portraits of the one they call Jesus. And they said they saw him. Ask the artist, "When you saw him in your imagination and you painted on the canvas, or you sculpted it, did you know then you are looking at the son of God?" If they say yes, well then you must know that you are God—because no one can see the son but the Father, and no one knows the son but the Father. Therefore, if you are looking at the son of God and only God can see the son, well, then you must be God. What are they going to say to that?

And Scripture cannot be broken. Read it in the 11th chapter of the book of Matthew: "No one knows who the Son is except the Father.

And no one knows who the Father is except the son, and anyone to whom he chooses to reveal him." So, I know in my own case, raised in the Christian faith as I was, and I call myself a Christian from my own personal experience of this great mystery, but I did not know from my mother's knee or in my school, because we had Bible reading and Bible study when I was a child. It was part of our schooling. We had to go to Sunday school. I was taught the Bible, raised with the Bible and there it is, but I didn't see it. And my teachers didn't see it. My mother didn't see it. My father didn't see it. And no one that I ever met, ever saw it. So, I didn't know it until it happened. It happened in me. And then I could not then make it fit in what they taught me. I had to go back and reread Scripture and there the whole pattern was there all along. But only the risen Christ can interpret Scripture. Only when David rises within me and calls me Father.

Now listen to the words: "When the time had fully come, God sent forth the spirit of his son into our hearts, crying, Father." What time has fully come? When you are born, the great load, the burden, the allotted span, not before you have borne it, the allotted span, can he come. And when you get to the end of the road and you have borne that burden, then the spirit of his son comes into you. And here he rises in you. You resurrect your own son. And that son is God's son. Therefore, you are God. That's when you gain the certainty that you are God. Yet, while you wear the little garment, you are still in a strait jacket and all you can do while you wear it is to tell it, try to clarify the atmosphere, and scrape off the barnacles from this ship that gathered them over the centuries.

Far from belittling Jesus, I place you where he actually is. He is God. He is not the Son of God. *He is God.* He is the Lord. A symbol of God, if you may say, but he wasn't born of any woman. The only woman of whom he was born, *I am.* That's the Jerusalem from above. *I am* Mary and birth to Christ must give if I in blessedness for now and evermore would live. So, each must bring forth the son. And it's the same son, only one son. And when you look at him, no uncertainty, no one need tell you anything. There you are looking at your son as though memory has now returned and you have suffered from total amnesia up to this moment in time when suddenly your memory returns and you know who you are. You're God, the Father.

It's going to happen to every child born of woman. Not one will be lost, not one. I don't care if you are a moron today, if you're brainless; that's only a temporary experience in this world. That brain that you have really, the true brain, that's not really addled at all. That's only some distorted aspect of life for a little while. Maybe you'll go through life spending fifty, sixty years in some distorted brain, but it's still not the brain of which I speak. Not that divine brain. If your child is not a balanced child, a demented child, I know it's a hard thing to bring up, and a hard thing to face in life, but that's not your responsibility. That little thing there that you call your child that is now demented behind it all, behind that mask, which is part of the burden that it bears, is the perfect being that is Jesus. And that Jesus in that, is *I am*. It was never tarnished. It was never soiled. No matter what it has done in the world, it was never soiled. And one day it will awake. Now when it awakes, it comes out of the tomb.

So, Paul could say, "I am crucified with Christ. Nevertheless, I live. *Not I*. Christ lives in me. And the life I now live in the flesh I live by faith in the Son of God who loves me and gave himself for me." And that son is David. Listen to the words: "I have found in David, the son of Jesse, a man after my own heart, who will do all my will." While the word Jesse means *Jehovah exists*. That's what the word means. So, Jesse is the father. What? Whose father? David's father. And who is Jesse? Jehovah. And who is Jesus? Jehovah. He is the Lord, but no one can say Jesus is Lord, except by the Holy Spirit. And who is the Holy Spirit? The remembrancer. When the son stands before you and memory returns and you are his Father and he is your son, then only by this return of memory, will you ever know. And so, no one can say that Jesus is Lord, and Jesus is the Father, for in spirit, David called him my Lord.

Why did he call him my Lord? Well, that's a title of Father. So, he called Jesus, my Lord. He is the, *I am in you. I am* in every being in this world. So, we will go up to Jerusalem. And all that was actually written about the son of man, which is the title that he used of self, will now be accomplished. So, I'm going up to Jerusalem because everything is going to happen in the skull. That's where Jerusalem is, the Jerusalem above. I'm going up to Jerusalem, not down. And all things said of the Son of man will now be accomplished. So, he goes up and the whole thing unfolds within the skull. That's where you awake. That's where you explode. When David comes out it's an explosion in your head. As though you put some dynamite to your head and the whole thing explodes.

And when it all settles, there stands David before you. He was buried in you. So, when he said to me, "I laid myself down within you to sleep." Who said that? The depth of my own soul. The Lord said that. I laid myself down within you to sleep. And as I slept, I dreamed the dream. I dream—and I knew exactly what he was dreaming. He is dreaming that he is I. And when the dream is over, we aren't two we are one. No longer will he simply treat me as something on the outside, an emanation of his. No more the emanation. He cleaves to me and we become one being. So, a man leaves his world, his father, his mother, everyone, and cleaves to his wife. And this is the wife, the emanation of God. Yet through his emanation, it's his wife until the dream is over. When the sleep is over, we aren't two. We are one.

And I know that when I awoke within me, I wonder, how did I get here? Who put me here? For this is a tomb. This is a sepulcher. And only one who thought me dead could have put me here. For this is a tomb and only the dead are placed in tombs. For, someone, I didn't realize then that it was a deliberate act on my own part. So, you are told in the same chapter of John, "No one takes away my life. I lay down myself. I have the power to lay down and the power to take it up again." And yet, over the centuries, we have condemned a race of people for taking away the life of one who never, as an individual, walked the face of this earth. He is in man or you couldn't even breathe. He's not on the outside of man, so someone can take his life. He is i*n man*. He's the breath of man. The spirit of man, the, *Iamness* of man. Man's own wonderful human imagination. That is Jesus. That's God. And so, to blame a race of people for doing what no one ever did. Listen to the Bible. The 10th chapter, "No one takes away my life. I lay it down myself. I have the power to lay it down and the power to take it up again. For I am the resurrection and the life." So, he entered death's door, the human skull, and laid down in the grave of man. And there he dreams the dream of life. And this is the dream of life. And one day it comes to the end, and he awakes where? In the tomb where he entered to find himself there. It was a long dream. Thousands and thousands of years he's been dreaming this dream. You didn't begin in your mother's womb seventy years ago or whatever year you may be. That's only a garment woven for you. You are eternal. You have no beginning and you have no end. Never was there a time when you were not nor shall there ever come a time when you shall cease to be. Beginning and ends are all dreams. It seems so real but they're all dreams. But you have no beginning, no end. *You are*. And that being is called in Scripture, God the father. But may I tell you something, you will not actually feel, *I am Jesus. I am Father*—that's what you feel. You don't feel Jesus. You don't feel God, you don't feel Jehovah. These are names given by man. But what you do feel is Father.

So, the great revelation of the New Testament is *God is Father*. That is the foundation of the entire thing. If you were not a father, then there's no child. So, the relationship of father-son is fundamental to the Christian faith. Without the son, there would not be a father. If there is a father, there must be a son. And if they search for a son and when the son is found, the father knows who he is, but not until the son is resurrected. So, in the Old Testament, in the 2nd Psalm, the 16th Psalm, and the 110th Psalm, they identify with resurrection. In the 16th Psalm, David is speaking and he's made to say, "Thou wouldst not leave my soul in hell." In confidence he knows he would not be left in hell; that he would be raised up because I will not take my steadfast sure love from David. That's my covenant with the people. I have made him a witness to all the people. I will not take my love from him. So, he dies and he's buried, but I will raise him up. And when the father raises up the son, then the smile is on his face because his son has returned from the grave. And David is the eternal son of God.

The resultant state of all the experiences that you as a man, which is God as man, experience in this world. So, God became as I am that I may be as he is. This is the story of Scripture. And it's all in the Old Testament, but not understood. There it is a blueprint. It's an adumbration. The New interprets the Old, not the other way around. When it happens in you, well, what a joy. I can't tell anyone the emotion that possesses you. And then you really are like one possessed. You walk in the dream of what happened and you cannot think of anything, not really. You may be diverted for a little while, a small party, a big one would bore you, a few friends, yes. A large crowd, no. It doesn't interest you A dinner party of a few chosen friends, yes. But to have an enormous crowd. No, that's nothing more than noise. Everyone's trying to, well, monopolize the entire picture, but a few chosen friends for a party, a delightful evening, with words where you're discussing reality, wonderful.

But after it happens to you, may I tell you, you can't think of anything but, and your dreams are not dreams anymore. Your nights are not what they were prior to that wakening. You wake and it's entirely different. And I can't explain to anyone who wakes every day of their life after a night of good sleep, that that wakening in the morning doesn't compare to this. It's something entirely different as though you had never awakened before in your life. That's what actually you feel like, something entirely different. And you look at all these things round about you. And here a thousand years, 2,000 years, 3,000 years ago, it was written there and it was all about you and you didn't know it. So, we are going to go up now to Jerusalem City and all that is written of the son of man by the prophets will be fulfilled, all will be accomplished.

Then he began to explain to them Scripture. And he said, beginning with Moses and the law and all the prophets and the Psalms, he interpreted to them in all the Scriptures the things concerning himself. Now, this coming Friday, if you do go to a part of the service, you'll hear the words on the cross. Every one is taken from the Old Testament. And you will know who you are in that sense. Hear the words of David for David's going to commit himself now to his father. "Into thy hands, I commit my spirit." This is now the 31st Psalm. "Thou hast redeemed me. Oh Lord, faithful God." Yet that is the final cry on the cross. When you read it in the book of Luke, "Into thy hands, I commit my spirit."

And he commits it into the hands of the father. He calls him, now, he calls him father, "Father into thy hands I commit my spirit." And these are the identical words of David in the 31st Psalm. So here, the entire thing unfolds within man. But something was said to me, just before I took the platform by a very dear friend of mine who is here tonight. Although he will admit to me and to everyone in the world, he is 101 percent American, but he cannot deny the fact that he has a 101 percent of the Irish background in him too. So, he gave me the definition of an Irishman. An Irishman is one who does not know what he wants and there'll be no peace on earth until he finds it. Not exactly his words. He told it much better than that, but that's the essence of it. He does not know what he wants and there'll be no peace on earth until he finds it. Well, that's the whole vast world. Ask him, what do you want? He doesn't really know what he wants because what everyone wants is to find the father.

And you can't find the father without the son. Basically, we are trying to find the cause of the phenomena of life. What makes things happen in my world? He told me, you know, years ago, long before he met me, he had these sort of daydreams of, well, talking to a crowd, maybe going on radio, maybe on TV. Clear out of the blue, someone came into his restaurant in Ojai and offered him a series of lectures, here, in New Mexico, possibly to send him into Arizona. She could arrange other things for him. And the whole thing is done, but he remembered these daydreams. Most of us don't remember. And when we are confronted with our own harvest, we deny it's our harvest.

So, I tell you, there is no such thing as an accident in this world, no. There is no such thing as a natural cause. Every natural effect has a spiritual cause. That is, an imaginal cause and not a natural. A natural only seems, it is a delusion of our fading memories. We can't remember when we set it in motion. He remembers that long before he met me in San Francisco that this happened back East, this daydream of his, and now, suddenly, out of nowhere, a seeming stranger comes into his world, listening to him in his restaurant, carried away with what he had to say, the way he said it, is moved to arrange this thing for him. He doesn't have to lift a finger to do it. It all will be done for him.

So, I say dream noble dreams, wonderful dreams. If they don't come to pass tonight, tomorrow or next week, you keep on dreaming them. But try to put yourself into the dream as though it's taking place, and try to live in it, be possessed by the dream and see the whole thing unfold within you, in this world of Caesar, always bearing in mind the real dream. It must come to an end only when it's fulfilled. And the story is the fulfillment when you awake, for resurrection is waking. It's not gathering dead bones together and putting flesh on it. It's simply awakening. You are sound asleep and you awaken like a man out of a deep, deep sleep to find yourself in a tomb. But you have the strength to break the bonds of that tomb and to come out of that tomb. And when they come to search for the body, they've taken away the body. They only knew you by reason of the body that you wore and that's taken away. They can't see you. "Him, they could not see." But he was fully aware of everyone round about him. And here, all the symbolism of Scripture is unfolding before him and he is the central character in the entire drama. They're talking about him. They aren't talking about Jesus. They're talking about you. You are individualized and you tend forever and forever toward ever greater individualization. They didn't call me by any other name. They didn't call me God. They didn't call me the Lord. They didn't call me Jesus. They spoke of me as Neville. *It's Neville's baby.* I was aware of being *I.* No loss of identity whatsoever. But then when David comes here is Neville, in this century I was born, the year 1905. Here, we have a recorded so-called history, a one born 1,000 years B.C. And he stands before me. And I know I'm his Father. And here we have words put into his mouth that the Lord said to him, you are my son.

And I know that I am his father. And only then did I gain the certainty as to who I am. So, you will not lose your identity. Yet, you are God, the Father. It is father that is being revealed. The sweetest name there in Scripture. He's a loving father, may I tell you. In spite of all the pain you've gone through and all the horrors of the world. For this is a nightmare, can't confine it only to the night, its daymare too, with most people. So, I tell you at the end, it's not a reward, it's simply victory. You had plotted and planned the whole thing before you entered the tomb. You prepared a way for your own return—to whom? To yourself. I came out from the father and I came into the world. Again, I am leaving the world and am returning to the father.

And that's the story of this week. So as far as Friday goes, Good Friday, save your tears. The crucifixion is over and it was a voluntary act on your part, which is God's part. You laid yourself down in a tomb for the purpose of dreaming the dream of life. And in that dream, you suffered, you knew you would, as you are told in the 24th chapter of the book of Luke. Again, you are told it in the 18th for that matter, but the 24th: "All foolish men and slow of heart do understand all that the prophets have written and said about the Christ." Was it not necessary that Christ suffer these things and then enter into his glory?

It's part of the training. These are the furnaces. "I tried you in the furnaces of affliction." Why? For my own sake. "For my own sake I do it, for how should my name be profaned? My glory I will not give to another. And my name is Father." That's my name. That's the name truly that is God's name of the world. And so, the word God, which makes the mind jump on the outside is not truly the name. We take the word, *Elohim*, and we translate it into God. We take the word *Yod Hey Vav Hey* and translate that, Lord. But the name that is revealed is Father. That's who this being is. This creative being is father and everyone is in search of the Father. And one day he's going to find the only one who can reveal him as the Father. And when he finds him, he finds his own son, David. Now that will come as an awful shock to the majority of people in the world. I would not take back one little iota. It's true. I am not speculating. I'm telling you exactly what I have experienced. It's not theory with me. This is all what I know from my own personal experience.

It was always there in that book called the Bible, but I had not experienced it, so I couldn't see it. So, you have eyes and you see not, and you have ears and you hear not. Because they're not yet bored. And it takes the furnaces to bore these eyes for you and to bore the mouth for you to bore the ears for you, that you may experience Scripture. And then the whole thing unfolds within you. It's all about you because it is all about God. And you are God asleep. And the day is coming, and may it not be too long, when you will awake in you as you. And when you will find your son that Scripture claims to be God's Son. And because Scripture claims it is God's son and you know it's your son, then you must be God. That's the story of the Bible.

Now, let us go into the silence.

Lecture XIV

Where and When Did It Happen?

March 31, 1972

Others spent some time in church today, listening to one or maybe all seven words of the cross. And I wonder what the attended really understood—the great mystery. For we are told when they came to the place called the Skull, there they crucified him. When they came to the place called the Skull. Where is it and what time? We cannot fix the cross in time or locate it in space. And it's a very great mistake in interpretation to ignore the out-and-out character of the supernatural nature of the crucifixion. In fact, all the great events in the life of Jesus Christ.

Let me share with you my own personal experience to show you cannot locate it in space and you cannot fix it in time. Remember, he's only fulfilling Scripture and the Scripture is the Old Testament. We turn now to a Psalm—the 42nd Psalm that was written hundreds of years before. If you didn't hear each of the [inaudible], you can't date it. It begins, "As the hart panteth after the water brooks, so panteth my soul after thee, oh God." My soul seeks and thirsts for God, for the living God. Now, he said, these things I remember, when I went to the throng and led them in procession to the house of God, a multitude being tested by God.

And let me share with you my own experience of that Psalm and you try to fix it in time or locate it in space. This night in question, I was leading an enormous crowd, a gay crowd, a very festive crowd, a huge multitude, and leading them to the house of God. And as we walked in this gay manner, a voice rang out from outer space. And the voice said, "And God walks with you." A woman at my side, to my right, she questioned the voice. And she said, "If God walks with us, where is he?" And the voice replied, "At your side." She looked to her left and looked into my face, and she became hysterical. She thought it was so funny. So again, she addressed the voice and she said to me, "Neville is God." And the voice answered, "Yes, in the act of waking." Then the voice spoke in the depth of my own self and no one heard it but the speaker. And the voice said to me, "I laid myself down within you to sleep. And as I slept, I dreamed a dream. I dreamed . . ."—and I knew exactly what the end of that sentence would be. He is dreaming that he is I.

But I became so emotionally moved by the voice speaking in the depth of my own being that I began to return to this level. As I returned, my hand, my head, the right side, and the soles of my two feet were nailed by a vortex. It was a vortex, a vortex, a vortex, a vortex, and each foot a vortex. Now, when did it happen? The test is passed. I laid myself down within you to sleep. And, as I said, "I dreamed a dream." Now it begins, these things I remember. If I remember, then it is passed. As Paul states, "I have been crucified with Christ." Nevertheless, I live, yet not I, but Christ who lives in me and the life I now live in the flesh, I live by the faith of the son of God who loved me and gave himself for me. Then he stated, "From now on, I recognize no one from a human point of view. Even though I once recognized Christ from a human point of view, I recognize him thus no longer." Paul, far from the dying side, no one more supported his vision than Paul. But Paul knew the whole thing was supernatural. When it pleased God to reveal his Son in me, I conferred not with flesh and blood.

The drama is a supernatural drama taking place in the soul of man. In the beginning of time, the crucifixion took place. That's when God became as we are that we may be as he is. God became man that man may become God. And that was in the very beginning of God. That was the crucifixion. *The crucifixion is actually God becoming man.* That is how what we speak of as Bethlehem *is man becoming God.* You cannot date them. But we have dated them, well, for church reasons. And today we speak of Good Friday as *a day.* In fact, we separate before and after. When Good Friday took place in the beginning of time, Bethlehem takes place at any moment in time. When it comes, it will come suddenly, unexpectedly. No one will know when he is born within you and you become God. But when he said to me, "And as I dreamed, I dreamt a dream." *I dream*—and I knew exactly what he was going to dream. He is dreaming that he is I. And when the dream of life is over, I will awaken as the dreamer. But then he's awake and I will be awake as the one who so loved me that he actually became and took upon himself all the weaknesses and all the limitations of man. And they are unknown. So, this day is called Good Friday. You cannot date it. Any attempt to date it and ignore the altogether supernatural character of the event called the crucifixion and try to explain it in some naturalistic way is to labor in vain.

God actually became that which you are and he is dreaming your life. So, the dreamer in you is your own wonderful human imagination. That is God. Man is all imagination. And God is man and exists in us, and we in him. The eternal body of man is the imagination and that is God himself, the divine body of Jesus. That's the divine body. And within us, we meet him morning, noon, and night by the misuse of our imagination.

So, here the suffering life that they spoke of today, and all the statements that their faith said today, are taken from the Old Testament. The first two are from Luke, the third from John, and the fourth from Matthew. Then we go back to John for two more. And then we end with Luke. So, in the beginning forgive them for they know not what they do. Not one really knows or he can agree. And the power is putting him through the furnace and suffering with him. Because as you suffer, if you didn't have an imagination, you couldn't suffer. Remove imagination and you can cut yourself in pieces and you couldn't suffer. So, God in man is the suffering one. He actually suffers everything that man thinks only he suffers. So, someone will say to me, it isn't God who suffers in my case. I am feeling the pain. I said, *who*? If I am, because that's his name, that's God's name forever and forever. "Go to the people and say, *I am* have sent you. For, this is my name for all generations." There is no other name that he has.

So, in the gospel of John, it is always, *I am*. Throughout the entire gospel, he's affirming I am the door, I am the shepherd. I am the vine. I am the true water, the living water. All these things the *I am* is speaking of, which is all in man. So here this night, millions celebrated this day and they thought they did God a service, which is all right. It's good to do something of that nature. So, they went out and they spent an hour, two hours, and spent three hours, and they heard these words from the cross and thought the interpretation given by the minister was the interpretation. The simple word, a word spoken of is not a word, but a competed sentence. It could be just, the shortest one is, "I thirst," well that's taken from the Psalm. In the very end, quoting now the 31st Psalm, but it's put into the mouth of Jesus on the cross. And he said, "Father into thy hands I commit my spirit." The completed verse in the 31st Psalm is, "Into thine hands I commit my spirit. Thou hast redeemed, oh Lord, faithful God." He said, "I've come only to fulfill Scripture." And all these words on the cross are taken from the Old Testament.

These things I remember for, may I tell you when it happened to me, memory returned. Walking in that procession to the house of

God, memory returned. But when did it happen? Not on earth, not here. What did she say to the voice? "If he walks with us, where is he?" When did the voice answer, "At your side"? And when she became hysterical, looking into my face—when was it and where was it? You can't fix it in time and you can't locate it in space. But I can tell you it happened, as far as I am concerned in an objective sense; they all seem objective to me. And the voice was objective, all to the last one; because everyone heard the voice. She heard it and could question the voice. Yet in the very end when it spoke only from within me: "I laid myself down within you to sleep." A deliberate decision on the part of my father and the purpose of laying himself down in me to sleep is to transform into himself as God the Father; that's his duty and to do it he put me through the furnaces. "I try you in the furnaces of affliction, for my own sake I do it." For my own sake. I will not give my glory unto another, and glory and I are identical in Scripture. "I will make my glory to pass before me, and when I pass by." So, he identifies glory with the "I". So, forgive me himself, which is his glory, he has to try me in the furnaces of affliction. And so, I go through hell in the shadow. And when he awakes, then I awake as the one who so loved me, he gave himself for me.

So, this is the great story that took place, not took place, but I mean that we celebrate today as having taken place 2,000 years ago. And it's not so at all. This is the eternal drama that is forever taking place. Something to be done absolutely and continuously without dating it. You can't date it. It has no reference to time, no reference at all to anything taking place here. It is always taking place. And so tonight, one, two, or maybe all of you, who knows, it'll be his will this night that he unfolds himself within you and reveals himself as you. Then it's his will, but no one can earn it. No one can force it. It will come and you'll see when the Father reveals himself. When people say, I saw God, you don't see God; God makes himself seen. You never see. He makes himself manifest.

If after the whole thing unfolded within, the few who see me unveiled, it's not because they came upon me and caught me by surprise. It was my deliberate choice to make myself seen. It's entirely up to me to make myself manifest after the whole thing unfolded within. You don't get anyone by surprise. I've made you a promise. I will keep that promise. I have kept it to at least a dozen that I have made myself seen twice, but you do not catch me by surprise. And so, when these events unfold within the soul of man, it is God unfolding because we are told, "Rouse thyself. Why sleepeth thou, oh Lord? Awake. Do not cast us off forever"—but he will never cast you off. But it seems so long when you are eager. We now go back to the 42nd Psalm. He likens "the little hart"—now hart is not H E A R T, it's the little fawn, the little deer, H A R T—"as the hart panteth after the water brooks, so panteth my soul after thee oh God." My soul thirsts for God, for the living God.

Now we tell people the same of the famine of the world. It will not be a famine for bread or a thirst for water, but for the hearing of the word of God. When that thirst is felt, nothing in this world can quench it but an experience of God. And that was an experience of God. When I heard his voice coming from without first, then coming within and I knew the "I" of the dreamer within was God. And I do not separate the dreamer within from the "I" when I awake. It's the same me. I can have a daydream, as I have a night dream, but that daydreamer and the night dreamer are one and the same. So, if I can think of the "I" in a dream, the night dream, the most wonderful picture, the most marvelous bridge of incident, and actually experience it, well then, the same thing is true when I awake. If I only know that the "I" when I awake is one with the "I" that is dreaming, I can now get my goal in this world.

Name the end. Go to the end. Experience the end as though it were true and let the dreamer in me build the bridge of incident and relieve me from where I am now to the fulfillment of that dreaming. When I get there, it will happen in the most normal, natural manner. It will externalize itself in my world. And I give all credit to the being within who is completing the dream. And when completed, these things will happen. This that I spoke of earlier preceded the resurrection. The resurrection comes about and it's not in some cemetery. It's all within your own skull. When they came into the place, which is called the Skull, there they crucified him.* In your skull. So go to bed a perfectly normal person, as you've done year after year, for as many years as you've lived, night after night, and something strange will happen while you're asleep. You will feel a vibration that you've never known before. The strangest vibration. And you may interpret it as I interpreted mine. I thought, I know nothing of the human form. I know nothing of this problem. And I thought to myself, well, now this is it. I don't see how I could survive this vibration. And I thought, knowing nothing about it, this must be what they call a terrible hemorrhage, but I couldn't see how I could survive this vibration. Apart from that, I began to awake and I awoke like I've never been awake before to find myself in my own skull. And I knew the skull was my skull, but I also knew it was the sepulcher. I knew it was a tomb and it was hermetically sealed. There wasn't the slightest little opening in that tomb. And I had one consuming desire: to get out, but I had a built-in wisdom as to what to do. I knew that if I pushed the base of my skull then something would give, that I could push myself through it and then come out.

When I did, I pushed it, and something moved leaving an opening. And I put my head against the opening and squeezed myself out, inch by inch by inch. And I came through that opening as a child comes through the womb of woman, and I pulled myself up. And when I came out, all the symbolism that you find in Scripture, especially in the book of Luke, surrounded me: the infant wrapped in swaddling

* Neville refers to the Biblical Golgotha (Aramaic), translated "place of the skull."

clothes, three men to witness the event, and the most fantastic wind. There was a storm and I interpreted the wind to be coming from the corner of the room, although I still felt it in my head. And one of the three who were present, he felt it and he was the most disturbed of the three. They all felt the wind. He went off to investigate the wind and looking down he saw the child, the infant wrapped in swaddling clothes, and he picked it up. And he looked into the little face; he announced what it was. And he said, "It's Neville's baby."

The other two in the most incredible voices asked, "How can Neville have a baby?" But they couldn't see me. I was invisible to their eyes. I was so alive, so awake. I've never been awake like this before. I can read every thought, their thoughts were objective. I heard what they said and their thoughts, not yet expressed, were objective to me. They couldn't conceal anything from me. And he brought the little infant and placed it on the bed. Then I took the infant up in my hand, and I said, looking into his face, "How is my sweetheart?" And the little child broke into the most heavenly laugh and then the whole thing dissolved. They dissolved, the room dissolved, the infant dissolved, and I found myself on the bed with this fantastically, indelibly imprinted upon my mind. I got out and wrote the whole thing in detail and mailed it to my wife. I went down the hallway and dropped it in so that there'll be a record that the story of Scripture is supernatural and is not secular history. It's something that's going to happen to every person in this world in their own good order.

But it is not something that happens only to one person, it is going to happen to all. It is God being born in man. That was his pledge to himself. And that man would actually become God. I was invisible to them—why? Because God is spirit. But it didn't rob me of the feeling of the part and understanding and wisdom that I did not enjoy when I wore the garment of flesh. Invisible to them. But I invite you, you are not invisible to the heavenly host, but they were not present. Only the three who came like the three shepherds coming and they saw it.

And then, 139 days later, a vibration similar to that one started in my head, this time at the top of my skull. Again, I thought, this is it. There's going to be an explosion with this. Well, there was. This time the whole thing exploded and then it all settled, sending me forward as God's son—not Jesus. David, as told us in the Old Testament. As David said in the 2nd Psalm, "I will tell of the decree of the Lord. He said unto me, thou art my son. Today, I have begotten thee." And then he tells it in the 89 Psalm, "I have found David. With my holy oil I have anointed him. And he shall triumphantly say, thou art my Father, my God, and the rock of my salvation." I did not know, born and raised in the Christian faith that I was and call myself a Christian. My training did not reveal this at all. And here I see David and there is no uncertainty as to the relationship. I know he's my son and I know that he knows I am his father. If I am his father and he is God's son, well then, who am I?

Everyone in this world is going to awaken as God the Father. There's no room for anyone else in the universe but God. For God is transformed in this wonderful creation into himself, and everyone will awaken as God the Father. So, it's the story of Jesus. Jesus is God the Father. You want to see the Father, and I've been so long with you Philip, and yet you do not know me. He who sees me has seen the Father. How then can you say, "Show us the Father?" I and the Father are one. Yet, I and the Father are one and the Father is greater than I, because he is the office of sender. I am limited, but when I return to myself, the Father, I am not in the office of the sent but in the office of the sender and the sender is greater than the sent though they are one. So, Jesus is not the son, he is the Father. David is the son. Did not David in the spirit call him, my Lord?

And "my Lord" is the title that the son always used to describe his father. He always talks of his father as my Lord. And when I tell you it is David, it is David. No one in this world would ever, I would say, dispute it. He can deny it now, but he would've had the experience. And when you have the experience, you can't deny it. I could no more deny that experience than I could deny now the simplest evidence of my senses, I couldn't. It's indelibly invested in us. So, all of you are supernaturally based. And yet men have been taught to believe they are part of secular history. It is not secular history. This being is born not of blood, nor of the will of the flesh, nor of the will of man, but of God. So, God became man that man may be born as God. And because God is a Father. If he's going to give himself to me 100 percent, then I must be a Father. Not just a Father, the Father of another son, but no, *that Son*. If he gives himself to me, tell me who are you? But he's a father. But what is your son's name? David. Well, if David is your son and you succeed in giving yourself to me, I must be, if you succeed, I must be David's father.

That's going to happen to everyone in the world. Not one will escape it, for it's not God's will that one be lost. Can't be lost. So, if you go through the furnaces, do not let anyone condemn you for it and say "serve you right" or this, that, and the other. Never. It is God's will. He passed through all the furnaces, but he did it for his own sake, for he could not give of himself until we are purified in the furnaces. And then he calls us out one by one, not in pairs. You're too unique. There is not one person in the world who can take your place. You are unique. The only one just like you. And so, in time, you are going to be called into the living temple, a living stone in the living temple until the whole temple is done.

So, we are told the curtain was torn in two from top to bottom and people looked in the synagogue for some curtain that was stolen. How could it be when the Scripture tells us we are the temple of the living God and the spirit of God dwells in you? If I am the temple of the living God, and the curtain of the temple is torn, it can't be something of the outside made with human hands. It has to be the temple that I am, and that too is the one that is torn in two from top to bottom.

You don't expect suddenly a bolt of lightning will cut you in two from top to bottom. At the base of your spine, you'll see a golden, pulsing liquid light, it's lit. As you contemplate it, you are going to know it is yourself and you would infuse with it. And then like a fiery serpent, you do the same thing to your own skull. But when you get there, it's going to reverberate like sound.

So, you tell the story in the third chapter of John, and as Moses lifted up the serpent in the wilderness, so must the son of man be lifted up. What did he lift up? A fiery serpent. And just as he lifted it up and called out to the shadow. No fiery serpent was lifted up in the wilderness. All these other shadows that you're told in the book of Hebrews, he was told to do this according to the reality. Build it according to the reality, but yours will only be a shadow, a shadow of the things to come. All this is a beautiful imagery, but although the words are figurative, the truth is literal. When it happens to you, it'll be literally true though, when you read it, the letter, the words used will predict lifting up a serpent in the wilderness.

Now, it all lifted up within you that created power within you that went down into generations will be reversed into regeneration and moved back up into heaven for heaven is within you, and God is in his heaven. For the kingdom of God is within and a kingdom means a king. And the king is within and you rise within yourself. One with God. And you play the part that you are predestined to play before that, the world. So, this is a glorious day, if understood. A perfectly wonderful day. In fact, all the way within, but there are only shadows and we mistake them for the reality. And they're not.

Now, this Psalm we quoted today is the 42nd Psalm. It's called a *maskil, a maskil of Korah*. The word *maskil* means in Hebrew, a special instruction and *Korah* means reality. True. That is really true. That which is real. So, it's a special reality or rather special instruction on truth, on reality.*

---

* In Scripture, Psalm 42 is called a "Maskil of the Sons of Korah"—the Hebrew term *maskil* sometimes means an interpreted or translated teaching or prophecy; *Korah* is a family name for descendants of Moses's rebellious cousin. Neville's interpretation here, particularly of the latter term, is nontraditional.

So, this is a Psalm that everyone should read and finally understand it. You have heard it this night. Take that with you when you read, for I'm telling you, the day will come. You too will lead them in procession. Don't think of Neville, and Neville alone got them in gay procession. Now you will play that part. And everyone will play that part. Everyone must lead them in procession to the house of God and everyone will hear, and everyone will have someone beside to question the outer voice. And then everyone leading them in the procession is going to hear the inner voice coming only to them. "I laid myself down with him into sleep. As I slept, I dreamed the dream." I dreamed and knew I was Neville without anyone coaching me what the sentence means at the very end. He's dreaming that he's I, you will say to yourself. And then you're going to know what the crucifixion is. It's not painful. It's sheer ecstasy, may I tell you. And if the memory of it brings back this ecstasy, just imagine what the original was. For these things I remember. For if I can remember something and become so ecstatic about it, just imagine what it was when in the beginning, we were crucified as God.

As Paul tells it, I have been crucified with God. And he confesses he never saw Christ Jesus after the flesh. He knows the whole drama was within himself. And because it took place within himself, he would not confer with flesh and blood. And all these are the great traditions put into historical form and men now worship an external Jesus, praying he is within. As you're told in the Scriptures, "Do you not realize that Jesus Christ is in you, unless, of course, you fail to meet the test." And then he gives us the test. And the test is so very, very simple. And here is the test. You've heard it several times tonight and only you can judge whether you've passed or failed. But I'll give you the test many times. This comes from the 5th verse of the 15th chapter of 2nd Corinthian. Test yourselves and see whether you are holding to the prayer. Do you not realize that Jesus Christ is in you, unless of course you fail to meet the test.

Now, you just heard the words *Jesus Christ* who tells it in the beginning, you think, if the word Jesus, or the word Christ, or the word Lord, or the word God, or the word Jehovah convey the sense of some existent something external to yourself, you fail the test. You haven't yet found it within. And I'll tell you, he is within you: your own wonderful human imagination; that is the Lord Jesus Christ.

So, if on hearing these words, you jump out and think of something external to yourself, existing, yes, but external to yourself, then you fail the test. As you walk there, walk in the consciousness of being this one, who so loved you, who became you. He is your own wonderful human imagination. Now you can test him in this way. If all things are possible to God, and he is within, and he is my own wonderful human imagination, certainly I should be able to test that. I will now dare to assume that I am the man that at the moment reason denies and my senses deny. But who is doing it? Who is making the assumption? *I am.* That's his name. And all things are possible to God. And he's just made an assumption. He's wearing this garment and responds to the name, Neville. When someone calls the word, Neville, he responds. But he is the reality that actually wears the garment. Now, I assume, well, I am assuming as God, I am assuming that I am the man that I want to be. I know exactly what I want. Well, walk as though you were, that's all he asked of him. When you pray, believe you have received and you will.

Believe that you have, not you're going to—believe that you have. Then, why not walk as though I have received? If I walk in the assumption that I am already the man that I want to be, though reason denies it, and my senses deny it, I should encounter that man. I will actually become that man, so that others can see I am that man. Well now try it. Take a noble concept of yourself, something new, something wonderful, something that you would like to live with. Assume that you are it and walk as though you are. Sleep as though you are. And then let the one within you, who so loves you that he became you, unfold you in that life. For eventually he is going to unfold you as himself. But in the meanwhile, in the world of Caesar, let him unfold you as the man, as the woman, that you would like to be. Make it noble, make it something lovely, always use your imagination lovingly on behalf of others. And certainly, on behalf of yourself. Nothing little, nothing that would take from anyone in this world; leave them just as they are. Don't rob them, leave them, think noble things of them, but for yourself dare to assume something wonderful and live in it just as though it were true. And I tell you from my own experience, it will become true.

Now let us go into the silence.

Lecture XV

Justified States

April 3, 1972

Tonight, we will take both the Law and the Promise. Just a little while on the Promise, that you may not be concerned. For I do know that so many people tell us that we must do this, that, and the other, or else. Well, you forget it.

God planned everything as it has come out and as it will be consummated. It is your Father's good pleasure to give you the Kingdom. You do not earn it; it's not your due; it's not a reward. It's simply a gift, unmerited. And therefore, you cannot lose it. This gift is irrevocable. So, no man can take it from you; no man can give it to you. So let no one frighten you. It is yours and it's coming on time. And the gift is nothing less than God Himself.

When He gives you the Kingdom, He gives you Himself. For the Kingdom is not a realm. The Kingdom is a character. It's a body. And that body is perfect. And wherever you are, clothed in that body, everything around you is perfect. No matter where you go, were you in the Petrified Forest, it would burst into the foliage. Were you in the desert, it would simply blossom like a rose. Were you in the midst of all broken members of society, they would all be in harmony. If you came into a world where they were blind, lame, halt, withered, instantly, as you glide by, eyes that were missing would come out of the nowhere and fill the empty sockets. Arms that are missing, feet missing, everything will be made perfect because you are present. That is God's gift, which is the gift of himself, which is his body.

One day you'll be clothed with that body. So set your hope fully upon the grace that is coming to you at the revelation of Jesus Christ within you. That is the unfolding within you of God and his Son. And this is the hope that makes it wisdom to endure the burden of this long, dark night of time. For as Paul said, "I consider the sufferings of this present time not worth comparing with the glory that is to be revealed in us."

We are told we are justified by his grace. Well, justification in Scripture is divine acquittal. You are completely acquitted, no matter what you have ever done, you are acquitted. So, when we are told, "Those whom he foreknew, he also predestined to be conformed to the image of his Son; and those whom he predestined, he also called; and those whom he called, he also justified; and those whom he justified, he also glorified."

So, justification is simply divine acquittal, and glorification is the gift of God Himself to you, so that man then matures when he becomes his own father. So, we say, "It is the Father's good pleasure to give us the Kingdom." In giving us the Kingdom, He gives us himself. In giving us himself, man becomes his own father. So let no one worry you; let no one in any way suggest that you've got to do something to earn it, you cannot earn the Kingdom. You cannot earn this gift. This is a gift, unmerited, and it's not your due. Were it your due, then it's not a gift. It's not given as a reward. You are made fit for the Kingdom, and your fitness for the Kingdom is the consequence, not the condition, of his gift. The minute he gives you himself, you are fitted for the Kingdom, and you wear the body of God. And everything in your presence, while you wear it, is made perfect. But, having given us the Promise, the Promise comes first in Scripture, then, we are told, he gave us the Law: the Law to cushion us, while we, as pilgrims, walk through the furnaces. And so, we have a Law. Man is not aware of the Law. Even the wisest of men, they're not aware of it

I'll go back now to 1949. I was in Milwaukee, and I gave a series of lectures on the Bible. And this couple, he was a physicist, the head physicist, of Allis-Chalmers. They're a huge, big manufacturing firm making these turbines, sometimes bigger than this interior, and he was the head of the chemical department, where they would send waters from all over the world who bought the turbine, and he would analyze the water to discover the problem that they faced; because the water, as it came through the stream, gathered the chemicals, and then the chemicals deposited itself within the turbine; and so they would send him samples of the water, and then he would analyze the water, and then send them the solution to their problem.

Well, being a trained chemist, and the head of the department, he didn't take issue with me, but he said: "Neville, I can't quite go along with you because as a chemist, it's in conflict with my training. You tell me that I can go forward in time, that you can move backward in time, that all things are, and everything is now, at this very moment. And yet you are telling me that you can make things change, and it is in conflict with my training." We have a law known, said he, and we call it *entropy*. And entropy means that the past is fixed and unalterable. You cannot change it. If that could be changed, it throws everything out of kilter in my lab. I must know the past is unalterable, like braiding a lady's hair, and the braided part, that's fixed. The rest is the future, not yet braided. We are waiting to see how it will develop from the braided part because that is completely fixed and unalterable. And you tell me it is not; that the whole vast world exists now, past, present, and future, and that you can go into these sections of time, in a world that is finished. Well, I can't go along with that.

That's perfectly all right. I'm not a chemist; I'm not a scientist, so I cannot argue the point with you. I only know my visions. And I teach vision as I have actually experienced it. And I can go into these spots. I have gone into these places and the past has not passed away. And it's fixed, as you say, but I'm quite sure one could go back and revise that past and change it.

And I can go forward into the future that I do know and set it up to walk across a bridge of incident; when I come to that point in time where I have entered, it takes on the color, the tone, and the reality that I assumed it to be when I entered that state.

Can't be done. But he was a very honest man, as most of these fellows are; they're trained to be honest. How else could they achieve what they do achieve in science unless they're perfectly honest with themselves?

Well, in the month of November, I received a letter from him and he sent me the science newsletter dated October the 15th. And it was all about the positron. And the one who wrote it was Professor Richard Feynman, he was then a professor of physics at Cornell University. Twenty years later, only last year, they granted him the Nobel Prize in physics for that paper.* It took them twenty years to recognize what he said as theory back in 1949. And if I can quote it, this is it: "The positron is a wrong-way electron. It's 'wrong way' in every sense of the word. It moves backward in time. It moves from where it hasn't been and speeds to where it was an instant ago. Arriving there, it is bumped so hard its time-sense is reversed and it moves back to where it hasn't been."

Now that is not Neville speaking; that is Professor Feynman. For that, he got the Nobel Prize last year. He said: "It's not only backward in that sense, but even its charge is backward. It's a positron; it's positive and not negative. And yet it is an electron."

---

* Feynman received the Nobel Prize for physics in 1965.

When they first observed it or rather had it as theory, they did not want to admit it, but yet it fitted in with Einstein's theory, mathematically, so they had to in some way accept it, but no one had ever photographed it. Then came someone who photographed it in their studies of the cosmic rays, and here it was the actual positron. It seemed as though two were developed at a certain point. And it wasn't, said he. That one coming back, which was the positron, should, if it is bounced, it should be deflected and continue on its course, but deflected course. On the other hand, if it's bounced so hard, it's not deflected; it's reversed and moves forward in a normal manner to where it hasn't been.

Well, I told him that I was sitting at home, and I would go into a section of time, even this year, for instance. This is now only April. I put myself in Christmas. I would feel the stores are all dressed for Christmas. I could hear the music of Christmas, all the carols. I'd walk through Saks Fifth Avenue in New York City, go into Best, go into the other, and I would feel all that I would feel if it were true that it's Christmas, that it's the month of Christmas. And then when I feel that it's all Christmas, then I would feel that things are as I desire them to be back in the month, say, of March or July, which was certainly not Christmas season. So, take a hot, hot day in July, and I'm feeling it to be cold, and snow on the ground, and all the dressings for Christmas. And then I would open my eyes, and bounce back, and shock myself because it seems so real to me that, when I came back and opened my eyes upon July, and it's hot, I thought, now, are you kidding yourself? No, when I went forward in time quite normally, waiting out the days, the months to the month of December, things happened as I actually had assumed that they would. I went forward and determined, predetermined, what would happen.

Well, when he sent me this, he wrote a sweet, lovely letter saying, Neville, I must confess: I didn't see it; no one saw it until Professor Feynman in his lab discovered this. But he discovered it by theory, and you tell me you know it by vision. You're not a scientist, and yet all that you said to me—which I could not believe, and even this moment it's difficult for me to believe, here comes the great professor, a theoretical physicist, and he is the one who wrote this paper. For that, he got the Nobel Prize last year. He worked on our atomic bomb; he worked on the hydrogen bomb. Then he asked the government to relieve him of the secrecy imposed upon him because of his position, and he came here to Caltech and taught at Caltech: theoretical physics. He said I want the freedom of imagination. I didn't want to be confined with the secrets of government so that I could not express myself. Leave me alone, all in theory. So, he goes blindly on with his mathematics and his theory, bringing out these concepts, all theory.

Well, mine is not theory. I go into these states. Now, look at it this way: see the whole vast world as infinite states, all states. If they are all states, and you are an immortal being, you are not a state; you are immortal, you enter a state and the state becomes alive. Therefore, you are not to blame if you enter a state unwittingly, and it's a horrible state. Man, not knowing, yet you are in a state; they condemn you. But you have to express the contents of that state.

If you enter the state of poverty, you have to experience poverty. If you remain in it, you must go and drink that to the very last drop: the dregs of that cup. If you go into any state and remain in that state, you are going to drink it to the very last drop. But you can get out of a state. You don't have to remain in it if you know it's a state. If you don't know it's a state, you identify yourself with the state and think that you're it. Man has identified himself with this little body, and he thinks he is it. So, the day comes he has to discard it because he's worn it out. And he discards it; all his friends are crying to think he died. He can't die. He is an immortal being who wore a garment of flesh, flesh and blood. That same being who goes into states: remaining in a state, and the state has to be expressed by him who resurrected the state. For I am the resurrection and the life of that state.

Now, you can change an individual, with or without his consent, if you so desire. Here is a story of a friend of mine. I persuaded him to give up his job here.* I knew he was a single man, and he would like to do what I am doing. So, I said, San Francisco, is wide open. I only go there once a year for four weeks at a time. Now I have reduced it to two weeks at a time. But I used to go, in the early years, for four weeks. I said they need someone badly who knows this law. You can't teach the Promise because you do not know it. You can tell it, but from hearsay, because you have not experienced the Promise. But you do know the Law. And you are presentable; you are a gentleman; you go up there, I will not give you any money, but I will give you my mailing list of five hundred; it's a live list, and you send out my list and when I go, I will tell them that I allowed you to have my list, and I will get behind you in that manner, but not in any other way. You've got to go on faith.

Well, he quit his job here, he has seniority of eight years in the place that he worked. He goes up to San Francisco, and he made arrangements to open. He had a little dog, a lovely little dog, and he was walking this dog one afternoon before he opened, and a man came over and greeted him and said, what a nice little dog you have. And then after the usual greetings, he said, can you help me out? I haven't eaten today. I'm out of work. And my friend said, no. I have no money, but I will do what I can, but I can't give you any money. The man couldn't understand that you can't give me money; what else could you do?

My friend did not move one step after he said "no" to the request. The man went off. He remained there until he imagined that man in his presence gainfully employed, happy in the job, and standing on his own feet. That was taking the story in the book of Acts: when a man came to John and Peter, and he could not stand on his own feet, and

* Neville is speaking of Freedom Barry.

he was begging at the temple door. And Peter said gold and silver have I not for thee, but such as I have, give I unto you. Rise and walk, and he rose and walked. It doesn't mean a cripple jumped up and walked. That's an entirely different structure that I do know is possible when you wear the garment of God. You couldn't come into the presence of anyone as a cripple. The minute you came by, he ceases to be a cripple. If he has no feet, feet come and fill the sockets. If he's blind, they come in and fill the sockets, and he is not blind. And you do nothing to do it. No compassion, you simply are so perfect that nothing imperfect can remain in your presence. But in this case, on this level, no one is going to actually jump up from the crippled state and start walking. But he takes a man who is crippled, who is standing on other peoples' feet by begging from them.

Well, a month later, he was walking his dog and he saw this man and he crossed the street, the man crossed the street and came over to him. He said I don't suppose you remember me. He said, "Oh, yes, I do. I remember you, just about a month ago, that you asked me for money." And he said, "Yes, and I want to thank you for not giving it to me and extended his hand to my friend. He said, had you given me the money, I today would be asking you for money. Because you did not give me, I was so embarrassed and so annoyed with myself that I put myself in that position, I went out the very next day and I got a job, a good job; it pays well, and it has a promise of growth. And I am very happy in the job. So again, let me thank you for not giving me the money."

He put the man on his own feet by representing him to himself as one gainfully employed. That's what I'm talking about when I tell you: *they're all states*. He took him out of one state and put him in another state. The man who is in the new state is the same man. You are an immortal being. You are changing only when you fall into a state. And others who knew you well in one state think, what has happened to him? You either go up, or you go down if they see a radical change, and they wonder, what has happened to him? He is affluent, he is this, he is that, or what has happened to him? He used to be and look at him now. And not a thing changed with the immortal being who occupies the state, other than the state, he changed the state. Man not knowing that he condemns the state when it's not the being you're looking at, you're looking at the state.

So, God forgives everyone—he justifies everyone because he knows they're only in states. And the Lord created all these states. These are the states. Well, that is what Blake meant, when he said, "I do not consider either the just or the wicked to be in a supreme state, but to be every one of them states of the sleep which the soul may fall into in its deadly dreams of good and evil when it left paradise following the serpent."*

Following the serpent: when man left that heavenly state of innocence, and came into a world of experience, of educative darkness, and experienced generation. For here we are generating, multiplying in these garments to clothe the innocent one who has come down. So, the whole drama is from innocence through experience to an awakened imagination. When the imagination completely awakes, that's the divine body, Jesus. That's God. And it takes all of this journey, we are the pilgrims moving through states.

So, I tell you, master the art of moving from one state to another state. You are not the state, you never have been and you never will be. The state, if you are going to condemn, condemn the state. But why condemn anything? Moving out of a state into another state. Move yourself out of one state into another state. So, others say it can't be done? Leave them alone. They'll say it can't be done. You go about your Father's business, moving from state to state as you desire it.

Now, it all starts with a hunger. It starts with a real desire on your part. And all these infinite states are simply to satisfy the hunger of

---

* Neville is quoting from Blake's 1810 essay, "A Vision of the Last Judgment."

men. So, you want to be good, as you understand good to be? You want to be wealthy, as you understand it? You want to be famous, as you understand it? All these are states. Go into the state before you are qualified. Go into the state and stay there. The state has all the things necessary to externalize itself. But you are the occupant of power. You have to go into the state and dwell there.

Now, as I go into it, let me remain in it. If I come back, like the positron, I'm simply going to be turned right around, I'm not going to be deflected, and continue my journey in the same direction, only deflected; I'm going to be so shocked—and everyone is shocked. When I go into a state and it seems like this, seems so real. When I open my eyes: well, here I am, back here. But that shock turns me around from my return to that motion forward now as an electron. I'm not a positron anymore. I was a positron when I actually started back in time, and when I reach this body, and the body is jolted when I open my eyes, then what I did there, I'm moving across a bridge of incident now, some series of events that leads me up to the fulfillment in what the world calls reality. But it was real when I occupied it in my imagination. That's when it was real. We exist in these bodies. We live in our imaginations. For our imaginations, these are the only realities. Imagination is God. That is the divine body, Jesus.

I used to sit and simply try it in my living room. I couldn't see the chair where I sat in the living room from the telephone in the hallway. I would sit at the telephone in my imagination, while my body was in the living room. And then I would assume I am on the telephone. Physically, I couldn't see that body. And then suddenly, I would feel myself back on the chair. And what a shock. And then from the chair, I would put myself back at the telephone. I would stand on the outside of the house and see it like this building, see it from the street, rather than from here, and assume while I'm standing here that I am looking at the building from the outside, and suddenly you are on the outside, and you're looking at it from the outside. Do it in your own home. Do it with anything in your room. And that gets you sort of in a state of moving. You become mobile, as it were. And it's easy, then, to occupy any state. And they're only states! So, when someone thinks themselves so important, it's only a state, but that's all right. That state, in itself, is important to them, and anyone occupying that state must do exactly what they would do. If I were in the state of Hitler, I would do the same thing Hitler did, because it's a state, and if I fall into it, knowingly or unknowingly, I've got to play that part.

So, he does not consider the just or the wicked to be in a supreme state but to be in every one of them states of the sleep which the soul falls into when it leaves paradise following the serpent; that serpent of generation. So here you can be what you want to be if you know that all these are only states. And in the end, you are justified. You're completely exonerated. You are acquitted, divinely acquitted.

So, let no one frighten you as to what you must do to earn the Kingdom. You do not earn the Kingdom. It's your Father's good pleasure to give it to you. And it's a gift that is not your due. It's not a reward for any good things you did. If you're in a state and you think that the good things you are doing—it's only the state. You moved into it, and I personally find it easier living in my world to be in a good state. I find it easier to be kind than to be unkind. If I'm ever unkind, it hurts me more than anyone who receives my dart, as it were. An unkind remark hurts me more than the one who received it from me.

So, I find it easier to be in that sort of a state. But eventually, you will completely awake with the gift, and the gift is God himself, There's nothing but God in this world; but nothing but God. Someone called me up and asked me about devils: that she went down to this Christian Science practitioner, who now feels she is hounded with devils. Well, they teach about devils, how the devil does this, the devil does that, but that's getting away from the first and great commandment, which is the great commandment: the *Sh'ma*, the confession of faith in the Hebraic world: *Hear O God, the Lord our God, the Lord is one.**

The minute you get away from that, you have a devil: there's another God, another creator, another something, and if you have two, you're going to have four, you're going to have eight, sixteen, thirty-two, and so on. Always come back to that fundamental state: there is only God, and God is your own wonderful human imagination. When you say *I am*, that's God. There is no other, and never will be another God. He is going to unfold himself within you, and completely awaken, and when he awakens, you are God. And then you'll be clothed in that heavenly garment, and I'm telling you, it's a heavenly garment. I can't describe it other than to tell you when you're in it, you're not standing on the earth. You're lifted off, as it were, and I can only describe it as air and fire. And when you glide by, and the sea of humanity, imperfect, you do not raise one little finger to change them. No compassion. Because they cannot remain that way when you go by. And as you glide by, everyone is made perfect, everyone. Not one is left out. Doesn't matter what he did to lose his eyes, what he did to lose his arm, to lose his legs, to lose his tongue. It doesn't matter what he did. In your presence, he cannot remain imperfect. And everyone is made perfect. That is the Kingdom.

So, it is your Father's good pleasure to give you the Kingdom. So set your hope fully upon this gift. And then you can endure the temporary ills of the world. Because we are moving through these things, and not every moment of time are we alert to these states, and we can fall into it by reading the newspaper; fall into it by hearing a news bulletin; fall into it by a little conversation with a friend, and there we slip innocently into a state.

But the state isn't concerned: you animated it, you made it alive when you entered it. Because you are the only resurrecting power in

* The prayer traditionally goes: *Hear O Israel, the Lord our God, the Lord is one.*

the world. You are the resurrecting, living power of the world. And that power is your own wonderful human imagination.

So, everyone here: put your mind at peace and don't think for one moment by being good, as the world calls good, by attending certain services, doing certain things, and observing certain things that there's something on the outside watching you and marking up some little thing in your favor. No, you're simply waiting for that appointed moment when he unveils himself.

So, you set your hope fully on the grace that is coming to you at the revelation of Jesus Christ within you, which is the Lord and his son. That is Jesus Christ: the Lord and his Christ. And Christ is the son of God. And no one can say Jesus is Lord, except by the Holy Spirit. And the Holy Spirit is the remembrance. Well, he doesn't really bring about that remembrance until the Son appears, and when the Son appears, memory returns and you know who the Lord is because you know who his son is. And you wear this little garment until, for a few more years. You take it off, and you are not in this world at all. You are in an entirely different world, where everything is perfect because you are perfect. And when you want to make yourself seen by another, you make that choice. They do not come in search of you and see you.

I'll give you one little story; and she doesn't come here anymore. And she may not be in the city, but she told me one night, quite innocently, she said, you know, I found myself asleep, I was very, very conscious, and I said to these people around me, do you know of Neville? And they said, yes. And she said, who is he? And with that, she said, I was whirled as though I was some meteor flying through space, thrown out, as it were, and woke scared to death.

You do not see one who has been born from above until he chooses to show himself. He must manifest himself to you, you do not go looking for him. Because unless you are born from above, you cannot enter the Kingdom, even though it is his good pleasure to give you the

Kingdom, it will come after your birth from above. Prior to that birth, he cannot give you the Kingdom. And one to whom he's already given the Kingdom is not in the world, though for a little while he is in the world telling the story, telling it from experience, and not from theory.

So, I'm telling you exactly what has happened to me. I share it with you. And it's going to happen to you, every one of you. So let no one, in any way, try to convince you that you must be a little better than what you are if you would get the Kingdom. The Kingdom is your gift. And listen to the words, from the 11th chapter of Romans: it is irrevocable. The gift and the call of God are irrevocable. You cannot revoke it and no one can revoke it. And your inheritance is not only God; we're told in the 4th chapter of Romans, you inherit the world. The world is yours, and all within it. You don't inherit some little portion of the world. You inherit God, and God owns the world, and the world is your inheritance. So, in the 16th Psalm, David is made to say, the portion of my inheritance is the Lord. That's his portion. He inherits the Lord. The Son inherits the Father. And so, a man matures when he becomes his own Father.

This is the great mystery of Scripture. And you will inherit the Father, for it is his will, and no one can break his will. It's your Father's good pleasure to give you. So, when you hear people bragging about how this one is better than the other one, forget it. They're judging states. So that man is richer because he's in a state that is richer than the other one that is poor, but the occupant of the rich state does not differ from the occupant of the poor state. And the occupant of the state tonight that is in jail does not differ from the judge who sentenced him. One is not better than the other in the eyes of God. In the eyes of God, all are acquitted. That's justification. We are justified by his grace, we are told. All are justified by his grace. And grace is an unearned, unmerited gift of God, and that grace is God's last, his final gift, which is love in action, and God is love. It's the gift of himself. And that's when he gives you himself; there's not a thing else to give.

He gave you himself, and the whole vast world is yours. So, we inherit the earth.

Now tonight, I hope you'll start practicing. Won't take you any time at all to try it. It costs you nothing. And it works wonders. You can sit here tonight, or you go home, put yourself in the state of affluence—what's wrong with that? Well, back in the 1920s, 1930s, we had a deep financial Depression starting in 1929, and do you know that you could go to Tiffany, and buy, say, eight glasses, beautiful glasses for a wedding present, cost you, what? Not more than seventy-five cents. A beautiful glass in a Tiffany box, the whole thing was in a Tiffany box, beautifully done. You'd go into Macy's, or Gimbels, and you'd buy something not comparable for a dollar, dollar-twenty-five. But the majority would not be seen dead in Tiffany. That was *style*. That was something beyond them. They wouldn't even walk in, they felt embarrassed to walk in. Yet you could go into Tiffany, the jewels are on the first floor; take the elevator to the third, where they had the lovely china and lovely glassware on another floor—and get a beautiful, gift-wrapped package from Tiffany—you didn't have to send two dozen, eight; that's enough. Eight beautiful glasses. And people would not go in. They were embarrassed to be seen in Tiffany. I'm quite sure the same thing is true with their branch here. And you could go to Tiffany and buy a lovely thing for very little, really. But people are trained: that means something that's classy and that, that and the other, and if you're in one state, you can't argue them out of it! You've got to get out of that state to be able to go into a state.

And if you tell them, you know, at one time in your life, a $12 suit, that's all you could afford, and all you thought you could ever afford. To get out of that state and pick something differently, and then you pay $250 for a suit easier than you could get $12 for the other suit! I know it happened in my own case. When I began to buy a suit for $250, it was easier for me to pay $250 than when I had to get out $12 for a suit that, if it rained, I had to start running, or I couldn't get out of it.

Now that is life, and you simply move from one state into another state. And the same being, I am not another being. I answer to the same name. You say, Neville, I answer; I answered then to the name, Neville. And yet I moved from one state to another state to another state. As you move from one state, what you couldn't do in one state, you find it so easy to do in the other state. I was in a state, for the longest while, where I couldn't eat meat, fish, fowl, drink alcohol, smoke, sex, well, I did nothing, but nothing. Then overnight, my friend Abdullah told me, "You're going to come back from Barbados and you will have died, you know." I said, "I will die?" He said, "I don't mean that you're going to die and be buried in Barbados or be buried at sea, but you will have died. All the things you haven't done in seven years, you'll be doing before you get back."

You know, he was true. And I couldn't tell you how it happened. I couldn't tell you how it happened. It just happened. In Barbados, I lived for three months in my mother's home and still lived as I did in New York City. And on my trip north, in ten days, I was doing everything I hadn't done in seven years. And I cannot tell you how it happened. I moved out from one state into another state, and it came to me as normal and as natural to do the things I did at sea as I did, in seven years, the things I didn't do.

So, I tell you: they're only states. All states of consciousness. And if you recognize that, you can forgive every being in this world, no matter what he is, or what he plans to be, or what he has done. Because in the end, he is going to be justified. He is justified by the grace of God, as we are told. Everyone is justified by the grace of God. He is divinely acquitted. And when God acquits him, who is going to judge him? And after justification comes glorification.

So, he begins with those whom he foreknew. Well, he foreknew us. For he chose us in him before the foundation of the world. And if he chose me in him before the foundation of the world, then he knew me. And those whom he foreknew, well, then, he also predestined.

He predestined them to be conformed to the image of his Son: that which reflects his glory, and radiates his glory, and bears the express image of himself. I am destined to be that: to be the express image of himself. And those whom he then predestined, he called. Call my sons from afar, and my daughters from the ends of the earth. Call them all, and he's calling us one by one by one, for we are so altogether unique. He can't call us in pairs. Call us one by one. And those whom he called, he also justified. And those whom he justified, he also glorified.

So, you are destined to be glorified with God, as God. And it will not, in any way, be stopped by anyone.

So, let no one frighten you. From the pulpits of the world, every Sunday morning, they try to scare the people to death. Set themselves up as the criterion of what people ought to be. In other words, look at me, they will say, and follow me.

I saw, in yesterday's paper, this son of a very prominent evangelist across the country, he's in Barbados, he's in all the West Indies, he's all over Europe, someone in Denmark wrote me three letters recently asking what I think of him. Well, I did not respond. I answered his first two letters, and then when he kept on trying to make this a conversation between us, and he mentioned this party, I did not answer. I never listened to the man; I've never read any of his works; but when I read in the paper yesterday, a picture of his son, who confessed that he was simply, he had sinned against his wife and his children, well, you know what he means. And then he sinned against God.

Then I went on to read that this man takes in, in tithes, thirty million dollars a year, in tithes. He tells them how they're serving God when they send him money and take in thirty million dollars tax-free. It's religion, thirty million. So now the son has now been removed from being the heir; the father is eighty years old, but he's still in control of that thirty million a year, tax-free. I wonder what he talks about.

So, that is big business. When you go into that sort of money, that's big business, and you have no room in your mind's eye for any spirituality—none whatsoever!

And you can take that greatest of all books, and make a mess of it, interpreting it as something that is taking place here within the secular world. It isn't secular at all! This story is profound, well, it's all spirituality. It's God's plan of redemption. It hasn't a thing to do with the secular world. And they're telling you the future of America, the future of Russia, the future of China, it's not in Scripture.

Lecture XVI

Consummation

April 28, 1972

No one knows how many civilizations must rise and fall before the end of the historic process on earth. But I can assure you that when it does come to its end, the consummation will be Jesus Christ, the pattern man. But no one knows how many convulsions will take place in this world before that end, but it will all be consummated in Jesus Christ, the pattern man.

Now, tonight, I want to share with you what I have experienced. I want to share with you what I've been sent to tell you and tell you I must and will. When we are taught in Scripture, that he who now is called Jesus Christ is here only for one purpose, and that is to fulfill the Scripture. Not to change governments, not to get involved. He leaves everything as he finds it. He's only telling of a pattern, a pattern that must be fulfilled in the individual to bring this historic process to an end within him. The Scripture must be fulfilled in me. Now, the only Scripture spoken of is the Old Testament. The New was not written. So, he's only speaking of the Old. Now we go back to the Old.

And here you read, "All the people of Israel came to David, and they said to him we are your bones and your flesh. And the Lord said to you, *you will be*"—bear the tense—"*you will be* the shepherd over my people, Israel. I have made a covenant with you that is everlasting, but you will be the shepherd over my people Israel, and you will be their prince forever." You'll read that in the second Samuel fifth chapter. It's also repeated in the book of Kings and also Chronicles. But the second chapter, the fifth and the second book of Samuel, the fifth chapter will give it to you. Now comes the thought of David as he's leaving the world. And these are the last words of David: "And the spirit of the Lord speaks by me and his word is upon my tongue." Now, here is David speaking. "His word is upon my tongue. He speaks by me."

Now we turn to the New Testament, which is the interpretation of the Old. He is not called David. He is called in the New Testament, the Christ. And in the New Testament, in the 14th chapter of John, he makes the statement, "The words that you hear are not mine, but the Father who sent me and the Father is the spirit"—the identical thought is conveyed in that statement. Prior to this claim that he makes, he said, "The day is coming, it hasn't yet come. The day is coming when you will know that I am in the Father and the Father in me and that I am in you." That day is coming. Then he goes on to say, "I will manifest myself to you." Then Judas—not Iscariot, but a Judas; he doesn't say who Judas is—"and he said to him, Lord, how is it that you will manifest yourself to us and not to the world?" And he replied, "He who keeps my commandments, my Father loves and I love, and we will come to him and make our home with him. He who has my commandments and keeps them."

Well, what are his commandments? Remember he cannot say anything that is not in the Old Testament. He's only come to fulfill God's word, which is in the Old Testament. He reduces 613 commandments to two; for the rabbis have taken the Old Testament and they've discovered 613 commandments; 365 are negative; 248 are positive; 613.

He reduces them to two, which you will find in Deuteronomy, the 6th chapter, and you'll find in Leviticus in the 19th chapter, and this is what he said to the one who said to him concerning the commandments. They asked him, what is the greatest commandment? He said, "Hear O Israel, the Lord our God, the Lord is one." That's the greatest. And one that is equal to it is this: "Love your neighbor as yourself." Now, the Christian believes that's an original one in the New Testament. It's taken from Leviticus, the 19th chapter, the 18th verse. For he's only going to fulfill Scripture. So, he takes 613 commandments and reduces them to two. If you hear these two and abide by them, I will manifest myself to you. And my Father and I will love you and we will come and make our home with you. But what is the first one? There's only one causation. I kill. I make alive. I wound. I heal. I create the light. I form the darkness. I make the wheel. I form the world. And there is no other God beside me. Never forget it. There's only one creative power. And I'll tell you who he is, your own wonderful human imagination.

God became as we are that we may be as he is. He allows us all the liberty in the world to create high or low, darkness or light, to murder or to give life. It's the same power. There aren't two creative powers in the world. That's the first commandment. And the second is equal to the first: "Love your neighbor as yourself," because your neighbor is yourself pushed out. There is nothing in this world but God, and God is your own wonderful human imagination. And everything in this world is God pushed out, bearing witness to an activity that is taking place within *us* of which we may be totally unaware; but it bears witness to what is taking place within us. So said he, "I will come and manifest myself to those who abide by my commandments." And he reduces the commandments to two. Do you really believe in that first confession of faith, it's called the *Sh'ma*. Israel's confession of faith. "Hear O Israel, the Lord our God, the Lord is one." There is no room for a devil. There's no room for a Satan. There is no room for any power in this world outside of God. All these are negations for the 365 commandments that are negative; 248 positive; all reduced to two. And the two are so simply stated to "Hear O Israel, the Lord, our God, the Lord is one." And: "Love your neighbor as yourself." Regardless of the pigment of his skin, regardless of his tongue, regardless of his background, he is yourself pushed out. So, whatever you are doing to him, you are only doing to self. The whole vast world is the individual pushed out to bear witness to the activity taking place within him.

Now listen to these words carefully. This is now from Peter's First Epistle, his fifth chapter: "And when the chief shepherd is manifested you will obtain the unfading glory of the crown." You will actually obtain this unfading *crown*. And it's a crown of glory and in the Scripture, glory is identified with God. You become God when the chief shepherd is manifested. In the Old Testament, the only shepherd spoken of is David. That is David. When he makes himself manifest to you, he reveals you as God, the Father. But God became you that you may become God. But you will not know, not in eternity, that you are God until that chief shepherd is manifested to you, who reveals you as his Father and his Father is God and he is the son. So, I am telling you what I know from experience. It is not written in any book that I've ever read. It is not recorded in any place where I have ever encountered it. I've never heard it from another man. But I have been sent to tell you what I have experienced.

When the risen Lord embraced me and sent me, and the words were "down with the blue bloods,"* meaning protocols, church protocols, all these extraneous things that keep from man the truth that God will reveal to man, all ceremonies, all rituals, all these things that hide the truth from man. And then it was revealed within me through actual experience. And I cannot restrain my words, I must tell it to you. Should I go tonight? At least you have a record right

* See *The Law and the Promise*, 1961.

now, knowing he's here, a movie, and you have a record of what I actually have experienced. He could only fulfill Scripture. And Scripture is the Old Testament. So, every word spoken of him that is real, go back. So, something new came when he said, "I give you a commandment, love your neighbor as yourself." Go back into the 19th chapter of the book of Leviticus, the 18th verse. "Love your neighbor as yourself," that's the command. Go back to the sixth chapter of Deuteronomy, named the greatest of all the commandments. And he names that sixth chapter, the fourth and fifth verses, "Hear O Israel, the Lord, our God, the Lord is one. By him, all things are made and without him was not anything made that was made." There is nothing but the one creator good, bad, or indifferent.

So here he sends himself into the world awakening man. And I cannot tell you how many civilizations must rise and fall. We think that we are permanent forever. England thought that. Russia thinks that. Greece thought it. Rome thought it. Egypt thought it. The ancient world thought it. And they have come and gone. And they will rise and fall. But in the end, the consummation of it all, will be Jesus Christ. Jesus being your own wonderful *I am*—that's the Lord. No one can say that Jesus is Lord except by the Holy Spirit, which is remembrance. And you can't remember that you are until the son reveals you as the being that you really are. So, Christ must come and Christ is the anointed one. So, rise and anoint him. Anoint whom? David. This is my chosen one. So, rise and anoint him. I have chosen him. So, Christ is the Son and Jesus is the Lord, *I am*.

So, they will come and make their home with you. If you have heard and accept the two commandments, those who have heard my commandments and abide by them, then I will manifest myself to him. This is now the son speaking. So, he speaks, although under the name in Scripture, as Jesus Christ, learn to discriminate, if the Son is speaking or the Father is speaking in that capacity, when he said my Father, then he's speaking as son. And so, the son is saying,

I will manifest myself to you. When the Son manifests himself to you, he reveals you as his Father for no one knows who the Son is except the Father. And no one knows who the Father is, except the Son, and anyone to whom the Son chooses to reveal him. He will choose to reveal himself to you when you accept and abide by the commandments—and there are only two. That there's only one creative power in the world, your own wonderful human imagination, and that is God. There is no other God. And the next commandment is, love your neighbor as yourself.

If any friend of mine tonight was accused of any crime in this world and they asked me, what should I do? What is your opinion? I would say forgive him. If my daughter, my wife, the dearest of my heart, had committed the most horrible crime in the world and I was called as a witness and the judge asked me, what would you do? What would I do? I would forgive her. I wouldn't care what anyone I love did, I want them forgiven. That's what he's saying. Love your neighbor as yourself. Am I going to stand in judgment and pass judgment? She is deserving of death. She's deserving of this, that, and the other. No, not as I understand Scripture, not as I understand the unity of being. I want to forgive every aspect to my own being for, in my own being, I caused it. I could not become aware of it were it not within me that it happened. It happened in me. Now I witness it and it bears witness to what I did within myself. The whole vast world is myself pushed out.

When I told this story years ago concerning my first wife, I was violently criticized. I only told it to explain a certain principle, but they didn't understand what I'm trying to say. And she criticized me, well, verbally in the most marvelous way, as she conceded, but it's perfectly all right, that was her right, it's myself pushed out anyway. But here was one, and I pleaded with the judge to forgive her; a simple little thing that she did, but it meant six months in jail. And I pleaded with that judge to please forgive her. You do not know the emotional strain under which she's been going, and she is eight years my senior, and therefore she must now be forty-five or forty-six, and going through the normal change of life that happens to women. Maybe it happens to men too, but it's an obvious happening in woman. Take that into consideration and forgive her. If you must sentence her, do it but then suspend it. He abided by my request. And she met me on the outside and said that's a very decent thing of you to do Neville; give me the papers for my divorce. Well, I didn't have any papers with me. So, I took her home to my place and I gave her the papers, a thing I'm told legally I'm not supposed to do. But I nevertheless gave them to her and I got my divorce in New York City. She only responded to my dear and deep need: I wanted a divorce. So, she was forced to do what she did based upon what I was doing within myself. I was sleeping in the assumption that I was blissfully happy and married to the girl to whom I am now married. And it's a heaven in this world with me, no matter what at the moment is happening to her, it still is a blissful state with me, blessed with the most glorious daughter. And she did what she had to do that I may get my freedom, for in those days the archaic law rested over New York City and you couldn't get a divorce by saying we are incompatible. You had to bring all kinds of the stupid lies of the world to do it. So, we didn't have to bring any, I simply got my divorce.

So, I'm saying that the whole vast world is bearing witness to what you are doing within yourself in your own wonderful human imagination, for that's God. There is no other God. God became as *I am*—that's his name—that I may be as he is. And he is God the Father, he is God the creator. There's nothing but God. So, I tell you this story is the truest story in the world. And how many countries must rise and fall, civilizations must come and go, I do not know. But I do know that whenever it is consummated, it's going to be consummated in Jesus Christ, the pattern man. That pattern must unfold itself in every child born of woman. And it will, it cannot fail. As it unfolds the day will come that you will accept these two commandments that there's only one causation in the world.

He didn't cause it, she didn't cause it, they didn't cause it. I am causing it. That's the only cause in the world. Are you big enough to accept that responsibility that no one in the world has caused anything that ever hurt you or praised you? You're doing it all within yourself and they only bear witness of what you are doing and have done. That's the first and greatest commandment. And the second is now, because of that, love your neighbors as yourself, for they only aid what you are doing within you. And if one has to go to jail to fulfill what you've done within you, *love him*, he's paying a price that you yourself have placed upon him. The whole vast world is the individual pushed out. It's an egocentric world for there is only God, and God is one. So, this is the story that I want to share with you. So, I've come into the world, said he, to bear witness to the truth. And the truth is your word. And your word can only be found in the day when these words were written in the Old Testament, and thy word cannot be broken. Now he goes and he finds out who is the chosen one to express the will of the Father and he finds it is David. And the whole of Israel came to David. And they said to David, we are your bones and your flesh. And the Lord said to you, you will be the shepherd of my people, Israel. And you will be the prince of Israel. That future, and even in the New Testament it is still the future because it's going to happen to the individual. It is not something that happens once and forever. It is taking place in the world.

So, when you go home, read that second Samuel, the 5th chapter, then read the 23rd chapter of second Samuel, and then find who that real shepherd is. Read Peter's first letter, the 5th chapter. You'll find it in the 4th verse. You don't have to go too far, the 5th chapter, the 4th verse. And he tells you when the chief shepherd comes and when the chief shepherd is manifested, you will obtain the unfading crown of glory. That is God himself. The minute he is manifested, you see him, the chief shepherd, and he's David and David reveals you as his Father and the Father of David is God. That's the story.

So, I tell everyone here, yes, you can have all the things in this world that you want, but everything. I don't care what it is. In the world of Caesar, it's simple, it's very easy. But let me share with you a little thing that happened to me today that I may remove from you a certain fear. A friend of mine came back just before I took the platform and allowed me to read a certain little letter, which I will not quote, but it's for his benefit too, to show you how in the world of Caesar they tried to scare you to death. I brought my wife home today from St. Vincent hospital. So, I went downstairs to the cashier to pay my bill. And she said to me, as she looked at it, she said, I think that you will owe thirty dollars. And then I didn't say anything. She said, oh no, your deposit, when you came in exceeds the thirty dollars because my wife is now sixty-five. So, she's on Medicare. And we also have Blue Cross. So Blue Cross and Medicare are supposed to pick up something like 80 percent of expenses. So, she said, no, you do not owe us anything. In fact, we owe you. I didn't ask her for any refund because we'd be going back for another six visits. I came home to find in my letterbox a bill from St. Vincent posted only yesterday. Today, they tell me that I owe nothing that they in fact owe me. And as I opened the letter, that is that little bill, that I owe them $5,403.63 cents. Well that amused me, the sixty-three cents.

So, I got on the telephone right away and I called the credit department and I asked to please give me the head man, whoever he is. I identified myself. I said I've just brought my wife home and you told me only two hours ago that I owe you nothing. In fact, you owe me something, which I did not collect. And now you tell me that I owe you $5,403.63 cents. Oh, wait a second. Then they go back. And would you hold a while? I said I will, willingly. So, they came back and they said that was a computer's mistake.

So, the computer went to town, all kinds of things over the years, the year and a half that I've been there, undoubtedly, I have paid them that much. And so, they are going to give it to me again because I've already paid out to the two hospitals over $14,000 before she became Medicare. Now that she's on Medicare, and these are billed in the month of March when she's already on Medicare in the month of February. So, I said, you know, my wife has Blue Cross plus Medicare and I can't conceive that ten days, only ten days in the hospital, that I could owe you $5,403.63 cents. So, she confessed. Then she said to me, don't worry, Mr. Goddard. I said, may I tell you something? I do not worry. I won't tear it up. I'm going to frame it just like a little laugh. I'm not going to tear it up. I'll take this little bill and frame it just for fun.

So may I say to my friend who came back tonight, don't let anyone tell you for one moment he can cut your ears off or any way incarcerate you. Forget it. You have caused everything that has happened to you. That little silly thing that came amused me. So that was my little amusement for the day. I brought her home and she came home and she's lovely, altogether sweet, didn't lose any weight, and she's strong. She has to go back for the normal things that must be done to her, but that came as an amusement because we both got a good hearty laugh out of it. And so, I will say to my friend, go down on the day that you are told to come down, but go with a laugh in your heart.

They can't do a thing to you because you caused it all and you can change it all. There's only one God in the world, only one creative power in the world, and that power is your own wonderful human imagination. Let them go all over the world looking for another cause and they aren't going to find it. They will only find one cause, and that cause is resident in everyone in the world, his own imagination. It's entirely up to us. If tonight you are fired, may I tell you, it could be a blessing because you dreamt bigger dreams than the present job could ever give you. So, if you are fired, in my own case, when I was fired from JC Penny. Twenty-two dollars a week, I was making and they fired me. I asked why, what have I done that is wrong? They said nothing, but we have a certain system here and when things decline in business, we let people out. And so, after a year-and-a-half in service, you have to go. I said, what will I use for money to pay for my rent? I was paying five dollars a week for my room. That's not our concern. Well, he realized I was completely green, so he gave me a little letter to Macy's, a friend of his who employed people. So, Macy's employed me at four dollars less. They gave me eighteen dollars a week.

So, then I determined I will not work for anyone but Neville in this world. I'm going to work here just long enough and then quit. So, I worked there for a year, and one day I said, you aren't going to fire me, I'm quitting. Worked that year. I'm still making eighteen dollars a week. So, then I quit and many a day I starved. Many a day I went hungry. I didn't have the money. Didn't have any food. But I wasn't going to work for anyone else in this world. I worked only for Neville. And then came my visions. And from then on, the Father gave me an outside source of income. And that was my story. So, I tell it and share it with you. You don't have to be afraid of anyone in this world if you know this principle. And take every one of this world as yourself pushed out. So, when I was fired from JC Penney, they were my friend but I didn't know it. Everyone who tried to put me down, they were my friend. When I went to a little school and they said, you'll never make a living using your voice. I resented that, but she was my friend because she fired me. She fired me to disprove her. If she hadn't said that I would have gone blindly on and not have done it. But she struck something in me that simply rose the fire in me. So, if someone can strike you to rise the fire in you, it's yourself because of your own activity. Within your own mind, you are dreaming noble dreams, all greater than your present job allows. And tomorrow you are fired. All right, it's a turning point in your good fortune, may I tell you, I know that from my own family's history. When we were completely down to the ground with no food or anything, there was a turning point in our family's fortunes. So, from nothing, with all these children, the family rose and today, well, you couldn't buy them out. If anybody wants to come today and buy them out, don't come under $50 million because you couldn't even interest them under $50 million. And we were fired out in 1922 with nothing; '22, we just celebrated our fiftieth anniversary, and from nothing. And you couldn't interest us unless you brought $50 million if you want to buy us out. And that's because they did not accept it as final, it was a challenge. If you're going to take a blow and go down with it, all well and good, not knowing the whole vast world is yourself pushed out. But I am telling you the whole vast world is yourself pushed out.

And everyone is only bearing witness to the man or the woman that you are. And you are your own wonderful human imagination, and morning, noon, and night, you are active imagining. And the whole thing is taking place in your outer world. And they're telling you who you are. So read it carefully. I have quoted tonight from just a few passages. Fourteenth chapter of John. It's a glorious book, John. But I took the 14th chapter. And then I took the fifth chapter of Second Samuel. I took the 23rd chapter of Second Samuel. And I took the 5th chapter of the First Letter of Peter. These are all that I have taken to weave together this thought that David is the son of God. And by David, I mean, he is the resultant state. God is the only reality, but in the end, he's going to manifest himself because he dwells in you. And may I tell you what's going to happen. There's going to be an explosion within your brain as it were, you'll feel the whole head explode. And when the explosion is over and it all settles, he who was within you, listen to the words: "The day will come that you will know that *I am* in my Father."

And when the Father explodes, he releases his son. He promised he would, and the son comes up and calls him Father. And the Father knows exactly who he is, but he also tells you—and you are in me. So, the whole vast world is himself pushed out. But the son is in the Father and the son is David. He is the great shepherd. So, when the chief shepherd is manifested, then you will obtain the unfading crown of glory.

Now, let us go into the silence.

Good. Are there any questions, please? I think you know that I am not closing tonight. I have asked for an extension of the month of May based on the needs of my wife. So, I will be here every Monday and Friday through the month of May. Same place, same time. Are there any questions, please?

Questioner: [inaudible]

Neville: We are sound asleep on all. We awaken. This is the most important level. This is the limit of contraction, the limit of opacity. And you break it from here. This is so important to become flesh and blood here. So, when they give me all these stories of abortions and these things, I don't go for it. It's not really a problem of people.* It's an economic problem and I am not an economist. We can produce so much food and so much wear and so many materials for building homes and so much of everything that it would frighten the mind, but how to distribute it under the present economic system? So, it is not a matter of explosion of population. It's simply an economic problem. And I am not an economist. I do not know under what systems such distribution of our abilities could be distributed. But I am told why, well, he was a grand, grand gentleman, I heard him speak in New York City—and that was George Washington Carver, who gave us the peanut butter and he gave us something like 600 byproducts of the Southern pine and the Southern peanut because they were going to see, not knowing what to do with it, the groundnuts. And he asked God, why did you make a peanut? And he said God said to him, go into your laboratory and I will show you why I made a peanut. And so, he went into his laboratory and meditated, and then he experimented, and God showed him why he made a peanut. In one little peanut he brought out something like 300 byproducts. So, we have peanut butter, peanut

* Neville is speaking here about the question of overpopulation.

oil, all kinds of things. And he stood before this wonderful group of men at the Waldorf Astoria, just about the year before he died, and he said, the very tie that I wear came out of the Southern pine, everything I'm wearing now, and the pigments on my tie, all this came out of the Southern pine. Hundreds of byproducts. And then he said, we could, from the Southern states, he meant the Mason Dixon line, that's what he meant by the Southern states, he said we from the Southern states could feed, clothe, and house the entire world, not America, but the whole vast world from the byproducts. Therefore, it is an economic problem. It is not a matter of children coming into this world. So, I have no answers for that. I can only tell you that I heard that great gentleman say that. I heard him on the radio. I was not physically present at the banquet. You had to be invited. And only those who were prominent were invited. So, I knew it was on and it would be on the radio. So, I tuned him in for the entire banquet and heard it at the Waldorf Astoria. In those days, we had no TV, it was simply radio and I heard that grand wonderful man say what I've just told you.

Lecture XVII

*Even the Wicked**

May 5, 1972

We have only to enlarge our conception of causality to excuse everything and forgive all. Now, let me just state one little thought from Scripture first before we unfold it. As we are told in the 25th chapter of Genesis, "In your limbs lie nations twain, rival races from their birth; one the mastery will gain, the younger o'er the elder reign." The first one is the sense man. I'm now looking at this room and all within it and that is the sense man. My normal apprehension of corporeal objects just like this room and the contents, I call sense perceived. That which is not present, and yet I perceive it, I call that imagination. That is destined to rule. That is the second man, the Lord from heaven.

The first man is of the Earth, a man of dust. The second is from heaven. So here we are in this world, and this is the world of this dual state within every child born of woman. And so, we have the physical man, the man of dust, and then we have the spiritual man, the man of imagination. That is the immortal man. When I see this picture of

* This lecture is also known as "The Duality of Man" and "It Is Done (In Your Imagination)."

the duality of man and how all things are created by this hidden man, I forgive everything in this world that the physical man does *for the physical man is only a state*. One being is playing all the parts. *The part played by the thief is the same being playing the part of the judge who judges the thief.* The part who is the murderer and the murdered, he's a part but the being within, he's one.

Now, let me explain it first in the beginning with a simple story. About eight years ago, I was in New York for a month, and two of my brothers, Victor and Lawrence, came up and spent two weeks with me in New York City. They're checked into the same hotel. They wanted to see everything they could within two weeks, and I brought them to fourteen shows. And sometimes they went even to an afternoon show. They wanted to see everything in the crowded two weeks. But the one thing my brother, Lawrence, wanted to see was the new presentation of *Aida*.

Well, the papers say it was sold out from the very moment that it was announced. Same music naturally, the same score, but new scenery. Something new about it. Now, this captured the imagination of all opera lovers and they all wanted to see *Aida*. The one thing he wanted to see was *Aida* but the papers had huge, big ads, not one seat is available. Come down and buy a seat for the other shows and this was the old opera house around 40th Street and Broadway. It ran from Broadway through 7th Avenue, the old Metropolitan. So, this morning we set out and I said, "It doesn't really matter, let us go. We have to go down and have lunch anyway. We will go and just see."

We got there and these huge, big signs on the outside: "No seats for *Aida* available," and they were plastered all over the Metropolitan. I went in and there were three lines leading towards the three windows selling tickets for the entire season, and there was no seat for *Aida*. I got into the first line. It was a very long line then I saw the third line from me moving more rapidly than the first and the second, so I moved over to that line. Then we all move rapidly forward. As we got to the window, and seemingly no hope of getting tickets, but before I left my hotel room, I simply assumed that I had the tickets for my two brothers. I didn't want to go. They wanted to see it, so I assumed that I gave them the tickets.

I got into this line. We move rapidly towards the window. As we got there to the window, a tall blond man, he must have been about six-foot-four, stretched his hand up over my head and diverted the ticket seller as he asked a question while one in front of me is buying seats, not for *Aida* because that's completely sold out, he is buying two other seats for some other opera. Then he departed after he diverted the man's attention. This man pushed on some bills under the window and then as the teller looked at the money—and this man is at the door now, the tall, tall blond fellow—and he's given this man the ticket and then suddenly he said, "For he only gave me three dollars. He should have given me"—and he mentioned the money he should have given. At that, he was bewildered, the teller was bewildered. I turned around and I screamed at that tall blond. I said, "Sir!" I screamed so loudly he couldn't stop, but the attendant, he turned around, I said, "Come back here. You're wanted." He came back like a little child being led by the nose. He came back and he said, "What's wrong?" And the man said, "This is all that he gave me. Two one dollar bills." Said, "Oh no, he didn't. He gave you two tens." Then I said, "No, you didn't. I was standing right here. I saw what you did. You gave him two one dollar bills. That's all that you gave him."

The man was flabbergasted. He was so completely dumbfounded, he didn't know what to do. I said, "I am standing here. I saw exactly what was done." Then he opened up his purse and here was a stack of ones and he had a twenty dollar bill and two tens. He said to the man, "Say when you discover your mistake that I gave you two tens." And the man said to him, "At the end of the season." And with that, it was closed, and the man then took out the money and paid for the tickets and took back his two ones.

Then I said to him, "I want two seats for *Aida* tonight and I want them in the horseshoe circle. I want them center." He said, "Yes, sir," and he took from what is called the VIP. They always keep a few out. Though the house is sold out, they always keep a few seats for those who are coming called the very important people. I am certainly not a very important person, but I saved him from the loss of twenty dollars and he quickly took the two seats out and said to me, "Twenty dollars." I gave him the twenty dollars and gave the two seats to my brothers.

Now, a state called a thief. These two men have chosen to be thieves in their world. They're con men. It's perfectly all right. God made everything for its purpose and even the wicked for the time of trouble. Read that in the 16th chapter, the fourth verse of Proverbs. "He made everything for its purpose, even the wicked, for the day of trouble." For the day of trouble may not be a war. I was troubled how to get these tickets. That's a moment of trouble and I simply assumed that I had them. I simply played my part in my imagination before I left my hotel room that my brothers are going to see this show this night of *Aida*, the new presentation of *Aida*.

They two, who have already given themselves over to the state of a thief, they had to actually come right into the line. I took the first line then I move over to the third line because I saw it moving more rapidly, so he comes over to the third line and plays his part beautifully. If he had not done what he did, I would not have received those tickets because I am not a very important person; but the man looked me in the eyes and thought here was an honest man. As far as he is concerned, I am an honest man who saved him from losing twenty dollars. And so, he quickly took out the two seats. I paid for them—naturally he didn't give them to me. I was willing to pay for my seats, but you couldn't buy them. All over the place, "sold out, sold out, sold out," all over the Metropolitan Opera. You could paste it on the wall; I mean a huge, big ad in the paper, "Aida is sold out." And I went that day and got those seats right in the circle in center row for my two brothers because one man played his part beautifully. He had given himself over to a con man. He finds it easy to make a living being a con man. There are those who are pickpockets. There are schools to teach people to be pickpockets. Do you know that? They come right out of the school and go into a profession. All right, that's their part. They play that part. Now, you play your part beautifully, and one of them can be instrumental in getting you what you want in this world. So, I wanted two seats for *Aida*. Were it not for a con man in that world, I would not have had those two seats.

So, he comes into the line where I was in the line, he comes forward, and just as I got to the ticket window, he puts his hand over my head to divert the man's attention. And the one in front of me who is buying two seats, not for *Aida* because you can't get them, he is buying two seats for something else. And he puts out two dollar bills instead of two tens, and then this man starts and I turn around as though I was inspired, and with my full voice I said, "Sir, come back here!" He had to come back. So, he came on back just like a little child and stood next to me, and he looked down at me. He wouldn't dare budge. Well, I said, "You didn't give him anything more than what he is showing you now. You've given him exactly what he's showing you"—because I was fair and I stood next to you. He was helpless. He couldn't hit me. He was many inches my height. I was five-eleven and he may be about six-five or more. A strong, strapping blond but he was impotent in my presence when I called him back.

He only played the part, so should I not forgive him? There are infinite states in this world and all you have to do is forget states. You play your part in every state necessary to make your part come to fulfillment at the moment that you need it. And so, we went out for lunch, and my brothers, Lawrence and Victor, they had their tickets and that evening, they went to see *Aida*.

So, "In your limbs lie nations twain. They are rival races from their birth, one the mastery shall gain, the younger over the elder reign." And the younger is the second and the second man is the man from heaven, and that man is your own wonderful human imagination who is God. And there is no other God. That is the Lord from heaven and the outer man that clothes him, he is under compulsion to fulfill the commands of that inner man. But everyone is falling into states, infinite states; to understand this world you must think in terms of states. He has made everything for its purpose, even the wicked for the day of trouble.

And so, use everything, but you don't have to think of which one will do it, forget it, who will play the part. I never saw that man before. Never saw his partner in their little crime before. That was their choice in life. There are those who have chosen to be pickpockets for the rest of their lives, so if they are caught in the act, all right, that's part of the game. They've chosen that part to play. Now, those who have chosen their part to play like Mr. Hoover who just departed this world.* He chose that part and there are others who chose other parts.

Either wisely or unwisely, we fall into these things; but when the inner man begins to awake, he selects his part wisely. It's entirely up to us, so I tell you, everything in this world that you want to be, you can be if you will know that there are only states. You move into the state because the occupant of the state does not differ from the occupant of any other state. The one who played the part that day of the conman to get two tickets for two dollars instead of twenty dollars and go on the street and sell them for fifteen dollars and make himself a quick few bucks.

The same occupant is God. God is playing all the parts, so all we have to do is simply to expand a little bit our conception of causality to actually excuse everything and forgive everyone in this world. I forgave him because he actually was instrumental in getting me the two seats for my brothers. Were he not playing that part at that moment, I would not have had the seats. But before I left my hotel room, I simply

* Neville is referring to President Herbert Hoover (1874–1964).

assumed that my brothers had their seats, and they were going to see *Aida*, and they came off thrilled beyond measure, so we went down at seemingly no hope.

I wasn't concerned about any hope. There were three long, long lines. After all you're selling out just for the show of the night. You're selling for the afternoon show, you're selling for the evening show, and for the entire season, and buy a month in advance, two months in advance. They're all there and so here are the lines and your three lines and three windows open. And what caused me to move to that moving window? The father in me. He knew which one is going to play what part because they're all in states and myself is fully aware of all the states in the world. And if you can play a part to aid me in the fulfillment of my dream, you will play it.

If I need a thief, there must be a thief somewhere. He was a thief and he played the part, better part in my getting the ticket than if he were an honest man. If he came up and played the part of an honest man, then the man would have said to me, he wouldn't know me, I'm not an important person, and so we have no tickets. Go into signs, "No tickets available." It's a sellout but it was not a sellout and a thief made it possible for me to get my two tickets.

So, when you see this, you forgive every being in the world, *everyone.* They're all playing their part, so don't condemn anyone because everyone will be instrumental in fulfilling your dream if you know this law. It's all infinite states but remember you are awakening to the reality of the second man. In this room, my simple apprehension of corporeal objects, the things on the wall, your hair, the chair, the house, this thing for a wedding tomorrow, all this preparation for a wedding. All this is to my sense man reality and I think of something entirely different, and that is called only imagination, and that is the second man.

Now, what do I want in place of what my senses are telling me? Let me now enter into that state and live it as though it were true and move forward in that state. Now, let me show you the difference now because we started with that statement from the 25th chapter of the book of Genesis. An idea that is only an idea produces nothing and does nothing. It must be felt, actually felt, so that it awakens within oneself certain sensations, certain motor actions, in order to be effective. What would the feeling be like if it were true? Dwell upon that until the feeling awakes within you these sensations, for *imagination is spiritual sensation*. That is the creative being in you. It's not just to entertain an idea. What idea? The idea must produce in you this feeling, which is a sensation, but it must be a *feeling*. What would the feeling be like if it were true? You dwell upon that until you catch that feeling.

As [Winston] Churchill said that the mood determines the fortunes of people rather than the fortunes the mood; the mood precedes the fortune. So, what would you want in this world of contemplating? What would the feeling be like if you had it? What would it be like if it were true? That is the story of Scripture. If I could only feel that I am already the man that I want to be, that I'm already the woman that I want to be, and feeling, then it's not only an idea, which as an idea without feeling will produce nothing, now, it has everything because in this story, he says to the second man, "Come close, my son, that I may feel you."

The secret is in the feeling. So, he's always out. He is the first man covered with fear, the outer man, and Jacob is the inner man, the man of imagination who is hairless. It isn't two little boys. These are only symbols. It's all in man, so come close my son that I may feel you. So, he comes close and deceives his father through feeling, so the father feels and he feels them just to be externally real. *You can do it.* There is no flower in your hand but you can feel the soft velvet feeling of a rose. You can smell a rose though it's not physically present. Try it. Try all these things with the inner man and when you can actually feel it so that you raise your imagination to the point of sensation, to vision, then the whole thing is done.

It's done in a way you do not know it's going to happen. If it takes a thief to aid you, then you forgive the thief. Should I not forgive that man who tried to rob that teller of twenty dollars when he did for me what no one else could do? I could go to all the brokers in New York City and they couldn't get me two seats. I could go to anyone and they couldn't get me two seats for my two brothers, and I wanted them to have the joy of seeing the new presentation of *Aida*, so I went myself prepared in my imagination that I had two seats. And it took a thief to be instrumental in getting me the seats. Should I not forgive him for the part he played?

He went to the door, this tall, giant of a man. He looked back at me but he wouldn't have the courage to come up and slap me. There was something in me that dwarfed him in his own mind's eye, so in spite of his height and his bigness and his strength, he couldn't dare strike me for I was speaking from a different level of consciousness altogether, so I didn't condemn him. He played the part he had to play and by playing it, I got the seats. So, all we have to do is simply to widen, just widen a little bit, our conception of causality to actually forgive all in the world, to excuse everything in the world.

They're playing their part. So tonight, you want a bigger job, you want more money in this world, you want—and you name it. Well, it may be a thief who is going to aid you into getting without knowing he is doing it. Don't judge him. Don't condemn him. Just simply—you go forward knowing that I have ways and means that the physical man knows not of. My ways, the inner man's ways, are past finding out, and you simply go forward in the assumption that you have already achieved what now is only a wish as far as the world is concerned, but you enter into the wish as though the wish is already fulfilled.

So, what would the feeling be like? "Come near, my son, that I may feel you," and so he comes close. He said, "Come nearer, my son." Then he said to him, "You know, your voice is the voice of Jacob, but your hands, your neck, and your scent, you have the feel of my son Esau." Esau is the outer world, so he gives emphasis to feeling. It transcends the voice. The voice was Jacob's but the feeling, that touch was that of an external world. He could feel the external world. It was a self-deception. He saved himself into believing that what he desired, he had.

It's not two little boys born of woman. All this is parable. *The whole story of the Bible is all parabolic*, telling stories that unless you have the depth to understand it, well then, you'll never really; but me I say you will, eventually you will, and you certainly do understand it now. So tonight, is a practical night. Do you know this night what you want, really what you want? Well, if you do, do the same thing I did in getting the two seats.

Do what I did when I was locked out completely from marrying the girl I wanted to marry. I simply assumed that she slept here, I slept here, and I went sound asleep, and in one week, my wife did an act which certainly I must forgive in the eyes of the world. She is condemned for taking what she did not pay for, and yet because of that act, I got my freedom. Then who is the culprit? Am I not? If there's any culprit, I am. If there's any culprit in this world, it is God.

There is nothing but God. God is doing all in this world. He created everything in this world, and so I fit in me, he is the second man, and the second man is my imagination, and that is God, for man is all imagination and God is man and exists in us, and we in him. The eternal body of man is the imagination and that is God himself. Well, if I in my imagination slept as though I am happily married to a girl that the laws of New York State said I could never get because of my entanglement with my first wife, and in one week she performed an act which was judged harshly by society and yet she was the instrument of my getting my freedom to marry the girl who now is the mother of my daughter.

How can I blame her to perform that act? She was in a state—and who did it? I did it. I did it by simply assuming that I was free and happily married to a girl that the state of New York said I could never marry because of these ancient laws that restricted my desire to get freedom in that state. So, you'll forgive everyone in this world for all playing their parts. In my own case, I have seen thieves, I have seen all kinds of people play their part; they were instruments in the fulfillment of my desire, so how can I ever condemn all? The last cry on the cross, "Father, forgive them. They know not what they do. Forgive them."

The whole vast world is playing until he awakes in that body. He is playing the part and he plays it automatically, unwittingly, for one who was awake, who knows exactly what he's doing, and so they all play their parts, for God in everyone is the same God. There aren't two gods. There's only one God—and that God is your own wonderful human imagination. When you say *I am*, that's God.

So tonight, you just completely boldly declare that you are the man, you are the woman that you want to be, and walk in that assumption as though it were true and then let all these sleeping states play their part. Now, I tell you, in spite of what they appear to be, they are sound, sound asleep. They do not know. He thought he knew what he did. He came right in into my line and played his part. I could have remained on the first line and waited and waited and waited, and no one would have played their part there. I moved over to the moving line and here he comes, and so how could I ever condemn him? How could I ever, in any way, feel other than thankful?

I would say to him, "Thank you because you played the part you had to play," like a play, so someone comes in on the play. The curtain goes up and here comes the monster, and he plays it beautifully. And the audience hisses and condemns him. If there's any condemnation of the part, where is the author? Send for the author for he wrote the part, and the author, if there's any praise, give it to the author. Any condemnation, give it to the author.

I know I've played a part, a second part, on a play on Broadway. And if I didn't get a hiss when I came on, if they didn't hiss me, I felt

I wasn't doing well. But I would say 99 percent of the time as I came on and started to play my part, the audience hissed. Then I knew I was really on my toes. I was playing the part well because I was a cad in that part and they couldn't restrain themselves especially with the matinees when they had children there. Lots of ladies and children, and they could not restrain their emotion and they were hissing for then I knew, "Neville, you're getting over all right."

So, I was thrilled with their hissing because I was playing only what was written for me to play. So, in this wonderful world of ours, we are infinite states, and everyone is in a state, but the one being in one state is the being in all states. There's only one player. God only acts and is in existing beings or name. He is in all the states and His name in all states is *I am*. So, someone chooses the part and he wants to be, well, a thief. He finds it easier. He thinks, "I'm getting up, going to work, and punching a clock, and punching it out." He feels it's better for him to live that life. All right. So, he has chosen that part, if he does it deliberately, for he might have fallen into it through habit of others and then it's unwittingly. All right. But he will also pay the price.

That is the thing he has to consider. He will pay the price because the part has a price with it; but in spite of that, he can be used in the fulfillment of your dreams. Now, many of you who have had, from your letters, dreams of death recently. May I tell you, it's a healthy, healthy sign. Dreams are egocentric. You cannot grow and not outgrow in this world. To outgrow is to die. You die to one state and you move into another state.

So, anyone dreaming of death, many of you have dreamt of my death numberless times, as Paul said, "I die daily." Every day, he grows. If he did not die every day well then, he didn't grow that day. So, death, when you see yourself buried or you see yourself in a coffin or you see these things in your dream, it's only a beautiful symbol of your growth. You are growing, that's why you see yourself buried, why you see yourself in a tomb. It's simply an expansion of consciousness, so you die to one state of consciousness as you enter a greater state of consciousness.

So, when people see themselves dying or others say, "you're dead," it has nothing to do with a little physical body because you don't die anyway, not really, for nothing dies. It's always an expansion and expansion and expansion, so when you do see yourself being buried, give praise. You have died to your former beliefs and these arcane concepts that you entertain which only enslaved you. Right now, someone introduces you to a new idea and you toy with the idea of accepting it, but you resist it for a while. Then suddenly, you see your body being entombed. It means it's gotten hold of you. These new ideas that will call you to an expansion of yourself, and so the old man dies that the new man may live.

A seed must fall into the ground and die before it can be made alive. If it does not fall into the ground and die then it cannot bring forth fruit. It simply remains what it was before. So, if it dies, it bears much fruit. So don't be afraid of any vision of death. *Death is the most glorious symbol in the mysteries of the expansion of consciousness.* Man is expanding and expanding and expanding in this world, and one day, his wonderful imagination will awaken, and that is God.

Then he sees a whole vast world as sleepers, all sleepers, and how can you condemn the sleeper? So, he played his part. He played it beautifully. I can see all these things in my world where people play some many marvelous parts, and they were sound asleep, and they thought they were so alert, going to get the better of me, and their attempts to get the better were exactly what I needed to move on. Just move on. They had no idea they're playing their part beautifully. So, I forgive all the thieves that came into my world, even those who took, actually took from my pocket by not giving me what the contract called for; I thank them because it simply allowed me to become all the more secure upon my own feet, and not think for one second that

I depended upon them or for anyone else in this world, so let them go their way.

They're all sound, sound asleep playing their parts. But this thing that happened, I would say about seven, eight years ago. It was so forceful in my mind. My brothers thought that I was very courageous with this giant over my head to do what I did. It wasn't any courage. At that moment, I saw what he did. And when I said to him, "You didn't do it at all. I saw what you did. You stopped two dollars there and there they are. You didn't give him any ten dollar bills." He opened up his purse and I saw all these ones, oodles of ones and then a twenty, and a couple of tens at the side. And then he pulled out the tens and gave them and took his two ones back. And then he went back to the door with the other partner of his and looked at me as though he could have killed me but he didn't have the guts to hit me. He couldn't.

If I were that big, he could have struck me, because I was speaking on an entirely different level, and on that level when I knew I was going to get my seats, that's all that concerned me. Here comes the two seats and the man said, "Yes, sir." He treated me as though I stood before him as the president and he thought, "Now, here is an honest man who saved me twenty dollars." I'm only playing the part. I only wanted two seats that night because that's all that my brothers could give because I had all these seats bought for them. All the shows for Broadway at the time within two weeks and every night after night and matinees and everything else. Got it right up to their heads in shows.

So, I'm telling you, if you know of this dual being within you, *in your limbs lie nations twain, rival races from their birth; one the mastery will gain, the younger over the elder reign.* Now, see that that younger one actually reigns and the younger one is your imagination. The older one is your sense man. The facts, these are the facts of life. What does my bank account—and I owe more than the bank account—have in it now? Well, now that is Esau's judgment.

Now, Jacob puts in fifty times what is there now. In my mind's eye, I deposited fifty times more than is there. How it's going to happen, I don't know. I don't know any more than I knew that day when I started out for the Metropolitan Opera, how I'm going to buy seats when the papers tell me you can't buy a seat. Huge big ad, "Save your time and don't come" or "Other seats are available but not for *Aida*." I go down only for *Aida* and I get them because of a seeming thief played by the part of God. For God plays all the parts in the world. There is nothing but God, and say *I am*—that's God.

That is the Lord Jesus within you. That is your immortal being that cannot die. He cannot die. That is your eternal self when you say, *I am*. Imagination is not some vague essence. It is a body, a reality, an infinite body that is so perfect when it's awakened that in its presence everything is made perfect. But while it is awakening, it exercises that power and draws into its world everyone that can play their part for its fulfillment of its dream.

So here I hope you heard it clearly. I hope I made it as clear as I can because tonight should be a very practical night that you will go out knowing who you are. You're a dual being. But the first man is of the dust, and to dust, he returns. That is the man of Earth. The second man is the Lord from heaven and He cannot die. That's your own wonderful human imagination. It cannot die but it sleeps. It sleeps embodied in this tomb and one day, it will awaken. As I've told you in the past, the symbolism of Scripture will surround you. It's perfect. It is true. Everything told to you in Scripture as to his birth, you are going to experience, and then your imagination awakens. And you'd trust no one but it, only this being within you do you really worship. Let them give all the medals and all the honors to this, that, and the other to the little earthly man. It doesn't interest you.

Lecture XVIII

Revelation

May 8, 1972

World of nature. Night after night, I teach and tell the story of him who comes from above this world of nature.

If you are here for the first time, it may seem strange, but you take it to heart and you dwell upon it and you will find it in the end far more practical than all the things that our scientists can give you. Well, this is revelation. I did not come by it through reason, it was all revealed to me. And the vast difference between revealed truth and science. Revealed truth is wisdom as defined in the Scripture. Christ is the power of God and the wisdom of God. Science is knowledge based upon experiments, and we've done a wonderful job in the world of science. But what I've been sent to tell you is not science. It's simply revelation. The revelation of him who is the same yesterday, today, and forever. There's no change in this being of whom I speak. He's called in Scripture, Jesus Christ, which is the Father and the Son. Jesus is the Lord and Christ, his Son.

Jesus is the, *I am*, in man. His Son, when you meet him, is personified and you will know him: the eternal youth, David. After 3,000 years, he hasn't aged one iota. If you knew of one and you take it as a chronological story and you know that he lived 1,000 B.C., you would expect an old, old, old person. And yet I tell you, when you meet him, he is the youth, the eternal youth, in his themes, and that is David. Have no concept about, "Will I know him?" Oh, you will know him, because he never changes. Jesus Christ is the same yesterday, today, and forever. That's why you'll know him. You will know Jesus because you will be Jesus. As you are told in John, that is the First Epistle of John, it does not get a prayer, what we shall be but we know that when he appears, we shall know him because we shall be like him. You will be the being called Jesus and Jesus is the Lord. And you will know him only when his son David, the eternal youth, reveals you as his Father, for David is the Son of the Lord.

Now, last night, as is my custom when my wife and I are separated either if I'm traveling or if she, as it is today, is in the hospital, I invariably call her and give her a thought for meditation for the night.* That is my habit. And so, having called her last night around eight, she can't speak but I asked for the floor and the head nurse and gave her just a thought and the thought was, "My state passes out, endures forever. Guess who I am?" And then I didn't say a thing. My wife would know exactly who called. I said to the nurse. "Go in and read this to her because she cannot speak to you, just go in and read it to her." And then I sat down next to my radio and turned on some lovely music. And then I took a theme, for as you are told, night brings council. And that's the proverb of all nations throughout the ages. If I instill my mind with something, then the night should in some way unfold it to me. And so, I took as my theme, those who sing my fall into division and my regeneration to unity. My generation into decay and death and my regeneration into this immortal state. I fall into division and I'm regenerated into unity. Well, during

* Neville's wife was Catherine Willa Van Schumus (1907–1975), also known as Bill.

the night I had this discourse, there were, oh, quite a few of us, as many, say, as we have here.

And there was one person present, a man, not any taller than I am, but much heavier. He weighed at least two hundred pounds, but strong, very strong physically. And he took issue with me. I was telling him, I'm talking to myself. The whole vast world is myself pushed out. It's all myself pushed out. And you are only an aspect of my own being. But he seems so completely free and independent by his attitude and his argument with me that it would seem stupid to persist in telling him that he is the outpicturing of something within me that I cannot leave in the grave; that I cannot leave anyone in the grave. I must raise them and bring them home to where I am, but he laughed ironically. And then I said to him, "What do you think is going to happen to you now when I awake?" And so, I awoke and he vanished, as they all vanished, and I was alone in my home. The whole vast world is myself pushed out and I have an obligation to take with me a certain number at this moment and simply not leave it behind and raise it. I cannot leave it in the grave.

And so, *I am* the resurrection and the light. I must prepare a way for my banished ones to return. And that way I will, for I am the way. There is no other way to the Father. There's only one way and the way is Jesus Christ, Jesus being the *I amness* of man that is the Father and Christ, the Son that is David, and only David can reveal you as God the Father. Then my mind wandered off to something that I discussed that day with a friend of mine who took me and my wife to the hospital. So, when we came back on the way out, we were discussing it in the car on the way home. And I thought of this Spaniard, and I wish I could read Spanish because if the English translation is as great as it is, what must it be in the original tongue of the Spanish tongue? He recently departed this world, but he must have had the most glorious concept because it's so poetically told. And he begins it this way. "This page will be no less a riddle than those of my holy books." And he only writes one page. "This page will be no less a riddle than those of my holy books."*

Then he starts it: "I who am the Was, the Is, and the Is to Come/ again condescend to the written word/ which is time in succession and no more than an emblem/ . . . These signs are dropped from My eternity." And then he starts this perfectly lovely, I cannot quote it exactly because it's a whole long page, but I'll give you the essence. And then he starts this wonderful story. *I knew*, first of all, he said, *I was born of a womb by an act of magic. I lived under a spell, imprisoned in a body. I knew hope and fear. Those twin faces of the uncertain future. I knew wakefulness, sleep, dreams, ignorance, the flesh; reason's roundabout labyrinths. I knew the friendship of men, and the blind devotion of dog. I was loved, understood, praised, and hung from a cross. I drank my cup to the dregs. I knew bitterness, as well. Sometimes homesick, I think back on the smell of that carpenter's shop.* Now, he tells you in the beginning, it's a riddle. *And this page is no less a riddle than the riddle of my holy books.* When you take that apart, your mind becomes *inflamed*, if you know the symbolism he has used on that one page.

I think back sometimes when I am homesick on the smell of that carpenter's shop. Well, the word carpenter, as you know, is associated with Jesus in the Bible. Is this not the carpenter's Son? Is this not the carpenter? Well, the word carpenter in Scripture, by definition in the concordance, the biblical concordance, means *to produce from seed, as a woman, as a tree, as the earth.* You produce it from seed. And here he is producing from the seed, the immortal seed implanted within. He has to drink his cup to the very end, drink it to the dregs and know bitterness, as well. He knew all these things, the flesh, for he became flesh and dwelt within us. He knew ignorance; everyone in

* Neville is quoting from and later paraphrasing the 1972 poem "John 1:14" by Argentine poet Jorge Luis Borges (1899–1986).

this world knows ignorance. He knows all the reasoning, this roundabout reasoning, and the labyrinthine states of reasoning. He knew the friendship of men, the blind devotion of a dog. All these things he experienced. And then he returned to where he was before, enriched by the experience.

So, I thought of those who sing our fall into division, and that I have experienced. And they also sing our resurrection into unity. That I have experienced. When that night at sea coming through the Caribbean Sea toward Mobile, Alabama, well, I was lifted up on high and moved in some strange, wonderful way, like a spiral, fiery spiral, but completely out of this garment, clothed in a garment of fire and air. And here I saw this enormous sea of human imperfection and I simply glided by, that's all I did. I had no compassion. I didn't do anything to change anyone in my world. But as I came by this huge sea of human imperfection, they were blind, they were lame, they were halt, they were deaf, they were dumb. You name it, they had it. And as I glided by, everyone was transformed into that perfection that I felt springing within me. And when I came to the very end and the last one was completely transformed, as all the others were, then that same heavenly chorus sang out, "It is finished." And then again, I felt myself imprisoned in this body. This body is a prison. And that enormous being, that glorious being that is perfect, is imprisoned in it for a purpose.

And the day is coming that you will completely drain the cup and you will drink it to the dregs. And when you've completed it, you will be lifted up and you'll return to the glory that was yours before that the world was, only enhanced by the experience of this world of death, for this is a world of death. Everything decays, everything dies in this world. So, you, the immortal being came down into a world of death and took upon yourself the imprisoned form called man. And here you move slowly imprisoned, restricted, and you've experienced death. You experienced decay and all the things that go with it. And one day you'll drain the cup. And when you've finished the cup, then you're restored to your original state, but greater than you were before the descent into this world. So, they sing your fall into this world of generation and they also sing it in your regeneration into the world in which you came—an actual choral group and they'll call you by name.

And you are the being spoken of in Scripture as the Lord Jesus, the Lord Jehovah, the Lord called God. There is no other God. There is no God but the *Iamness* within you. There is no other God. And he prepared the way for his banished one, for all the banished ones, to return. And the only way back is through his Son. Until you find his Son, you can't get back because you don't know who you are. You will only know who you are when the Son of God calls you Father, then you will know you are God the Father. Outside of that, you will never know it. I can tell it to you from now to the end of time and maybe you will believe me and maybe you'll be hopeful. But as he said earlier in this one page, *I knew hope and fear.* Those twin pieces of the uncertain future. I hope he's telling me the truth, and yet it's mingled with fear.

Have I done the right thing? You've done the right thing. You've gone through all of these things that he mentioned on that page. You've known the flesh and the weaknesses of the flesh. You've known the friendship of men, the blind devotion of the dog. You've known all these things. But in the end, after you have drained the cup, you will turn up. "For there is a river that makes happy the city of God. There is a river and that river flows down and it flows up." Read it in the 46th Psalm. This river, you're told, God is in the midst of it and it shall not be moved. And that river is within you, it's not a thing on the outside. It's the Nile. It's not any river in the world outside of man. The whole vast world is man pushed out. And that river is within you. And it comes down from above. I am from above and that to which I go, it is from below. I come down into the world of generation to experience generation, which leads me into decay and death. And having played it all, then I turn around, I move up once more to the top, bringing in with me the sum total of the experiences of my descent into the written word.

He said, I now descend into the written word to make it alive. The written word is his holy Bible, his holy word. It's a sealed book for anyone who only has reason about how wise he is in this world. As you read it, it's a stupid book. They take it as history and it's not secular history. It's the eternal history, something that is taking place forever and forever without change. That David hasn't changed in the unnumbered years and neither has the Lord. The same Jesus Christ. The same yesterday, today, and forever. There is no change.

And you think of someone today, if you met Abraham Lincoln, people think of Abraham Lincoln, as he lived a hundred years ago, but hasn't he aged in our world? Would you expect to meet the same man that was assassinated? Wouldn't he have aged? Well, not in God's history. David remains the eternal youth and the Father is the eternal Father, the *ageless* one without beginning, without end. And David never goes beyond the eternal youth bearing witness to *your Fatherhood* for you are God the Father, but you don't know it yet. You are sound, sound asleep, as the man in my dream of last night was sound asleep and seemingly from his argument, independent of my perception of him. But I knew what I was doing. I was in complete control and I knew wakefulness and sleep and dreams and ignorance and the flesh and all these roundabout, labyrinthine ways of the reasoning mind.

So, I know exactly what I'm looking at. But I knew I could not leave him, only for a moment I would explain. And then I said, "And when I now awake, where do you think you will be?" So, I awoke and the whole thing vanished to return where, to leave him on the outside? No. To return to me. All that I behold, though it appears without, it is within, within my own wonderful human imagination of which this world of mortality is but a shadow. It's this shadow world. All these are but signs dropped from my eternity and they're telling me something, everything is telling me something. So, he begins his wonderful page and he said, they are only emblems, and you know what an emblem is? An emblem is simply a visible object, which reveals something other than what it appears to be.

You go to Washington, D.C., and you wonder, "I wonder if the president is in the White House?" Well, look to see if his emblem is flying. If it's flying, he is in residence. He's not the flag and you're looking at a flag, but it conveys a different idea. When he is in residence that flag flies; when he is not, it is lowered. So, you see a flag and to the average person, it's only a flag and they see an emblem. So that's the President's emblem. But they do not know what it signifies. It signifies his presence when it flies over the White House, like a battleship that carries or maybe it could be a destroyer, it could even be something less than the destroyer who carries the admiral of the fleet, depending on where he wants to be centered. And the admiral's flag is flying. And if it's there, that's where the admiral is. So, these are emblems, these are signs dropped into this world of death from my eternity.

So, I who am the one, the is, and the is to be, descend to the written word to fulfill the written word. For they're only emblems and no one knows the meaning until the living word descends for "the Word became flesh and dwells within us." And as it became flesh and dwells within us, it gave meaning to the word. For the word that we translate *logos* is translated as *the word*. "In the beginning, was the word and the word, which was God, and the Word was God." That word *logos* meant when it was used 2,000 years ago, what we mean today by the word *reality*. So, reality comes down—you can't change it, it's forever, and then assumes flesh. And the Word was made flesh and dwells within us.

Now, to the scientific mind and the philosophic mind, these rational minds, it doesn't make sense, so let them go their way. It's perfectly all right. And if we confused the wisdom of revealed truth with the knowledge of science, then we are in deep water. You'll never, never understand it. So let them go their way. Eventually, they will have all that they can possibly do in what is known as knowledge. It hasn't gotten them anywhere. So, we get more and more gadgets, more and more things, more and more things to destroy the world, whether we pollute it or we destroy it by bombs or do anything with it, we're getting more and more. The rich get richer and the poor get more of their own poverty. And so, we go on and on and not a person has arisen to solve the knowledge of man. It doesn't matter because we aren't here for that purpose. We came dumb into this world. We are immortal beings to drain the cup to the very dregs and to experience what it is to be in a world of death and decay. And the choral group sings your fall, may I tell you. They sing your fall into division. When all of a sudden it all comes out in a world and you see a world not knowing it is yourself pushed out. They sing your fall into division. And all that is contained within you is completely externalized as a world that differs from you and you don't know it,

But they also sing your resurrection into unity when you bring them all back and they're all redeemed within you. So, this is the story that I have been sent to tell you. I am not making it up. I am not manufacturing it. I am telling you exactly what has been revealed to me. And so, when I called her and gave her just a thought for the night, I know it would amuse her and she would know exactly who it was, who had sent his love relative to her in yours forever. And this morning she went under the knife, but through the night she could dwell upon it until she, from sheer exhaustion, would sleep. And so, then I turned to this scene of unity in division. And they sing my fall and the chorus is altogether heavenly, may I tell you. And when they sing your resurrection into unity, what a choral group. And then you come to the end of it all before you begin to tell it, and you feel yourself at the very end, when the last one is completely transformed into perfection, and then you feel yourself imprisoned in a body.

So, this Spaniard was telling it in the most beautiful way. I only wish I could read Spanish to read it in its original tongue, but the translation into English is so altogether beautiful that I accept that and take it for what it is. But he wrote it in his own tongue and this is only translation. And he based it on one little thought, the 14th verse of the first chapter of John. "And the word became flesh and dwelt," as he said, "among us." But the word *among* is really the preposition *in* and *dwelt in us*. That's where he dwelled. Christ in you is the hope of glory. Do you not realize that Jesus Christ is in you? If he is seeing me, where am I looking for him to come? He cannot come from without. There *is no one* coming from without. It's all from within my own wonderful imagination. And that's where God is.

So, "There is the river that makes glad the city of God. And this city, he dwells in the midst of this river and this city and it shall never be moved." His most, I would say, high habitation, we are told, the habitation of the most high. Then in that same 46th Psalm, it tells us, "Now be still and know that I am God." A man is still and he can't even still his mind, so putting you in a straitjacket is not going to make you still. Can you still your mind to the point where it actually is so still that you can have the revelation? The mind is so busy all the time, trying to work out something, trying to defeat what the other fellow said, trying to disprove him. And that those who will come here for the purpose of disproving, like the pictured being last night, and he, my own being pushed out, he is going to challenge my right to say that they're all myself pushed out. And he was big and strong, not taller than I am. I'm 5' 11" and he was the same height, but strapping, about 200-odd pounds, a giant of a man. And he was insolent. But he's myself looking for the challenge. And I said, all right, wait and see. Now, if I awake, where do you think you will be? And so, I awoke and I was alone. I only out-pictured it in my dream. It's an egocentric world beautifully told in dreams. And here I am, outpicturing my own being. And that one to be redeemed. I have to take him back. I cannot leave him in the knowing grave. So, I have prepared the way for my banished ones to return. And there is no other way. To return to what? To God, the Father. And who is God, the Father? The "I am in you." That's God the Father. You'll never get back and know that I am he until his Son stands before you and calls you Father. And that Son is David of biblical faith. And when you see David, he hasn't aged. He is the eternal youth. Eternity is personified as youth. Men not knowing that, they personify eternity as an old man with a sign gathering people. That's not the true personification of eternity. It's youth. The Ancient of Days, yes, has no beginning, no end. And yet you can't call him old, you can't call him young. He is the Ancient of Days. When you stand in his presence, here is the Ancient of Days, Infinite Love, that's what he is. He embraces you, incorporates you into his being, and you are one with the Ancient of Days, who is the Lord God, Jehovah. And that is Jesus. And now he sends you into the world to finish the cup.

And now you'll drain it. And you will drain it to the very end. And you will know bitterness as well, for joy and woe are woven fine, a garment for the soul divine. It's not all joy, it's not all woe, it's not all sweet, it's not all bitterness. In the Hebraic marriage ceremony, there are two glasses of wine, one sweet, one bitter, or be it dry, but it's always more of a sweet, and then they drink it. And when they drink it, then the rabbi steps upon the glasses and crushes them. That's the end of the drama. That's all symbolism, beautiful symbolism, but that's the story and that's life.

So, I am telling you what I know from my own experience. And this tonight may seem far out. And yet I tell you, if you dwell upon it, while you are dwelling upon it, trying to unravel the riddle, earthly things are taking place to your advantage. You put all your mind into unraveling a job, how to get more money out of it, how to make more out of it. And all these things are a waste of time. "Seek ye first the Kingdom of Heaven and all these things will be added unto you." Your heavenly Father knows your needs. So, seek what he offers you. Leave these things alone and they'll all add up in the end, you are amazed how it happened. It all comes into focus and you are reaping earthly benefits by giving your attention to the heavenly story.

So here, by simply dwelling upon it, the answer came during the night, the out-pictured self, the one opponent always opponent, and then to your own satisfaction, because there's no one else to satisfy, you awoke to find they all vanished anyway. And where do they go? They can't go off into space. They return to you, for one night you push them out and commune with them to explain what's taking place within you, for only one man fell. And he carried with him all. Read the 82nd Psalm. "And one man fell and that one man carried all." And then in the fall, he became fragmented. And this is the fragmented one man pushed out in the world. And that one man has to return redeeming himself. And that one is God. And there's nothing but God. So tonight, dwell upon it, as I did last night. And if today you had a problem and it was a financial problem or some little problem in your household, it will all be solved. It'll be resolved, but to put all of your attention upon that little problem and work on it in this little square of knowledge, where are you going to get it?

While you are doing God's work, Caesar's world collapses and reforms itself in harmony with what you are doing within you. I know from experience that's how it works. So here I can pinpoint that page. I know the man's name, if I pronounce the Spanish correctly, it is Jorge Luis Borges. For those who speak Spanish, it's J O R G E and then Luis L U I S and B O R G E S who departed this world only recently. He writes beautifully. His prose is really poetry and his native tongue is Spanish. Well, I can't speak Spanish or read Spanish, but if the translation into my tongue, which is English, is as beautiful as it is, what must be the original, because don't tell me that translation does not lose something in the inflection, in the mood, in the translation because they do.

When someone tells me that they can translate Shakespeare into German and make it more beautiful than you can in the original tongue of English, I start laughing, any more than I would take the great German poets when they were thinking in those words and then translate them into English and expect the English translation to equal it. No. If one could read Hebrew with understanding, I'm quite sure that the Psalms would be so altogether different. Yet we have a marvelous translation in English, but if it's so great in English, just imagine what it must be in the original tongue, when this inspired being is penning his words.

So, I tell you, when you go out tonight, dwell upon it. When you say *I am*, that's God, there is no other God. And you will laugh at that thought if you are here for the first or second time. And it seems arrogant. Here is a little man on a platform trying to persuade me that my own wonderful human imagination is God creating the universe and sustaining it. And so, you laugh. It's perfectly all right. I will not retract one word that I said. I only wait and time will prove me true. You will discover who you are. And when you discover who you are, you'll discover that you are the being I tell you that you are. You are God, the Father, but you will not in eternity know that you are God the Father until his Son, David, calls you Father.

There is no other way of knowing it. So that's the way that man returns. So, I have prepared the way for my banished ones to return. And I am the way. The way to what? The way to the Father. So, when you see me, you will know the Father, for the minute you see me, then you'll know you are the Father. That's what he's saying. You cannot see me and not know the Father, for it takes the Son to reveal the Father. And you aren't going to see Jesus. You are going to see David because *you are the Lord Jesus.* That's the one that came down, bringing with him his Son who will do all his will. And you have done his will. You've played all the parts. And in the very end, when you've drained the cup, right to the very end, all of it drained, leaving just the dregs, and had both the bitter and the sweet, then you will awake and you'll depart this world not to be restored to life in a world just like this, as the whole vast world will be. You will ascend to the point where you were before your descent. But no one ascends into heaven but he who first descended. There's only one way down and one way up.

Lecture XIX

God and I Are One

day unknown, 1972*

If I could persuade you to believe what tonight I hope I, well, I will try to. Your entire world would change. You hear the word, God, the word Jehovah, the word Lord, the word Jesus, the word Christ, and you think of something other than yourself. One that is greater, one that you would worship. Tonight, it is my purpose to show you that God and the *I* of man are one. When you say *I am*, that is the God of Scripture. Confined as you are, you think, how could it be? God created the universe and sustained it. And here I am like a little worm, threescore and ten years and then I vanish.

And now, let us turn to Scripture. We turn now to the 16th chapter of Matthew. And the question is asked of the disciples, the followers, those who have him. And you say to them, "Who do men say that the son of man is?" And they reply, "Well, some say, John the Baptist come again. Others, Elijah, others, Jeremiah, or one of

---

* Although I have, as of this writing, been unable to date this lecture it is ordered last in this volume because Neville references a news event that occurred in late May 1972, about four months before his death.

the prophets." Then he said to them, "But who do you say that *I am*?" And the spokesman called Peter said, "Thou are the Christ, the Son of the living God." You say to him, "Blessed are thou, Simon Bar-Jonah. For flesh and blood could not have told you this, but my Father who is in Heaven." For here he equates the son of man with the *I* of man, not the organ that sees or through which you see, but your sense of awareness, that *Iamness*, when you are aware of being, your consciousness, your human imagination. So, he equates the two, the son of man spoken of in the Old Testament and brought forward into the New is nothing more than the "I" of man. And he calls it the Christ and defines Christ as the Son of God. Now we find Christ being defined in the New Testament as the power of God and the wisdom of God. So, the "I" of man is the power of God and the wisdom of God.

If a man does not know it, well, then he will not exercise that power. He will not exercise that wisdom. So tonight, I am trying to persuade you that when you say *I*, before you say anything, that that is the power and the wisdom of God. You can't separate the power of God and the wisdom of God from God. So, you will say at the end, *I* and my father are one or he is called the son of God. Now, we are called upon to test this. If it be true, can we test it? I hope you'll put it to the test when I tell you that your own wonderful *Iamness* is God. Though prior to that, you believe that you're a little something, moving across the earth for a few years, seventy years, and then you will vanish, in the hope of some restoration, but a hope, no assurance.

Well now, I'm going to tell you that you really are God. Your own wonderful consciousness, your human imagination—that is the God of Scripture and there is no other God. Imprisoned as you are in these bodies of flesh, you did it for a purpose. Now let us see what it tells us about this Son of man that is now equated with the *I* of man. No one has ever ascended into Heaven, but he who descended from Heaven, the Son of man. You'll read that in the third chapter, the 13th verse of

John. So here we find you are a preexistent being. No one can ascend into heaven, but he who descended from heaven, the son of man. Your ascension in the next verse, the 14th verse, is showing you how you ascend. As Moses lifted up the serpent in the wilderness, so must the son of man be lifted up.

That's all imagery and yet it is true. You descended into generation, in a world of death, where everything begins; it waxes, it waves, and then it disappears. But there's something in you, sewn in this garment, that does not die. That is preexistent and its home is Heaven, which is harmony. You gave it up completely. You aren't pretending that you're a man. You descended into man. You became man with all the weaknesses, all the limitations, all the restrictions of man, to experience this world of death and decay. There will come a moment in time that you will ascend from this restriction, taking with you the experience that is yours because of this restriction. And you will ascend in the same manner that Moses lifted up the serpent in the wilderness. That was an adumbration. That was a foreshadowing.

You will rise from the base of your spine, up your spine into your own skull, for Heaven is within you. And you rise like a fiery serpent, without any loss of identity, the form you wear, I hesitate to describe it. I will tell you that your face is human, your hands are human, and your voice is human. But do not ask me to describe the body that you wear. It's infinite power, infinite wisdom, and yet it is a form. You are that fiery being that descended. Not because of anything that was wrong when you descended, the fall is not because of any mistake on our part. It's a predetermined plan to come down into the world of death and decay and overcome it. If coming down, wearing these garments, we knew who we were, pretending that we were men, we could not accomplish it any more than an actor on the stage, pretending that he is Hamlet, can actually play that part. He has to actually assume it but even then it is still, with a little something in his mind, he knows he is the great actor who tonight will go home, to his lovely home and he'll take off the garment and hang it up once more and tomorrow he'll replay the play. You don't do that in this play of God.

You don't take off the garment, you wear it for your three score and ten, and if by strength, your four score or maybe even longer or shorter, but the *I* of man is the God of Scripture. Put it to the test. Let me now, first of all, before we go into the testing of it, make clear what I said on the last lecture night, Friday night, prompted by a question that was asked here. For I had said in the previous lecture that there are ranks in Heaven as there are on earth, for this is only a copy. Everything here is a shadow, it's a copy of eternal realities. And in the 12th chapter of First Corinthians, Paul describes the eight ranks. He does it many times, but he never changes the first two. The first is always the apostle. The second, the prophet. The third, the teachers, and then he goes on, miracle workers, healers, helpers, administrators, and the speakers in tongues, but he never changes the first and second, the apostle and the prophet. You might think because I told you *I am* sent—and the word sent means an apostle—that I am appropriating unto myself a certain first rank. But now to put your heart at peace, I'm going to quote the 11th chapter of Romans. "As a whole, for there are always remnant of whole, and the remnant simply means the elect of God."

You're not elected because you are born by accident into some ethnic group, it hasn't a thing to do with that. A descendant of Abraham after the flesh is not necessarily the elect of God. You are chosen from any race, any nation, any religion. Well, how the choice is made, no one knows, it remains the Father's secret, but Paul qualifies it in this manner, "There is a remnant to this day called by grace." And if by grace, then it is not on the basis of work. Otherwise, grace would no longer be grace. Therefore no one who is called and sent can brag. If he brags, he is not the sent, because it's all by grace. He didn't earn. It is not by merit. It is simply a secret known only to the Father. So, when we are called, incorporated into the body of infinite love, who *is* God, and then sent, let no one who is sent raise a finger to brag, to boast, for it is all by grace. Read it in the 11th chapter, the fifth and sixth verses of Paul's letter to the Romans. So now I have stated that.

So do not think for one moment, when I tell you I have been called and think that in any way I am trying to act superior, for there is no intrinsic superiority to those who are called. Now, he uses it in an analogy, which I do not think is adequate, but you can read it in the book itself. He uses the analogy of the human form. Not our head, eyes, nose, teeth, and so on, but that is a weak analogy. Nevertheless, he uses that to show you the different parts in one body. But now to come back to make this a very practical night. Believe me, that when you say *I*, before you say I am John, I am Bill, I am this, I am that, I am the other, you are declaring yourself *to be* and that sense of being is God; that's God. Now, what are you going to put on it? All things are possible to God, all things. You could say now, as you're seated here, after first affirming that "I am." You can then assume that *I am*, and your name is exactly what you want to be. If you believe what I tell you about your own *Iamness* and remain faithful to what you have assumed, that assumption will harden into fact.

When you pray in the true sense of the word, you do not pray to any external God. That was my command when I was sent. "Down with the blue bloods" hasn't a thing to do with the social structure of the world.* It has only to do with church protocol, all external worship, all ceremonies, everything that leads the individual outside of himself. To put a little cross on the wall and then bow before it, and see it as something external, is not what Scripture teaches. Buried in the Old Testament there is a pattern. So, he said taking the twelve, we're going up to Jerusalem and everything written about the Son of man, which is the *I* of man, will be accomplished. But they did not understand what he said.

* Neville recounts the experience of hearing these words in his 1961 book, *The Law and the Promise.*

It was beyond their ability to grasp. He's going up. And only the one who has experienced Scripture, which means, he has actually resurrected the pattern, playing the part that is the central part of Scripture. He resurrects the pattern all within himself. He plays all the parts. He is the one who is born from above. He is the one who comes out of the grave, unassisted. He is the one who three witnesses bear witness to his birth from above. He is the one they cannot see because he's now spirit, yet more real than all the flesh in the world. He is the one who actually sees his Son, David and David calls him Father and he knows he's David's Father. And David knows that he is his Son.

He's the one whose temple, the body, is stripped in two from top to bottom. It is he now who ascends like a fiery serpent from the base of the spine up into the skull. He is the one on whom the dove descends and lights upon his hand like Noah in the ark. And as Noah brought the dove into him, you bring the dove to you, for man is the ark of God. And as the ark contains all things within itself, man contains within himself all things. Everything—he creates from within himself. In this pattern, the individual awakens within himself. And who does it? The *I* of man. And that is God.

Now tonight you can test it as you are called upon to test it, test yourselves and see, do you not realize that Jesus Christ is in you? Unless of course, you fail to meet the test. Examine yourself, to see whether you are holding to the faith. What faith? To have someone tell me that I am a Christian or I'm a Jew or I'm a Mohammedan and holding to that faith that they talk about? No. The faith that I'm talking about tonight; that your own wonderful *Iamness* is God. Test it to see if you're holding to that faith. If you are holding to that faith, and all things are possible to God, you should be able to prove it in the testing.

She's not here tonight. She promised she will write me a letter, having told me the story on Friday, but I know she finds it difficult to express herself in writing. She can paint and paint and paint and do all kinds of lovely things in painting and drawing. But when I said to her, please write it that I may tell it to my audience before I close; that I have no future plans after I close on the 29th. So, I would like to share your experience, to encourage everyone in this world to do what you did. Well, the letter didn't come. I can see her struggling over one page and rubbing out a line because she didn't spell the word correctly and going over the next one. But she can take a piece of canvas, a piece of paper, and do miracles with it. But because she's restricted in writing a letter, she didn't send the letter.

But the essence is this. She is now a divorced girl with a little boy, a handsome little fellow. Well, when you're living alone and you need money and you have a child to support and you have a home, all the things, and the money isn't coming in, then you're up against it. She said, "I blew my top," as you are told in the Psalms to do. "Then I applied this principle and I assumed that I had exactly what I needed plus and plus. Then I got a call from First National City Bank of New York City." Now that is the second-largest bank in our country. Bank of America comes first, they're second, and Chase Manhattan is third. "Giving me an order"—she has no agent, this is an unsolicited statement—"an order for $5,000," which she can execute and deliver within a month. Well, the First National City Bank of New York is not going to be hard-pressed to pay her immediately $5,000.

If she called them and told them to pay in advance, they would willingly pay in advance. And she said, I can execute that order in one month, but I want the detail I had hoped she would send me as she promised last Friday, but knowing her restriction concerning the use of words, you can use the brush and use the pen and use the pencil, but she's limited in the use of words. Eventually, she will send it, but I'd hoped to have it by tonight, so I could give you exactly what she did, but this is what I do. Having convinced myself through experience, I have come to the conclusion that because I am aware that *I am*, that that is God. For if by him all things are made and without him is not anything made that is made, and I start from scratch only imagining a state and then I boldly assume that it is real, that I actually experienced that state now. And then in the not-distant future, that state crystallizes in my world. Well, then I have found God. I have the source of the phenomena of life. My only concern then is to share it with others and tell and tell them for they are all one, we are one. No one is greater than the other. Not fundamentally. In his claims of what he is in the world of Caesar, he has more money or he has so and so, and so and so, but basically, the same creative power in the man tonight behind bars serving life is the same creative power of the one who sentenced him to life, is the same being, there is only one God. *Hear O Israel, the Lord, our God, the Lord is one.*

And the word translated the Lord is *Yod Hey Vav Hey*, properly translated is *I am*. When you go unto the people of Israel and they ask you, "What is his name?" And you claim that the God of Abraham and the God of Jacob and the God of Isaac sent you. You say onto them, "*I am* hath sent me. That's my name forever. And by this name, I shall be known throughout all generations." But man finds it difficult keeping the tense. And so, he speaks of *thou art* or *he is*, and he never actually comes down to the fundamental and knows that *I am*. I am the cause of the phenomena of my life, good, bad, or indifferent. I have to live with it and change my assumptions if I would change the world in which I live.

But now can I help a seeming other? I say you are myself pushed out. Can I help another? Yes, because there's only one. If your request of me comes within the framework of the golden rule, something that I would like done to me, then I can willingly help you. If you ask of me that which does not come within the frame of the golden rule, do not ask it of me. I grant you complete freedom to go elsewhere and go to anyone who will tell you they can do it in spite of what he said. Go ahead. But if anyone asks of me any request, all that I do is this, it's so simple. We are told in Scripture, that whatever we ask of him, knowing that he hears it, it shall be done for us. If we know he hears it. For can you imagine you seated here on the surface of your being, a rational being, knowing something that the depth of your own being that encompasses you doesn't know? So, you know and you think, well, he doesn't know. Well read that in the story of Ezekiel. You'll read it in the 38th chapter. "And these are the elders of Israel that went into the dark room and they are carving on the walls, all gruesome things. And they said within themselves, the Lord does not see it." And the Lord is speaking to his prophet Ezekiel. And he said the elders of Israel say that I do not see them—and watch what they're doing, making all these abomination things within the great caverns. They will all reap them because I see everything that the elders of Israel see, but they think because it's dark and it's a cavern no one knows what you do, that God doesn't know.

I have said time and again, that there is no fiction in this world. You might have heard the story and read the story concerning the seajacking of the Queen Elizabeth. You might have read the article in *Time* that some girl at Hunter College wrote that story in detail.* And she was so shy when it came to the point to be read, she could not read it. She's a shy, sweet lady with a gift of writing. She wrote that in detail, including those who seemingly participated, a terminal case of cancer, and one who is running away from the Law, who has not a thing to gain, and therefore is quite willing to blow the Queen Elizabeth with the 2,200 souls aboard, and everything is completely in detail in her fictional story. Imagining creates reality. There is no fic-

---

* In the episode that Neville describes, in May 1972 a hoax bomb threat was made to the passenger liner Queen Elizabeth 2 which echoed the short story of a writing student, Barbara Shalvey, whose work was read aloud to her class at Hunter College the day before the ship's launch. A *New York Times* article of May 20, 1972, "A Short Story Foretold Queen Elizabeth 2 Plot" by Joseph Lelyveld reported: "Interviewed yesterday, Miss. Shalvey said she thought it was just a wild coincidence when she heard of the threatened hijacking Thursday afternoon. She said she had experienced similar coincidences. For instance, she said, she wrote a story recently about a child who stabs a groom at a wedding with the knife that was used to cut the wedding cake, only to read in a newspaper of a woman who stabbed her husband with a knife she had used to cut his birthday cake." *Time* magazine also covered the incident in an article of May 28, 1972, "The High Seas: A Queen's Ransom." The FBI later arrested the hoaxer who had made similar threats against Pan American Airways.

tion. So, someone expressed her thought and called the captain while at sea and demanded a million dollars and would settle for $350,000. Well, it must have cost them, I should say, more than a million to stop that huge hulk in Mid-Atlantic and then feed 2,200 people four times a day for the extra meals that they would have coming to them, plus all the things that you put it all together, it would cost more than a million dollars, and a little girl possibly writing this for her Ph.D., or writing it for some reason, and she writes it in detail. They gave her name, so you can contact her. They gave the school, it's Hunter College in New York City. And everything in detail is told in that story. So, I tell you, you sit down and write fiction. Need not put it down. My friend wrote fiction. She had a large sum of money coming in and she went to town within herself and she wrote in herself and blew her top, as it were.

Thank you. Thank you. Didn't drink enough tonight.

So, she, in the depth of her own being, conjured the sum of money that she needed, beyond, always go beyond. So, we are told in the Psalms, "Be angry, but sin not. Commune with your own heart upon your bed and be silent." Yes. Blow your top, but do not let the sun go down upon your anger. Be silent as you commune with self, you don't commune with another. For the self of man is God. So be angry, but sin not, commune with your own heart upon your bed. Start communing with another and then you actually know exactly what you want. And in that state fall asleep. And in a way that no one knows and you in your surface mind you do not know, it will all come to pass. Everything in the world is created this way but man does not know it. Who knows tonight who is treading the wine press that is going to cause a change of mind in tomorrow's world? But when they do it, they are intent in the doing. "If you are lukewarm," you are told in the Scripture, "I'll spew you out. Would that you are either hot or cold, but because that you are lukewarm, I will spew you out." You can't do anything if you are lukewarm. You must be intense about it. You want to be rich, all right, you can be rich. You want to be known. You can be known. No matter what you want but you must be intense about it and then commune with your own heart upon your bed and then let it drop. You'll read that in the 4th Psalm, the Psalm of David.

So, I say to everyone here, believe me, your own wonderful *Iamness*, your consciousness, your wonderful human imagination. That is God. And all that you behold, though it appears without it is within, in your imagination of which this world of mortality is but a shadow. So, you can change the shadow if you change the object, for you are the light. He said, "I am the light of the world." Change the object that you are holding within yourself and identifying yourself with it. Change that object. You're lighting up and you'll cast a new shadow upon the world. So, you say, *I am* and you name it. And then you say, *I am* unemployed. No, *I am* gainfully employed, making more than I've ever made before. Don't ask yourself how, why, and through whom—that is not your conscious reasoning mind's concern.

If you take the intellectual background, the educational background, of those who are making top money in the theatrical world, I doubt that they could pass any college examination. I don't think they could pass any entrance examination to college. Yet, they're making a million dollars, two million dollars a year. Do you think Bob Hope could pass today's examination for entrance into college? But all of his material is written for him anyway, he can't even write that. But he has millions. All right, because that's how he dreamt, may I tell you? I know the background of the man. A friend of mine who has now gone from this world, played in vaudeville with him. And he would borrow from my friend every week, a sum of money because he had to go to that post office and buy a postal money order and send it to his bank. He borrowed money that was interest-free because he was sending in money that was not interest-free. He had to send a certain sum of money every week and he would send it into his account. And borrowed from my friend, Harry Webb who had a band and they played together, not in the same act. Harry had his own act. He has a small band. And Harry was the outgoing personality who didn't care about money. And so, he wanted money, Hope wanted money, he would loan him the money. He always paid it back the next week and borrowed it again because he had to have so much in that bank every week. And when they would go into a restaurant and food was leftover like bread and butter, who took it all home? Bob Hope. Bob took all the buns, all the rolls, everything that was there uneaten, he paid for it and you paid for it. "You don't want it, Harry, do you?" No. All right. So, he took it home. So, he has $400 million, so they claim. That was his goal in life.

If that's the goal, have it. I speak of another goal. The goal of awakening to who we are. When man awakens from this dream, the whole vast world and all that it contained is as *nothing* to the being that you are. You came down from Heaven where the whole is yours. As you're told in the 50th Psalm, "If I were hungry, I wouldn't tell you, for the world is mine and all within it. The cattle on a thousand hills are mine." So why should I tell anyone of my need when it's all mine anyway? I would slay and eat. When you are awakened, you don't ask anyone. If you awaken from this dream of life. But while you are in it, all right, we are one. This little hand of mine, if it begins to itch here now, it's easier for me to take this hand that is not attached to this and scratch it than to try to bend this thing out of shape, to scratch the back of it. I could rub it here, but why not? This is easier. And take a part of my own being to ease the itch.

We are all one pushed out. So, you can do it. Ask anyone that you trust. May I tell you, he isn't, if he knows how to pray, he isn't going to burst any blood vessel. He isn't going to get down on his knees and pray to any external God if he knows how to pray. He isn't going to beg of anyone in this world. What he will do, he will simply represent you to himself as one telling him that you have what you asked of him. And when he is satisfied that you told him that you have it, don't ask the second time for the same thing, because he's not going to listen to you. He heard it, he is still hearing it, and he will continue to hear it until that which he has heard is perfectly externalized.

So don't think you need several treatments. That's a lot of nonsense. Treatments for what? It either is or it isn't. So, when they start getting you on the hook and say, now I think you need more treatments, you need more treatments. She or he or the crowd, they do not know what they are doing. When you pray, go within and close the door of the senses, deny all that seems so obvious. And your Father who is within will reward you openly. But commune with self for you and the Father are one. So, you commune with self. And what did he tell you? Exactly what was asked of you. He heard it and he has all the ways and means that you, on the surface of your being, know not of. He will do it. If you ask anything of one if it comes within the framework of his code of ethics. Don't ask anyone who knows how to pray something that does not come within his golden rule, do onto others as you would have them do unto you. Just as simple as that. And most of the requests would come within that rule. And so, you simply hear it. And then you drop it completely. And in the depth of your own being, you are still hearing it. And the Father knows all means, all ways, and so he singles out the best way to externalize it.

Here in New York City many years ago, this lady, a lady of considerable means, she left her home in New York City and went off to Paris with her two children, leaving her home and her maid. Before she returned the maid took all of her furniture and took it away. When she returned the apartment was there, rent was paid every month, but there was no furniture, not a thing in it. She employed a private agency, told the police department, told all the authorities in New York City, and plus her private agency. At the end of a few months, they did not turn up one thing concerning that stolen property. She came to see me, I said, all right, you're seated there and I'm seated here in my apartment. Now you are not seated in my apartment. You are seated right now, close your eyes, you are seated in your own apartment. And you had a grand piano. She said, no, I had a piano, but it wasn't a concert grand. It was grand but not a concert grand. And on it, I had my pictures of my two children. And I had pictures on the wall. She told me what they were. And the furniture. I said, all right, refurnish that place as you left it, you have a memory. She did. Now when I stop talking, it's because you have refurnished that place to me. Now you're going to go in and you aren't going to see your apartment from my apartment, *you are in your apartment*, and you can feel your chair and get off your chair and feel the piano, and see the children, the pictures of the children. And that's what you're going to do. She agreed she would do it. And then we simply broke the spell. What did it take? Two minutes, three minutes. That week she went to her bank on Madison Avenue. As she was coming out of the bank, she had a past history of her little mental state, where she was put away for a while because she needed psychiatric treatment. And the bars on this window reminded her of her past history and therefore addled her for a while.

So, she came onto Madison Avenue and turned south instead of turning north where she should have. When she discovered her mistake, she was at the end of the block. When she got there and discovered her mistake, she looked down and two very familiar ankles were standing right before her. She came up to the face, that's her maid and the maid started to scream. She went over to the maid and grabbed her before the light changed, and hailed the oncoming taxi, said, you are taking me right now, and the maid who could have killed her, she was so big and strong, was so reduced to impotency because of the discovery. And the maid took her to the place where she had stored that furniture. She said I'm not bringing an action against you. I want my furniture. And she got it back into her own apartment within the week. A seeming mistake was the way the Father led her. All I ask is to go to the end. If I go to the end and give thanks to the end and for the end, it's done. Now, let the one in the depth of my own being devise the best means to take me to that end. The end is where I start. The end is my beginning. And that is a story that I know from personal experience.

So do not attempt to devise the means and tell the one that you ask to pray for you how it should be done. He will lose all interest and turn his back and say, go elsewhere. You don't go into a doctor's office and tell him what he should do. If you go to him, because you trust him, well then, you're either going to trust him and continue or you're going to leave him. Well, if you go to someone that you really believe who knows how to pray, don't tell them how to do it, and what means should be employed in order to do it. He is going to go to the end if he knows how to pray. The end is where we begin. In my end is my beginning. And we're always ahead of our evidence. So I go to the end, I see the whole thing done, and then drop it and let it happen in my world.

So, to come back, the *I* within you now, when you say *I*, no matter how little you have thought yourself so far, may I tell you, you are the infinite God. And when the story of Jesus Christ repeats itself within you, you will know *it's all I.* No one called Jesus is going to appear. He's not going to push any stone away from you when you come out of that tomb. And then you'll know the words of John, "In that day you will know that I am in my Father, and you in me, and I in you."

Neville Goddard Timeline

1905—Neville Lancelot Goddard is born on February 19 to a British family in St. Michael, Barbados, the fourth child in a family of nine boys and one girl.

1922—At age seventeen Neville relocates to New York City to study theater. He makes a career as an actor and dancer on stage and silent screen, landing roles on Broadway, silent film, and touring Europe as part of a dance troupe.

1923—Neville briefly marries Mildred Mary Hughes, with whom he has a son, Joseph Goddard, born the following year.

1929—Neville marked this as the year that began his mystical journey: "Early in the morning, maybe about three-thirty or four o'clock, I was taken in spirit into the Divine Council where the gods hold converse." (lecture from *Immortal Man*, 1977)

1931—After several years of occult study, Neville meets his teacher Abdullah, a turbaned black man of Jewish descent. The pair work together for five years in New York City.

1938—In February, Neville begins his own teaching and speaking.

1939—Neville's first book, *At Your Command*, is published.

1940–1941—Neville meets Catherine Willa Van Schumus (1907–1975), also known as Bill, who is to become his second wife.

1941—Neville publishes his longer and more ambitious book, *Your Faith Is Your Fortune.*

1942—Neville marries Catherine, who later that year gives birth to their daughter Victoria. Also that year, Neville publishes *Freedom for All: A Practical Application of the Bible.*

1942–1943—From November to March, Neville serves in the military before returning home to Greenwich Village in New York City. In September 1943, Neville is profiled in *The New Yorker.*

1944—Neville publishes *Feeling Is the Secret.*

1945—Neville publishes *Prayer: The Art of Believing.*

1946—Neville's friend mystical philosopher Israel Regardie profiles him in his book *The Romance of Metaphysics.* Neville also publishes his pamphlet *The Search.*

1948—Neville delivers his classic "Five Lessons" lectures in Los Angeles, which many students find the clearest and most compelling summation of his methodology. It appears posthumously as a book.

1949—Neville publishes *Out of This World: Thinking Fourth Dimensionally.*

1952—Neville publishes *The Power of Awareness.*

1954—Neville publishes *Awakened Imagination.*

1955—Neville hosts radio and television shows in Los Angeles.

1956—Neville publishes *Seedtime and Harvest: A Mystical View of the Scriptures.*

1959—On July 20, Neville undergoes the mystical experience of being reborn from his own skull. Other mystical experiences follow into the next year.

1960—Neville releases a spoken-word album.

1961—Neville publishes *The Law and the Promise*; the final chapter, "The Promise," details the mystical experience he underwent in 1959, and others that followed.

1963—On January 1, Neville describes the Holy Spirit descending upon him in the form of a dove, bringing his complete and final union with God.

1964—Neville publishes the pamphlet *He Breaks the Shell: A Lesson in Scripture.*

1966—Neville publishes his last full-length book, *Resurrection*, composed of four works from the 1940s and the contemporaneous closing title essay, which outlines the fullness of his mystical vision and of humanity's realization of its deific nature.

1972—Neville dies in West Hollywood at age sixty-seven from a hemorrhage after a rupture of the esophageal veins due to liver damage. He is interred at the family plot in St. Michael, Barbados.

About the Authors

Neville Goddard was one of the most remarkable mystical thinkers of the past century. In more than ten books and thousands of lectures, Neville, under his solitary first name, expanded on one core principle: *the human imagination is God.* As such, he taught, everything that you experience results from your thoughts and feeling states. Born to an Anglican family in Barbados in 1905, Neville traveled to New York City at age seventeen in 1922 to study theater. Although he won roles on Broadway, in silent films, and toured internationally with a dance troupe, Neville abandoned acting in the early 1930s to dedicate himself to metaphysical studies and embark on a new career as a writer and lecturer. He was a compelling presence at metaphysical churches, spiritual centers, and auditoriums until his death in West Hollywood, California, in 1972. Neville was not widely known during his lifetime, but today his books and lectures have attained new popularity. Neville's principles about the creative properties of the mind prefigured some of today's most radical quantum theorizing, and have influenced several major spiritual writers, including Carlos Castaneda and Joseph Murphy.

Mitch Horowitz is a PEN Award-winning historian whose books include *Occult America*, *One Simple Idea*, *The Miracle Club*, *Daydream Believer*, and *Uncertain Places.* His book *Awakened Mind* is one of the first works of New Thought translated and published in Arabic. The Chinese government has censored his work. Twitter @MitchHorowitz | Instagram @MitchHorowitz23

CPSIA information can be obtained
at www.ICGtesting.com
Printed in the USA
JSHW020835041022
31286JS00001B/1